PSYCHOLOGICAL ASPECTS OF LEARNING DISABILITIES & READING DISORDERS

McGRAW-HILL SERIES IN SPECIAL EDUCATION
ROBERT M. SMITH, Consulting Editor

Cartwright and Cartwright:
DEVELOPING OBSERVATION SKILLS

Haring and Schiefelbusch:
TEACHING SPECIAL CHILDREN

Ross:
PSYCHOLOGICAL ASPECTS OF LEARNING DISABILITIES
AND READING DISORDERS

Smith:
CLINICAL TEACHING: METHODS OF INSTRUCTION
FOR THE RETARDED

Smith:
INTRODUCTION TO MENTAL RETARDATION

Smith and Neisworth:
THE EXCEPTIONAL CHILD: A FUNCTIONAL APPROACH

Worell and Nelson:
MANAGING INSTRUCTIONAL PROBLEMS: A CASE
STUDY WORKBOOK

PSYCHOLOGICAL ASPECTS OF LEARNING DISABILITIES & READING DISORDERS

ALAN O. ROSS

Professor of Psychology
State University of New York at Stony Brook

McGraw-Hill Book Company

New York   St. Louis   San Francisco   Auckland   Düsseldorf
Johannesburg   Kuala Lumpur   London   Mexico   Montreal
New Delhi   Panama   Paris   São Paulo   Singapore
Sydney   Tokyo   Toronto

By the same author:
Psychological Disorders of Children: A Behavioral Approach to Theory, Research, and Therapy

PSYCHOLOGICAL ASPECTS
OF LEARNING DISABILITIES AND READING DISORDERS

1 2 3 4 5 6 7 8 9 0 D O D O 7 9 8 7 6 5

Library of Congress Cataloging in Publication Data

Ross, Alan O
   Psychological aspects of learning disabilities and
reading disorders.

   (McGraw-Hill series in special education)
   Includes bibliographical references and indexes.
   1. Learning disabilities.   2.   Child study.
I.   Title.   [DNLM:1.   Dyslexia.   2.   Learning
disorders.   LC4661 R823p]
LC704.R68   371.9'2   75-20254
ISBN 0-07-053845-X

This book was set in Times Roman by National ShareGraphics, Inc.
The editors were Stephen D. Dragin and Barry Benjamin;
the cover was designed by Pencils Portfolio, Inc.;
the production supervisor was Charles Hess.
R. R. Donnelley & Sons Company was printer and binder.

To Judy and Pam

Contents

Preface

Learning disabilities are a serious problem: serious in terms of the distress they cause children and their parents; serious in terms of the number of children who, thus affected, fail to benefit from the academic opportunities which serve to educate their peers. Estimates as to the number of learning-disabled children vary and depend in part on how learning disabilities are defined and identified, but their prevalence is put by some to be as high as 20 percent of the school-age population. Even if one takes the lowest, most conservative estimate of 4 percent, it is clear that learning disabilities represent a challenge to those who are concerned with the education of our children.

Educators have been aware for some time that there are children in almost every classroom who, though otherwise normal, achieve at a level that is below their presumed potential. For some of these children the difficulty is limited to one subject matter, such as reading; for others it is more prevasive, with performance hindered in several areas.

At first these children were known as underachievers; then people seeking a cause for the problem spoke of minimal brain damage. Later, when no brain damage could be demonstrated, the phrase "minimal cerebral dysfunction" was coined. Most recently, the term "learning disability" has attained wide acceptance. The problem of these children has been described as hyperactivity, impulsivity, distractibility, or short attention span. Labels such as "hyperactive child syndrome," "psychoneurological learning disability," "perceptual handicap," and "specific learning disorder" continue to have currency.

I once proposed and used (Ross, 1967, 1974) the term "learning dysfunction," but I believe that there is much merit in agreeing on one term. Thus, at the risk of confusing those who are familiar with my earlier writing, I have decided to adopt "learning disability" to designate the problem under discussion. This term owes its wide acceptance to Samuel Kirk, who suggested its use in a talk to a conference sponsored by the Fund for Perceptually Handicapped Children and held in Evanston, Illinois, in 1963.

The problems of the learning-disabled child lie in the areas of perception, attention, memory, association, and information processing. Psychologists have investigated these topics for many years, yet the results of these investigations have rarely found their way into the literature on learning disabilities. The classroom teacher's practice has therefore remained singularly unaffected by whatever knowledge psychology might have to offer. It is as if the problems studied in the psychological laboratory and the problems found in the classroom existed in two lands whose inhabitants spoke different dialects, lands which were separated by a body of water that was crossed by only an occasional boatsman.

This book was written in order to provide a bridge between the laboratory and the classroom. It is my hope that over this bridge those concerned with learning-disabled children will enter into commerce with those who do research on learning; thus both may discover that their dialects are not so different and that it is possible to benefit from each other's work. Such transaction should be of advantage not only to the learning-disabled children and those who seek to teach them but also to those who seek to understand the basic processes of human learning.

In trying to relate laboratory findings to classroom practice, it is often necessary to extrapolate implications from results of research studies which did not have the problems of the classroom as their focus. Research is often conducted on children, topics, and concepts that are only indirectly relevant to the children, topics, and concepts which the teacher of learning-disabled children encounters in the classroom. In the metaphor of the bridge, one finds oneself in the position of the bridge builder who seeks to connect two roads which do not terminate on directly opposite sides of the river because they had been laid out without a river crossing as part of the plan. In such a case, the bridge cannot follow the most direct route; it may have to be provisional and to be used with caution until the roads are relocated so as to serve communication between the two shores in the most direct fashion. Such will be the case once psychologists conduct more research on learning-disabled children and educators come to look to such research as an aid in solving their problems. It is my hope that this book will contribute to this development.

As I explored the diverse literature related to learning disabilities, two points clearly emerged. One was that we know far more about reading, reading acquisition, and reading disabilities than we do about the various other academic tasks and children's difficulties related to these. As a result, I have used reading disabilities as paradigmatic of all learning disabilities, devoting an entire chapter to that topic. Since reading disabilities are both more frequent and more handicapping than other academic disabilities, this somewhat biased emphasis seems justified.

The other point which became apparent as this book took shape has to do with the recurring theme of selective attention, a topic which appears in several chapters and in different contexts. Though I had not set out to find a unifying theme, much less a basic cause of learning disabilities, it does seem that there is one cognitive function with which most learning-disabled children have difficulty and which, in fact, might serve to define learning disability: the

...o sustain selective attention. I thus propose that learning-disabled chil-
...i have in common a developmental delay in the acquisition of effective use
...i sustained selective attention and hope that others will find some merit in
this formulation.

When one writes nonspecifically about a child who is learning-disabled,
one is constantly reminded that the English language demands that one designate a gender for this child whenever a pronoun is required. It would obviously be desirable to say "he or she," and I have tried to do so as often as it
seemed reasonable. At times, however, I have reverted to the use of the mascu-
line pronoun, as I had done before I became fittingly sensitized to this issue.
One excuse for what may seem to some like chauvinism is that the majority of
learning-disabled children are indeed boys. The other excuse is easier style and
smoother syntax. I hope that this disclaimer makes it clear that when I refer to
a child as he, I am in no way disparaging girls.

Again, as I have on previous occasions, I should like to express my fond
gratitude to Ilse Wallis Ross, my wife, whose loving support and encouraging
interest contribute immeasurably to my work and whose professional sophistication and experience do so much to help me in my endeavors. My daughter
Pam made a valuable contribution to the writing of this book by assisting with
the literature search, and her help is greatly appreciated.

ACKNOWLEDGMENTS

For granting me permission to quote from their writings, I am indebted to Drs.
Virginia Douglas, Roscoe A. Dykman, Jerome Kagan, Laura Schreibman,
Gerald M. Senf, L. Alan Sroufe, Lewis Vande Voort, and Peter H. Wolff.
Corporate holders of copyrights who let me quote from their material by
permission and whose courtesy is hereby acknowledged are the *Canadian Jour-
nal of Behavorial Science, Journal of Behavior Therapy and Experimental Psychi-
atry,* Grune and Stratton, Holt, Reinhart and Winston, Pergamon Publishing
Company, Prentice Hall, Syracuse University Press, John Wiley & Sons, and
The Society for Research in Child Development.

Alan O. Ross

Chapter 1

Learning Disabilities

The Term

"Learning disability" is a term which calls attention to the fact that there are children attending school who have trouble learning despite the fact that they have no apparent physical, sensory, intellectual, or emotional defect. Such children had for years been ignored, misdiagnosed, or mistreated and their difficulty had been variously designated by such terms as "hyperactivity," "hyperkinetic syndrome," "hyperactive child syndrome," "minimal brain damage," "minimal cerebral dysfunction," "learning disorder," or "learning dysfunction."

   With the introduction of the term "learning disability" (Kirk & Bateman, 1962) and its wide acceptance in both professional and lay circles, some order has been brought into this field; this can only benefit the children with whom we are here concerned. At the same time, one must not overlook the fact that this term covers a variety of children with different kinds of problems who have in common only that they share difficulty in learning under ordinary classroom conditions without showing a clearly identifiable reason for this difficulty. One should also remember that a learning disability may be general, and thus cover many areas of academic subject matter, or that it may be specific, so that a child might have no trouble learning except in one subject such as reading, spelling, or arithmetic. Learning disability thus subsumes a variety of children, and no one teaching or treatment method can possibly provide the answer to their problem.

Among children designated as learning-disabled, many seem to have trouble selecting—from among the mass of sensory stimulation impinging on them—that stimulus which is relevant to the task at hand. Others may well perceive stimuli in an atypical fashion, and still others seem to code information in an ineffective or inefficient way. Some of these children seem impulsive, some hyperactive, some distractible, and some undermotivated. There are those who have detectable abnormalities in brain functions and others who have secondarily acquired low self-esteem, expectations of failure, high anxiety in the face of learning tasks, or such behavior problems as aggression or withdrawal. A great deal of research is needed before one can know how the category learning disability should be subdivided in order to achieve greater homogeneity.

Faced with a category which covers such a great variety of children, some are tempted to conclude that the term "learning disability" is meaningless and should be discarded—that no two children are alike, so that the only feasible approach is to treat each child as a unique case. Such a radical step would seem to be as counterproductive from the standpoint of helping the individual child as would be the opposite approach according to which all learning-disabled children are to be treated alike. In order to decide whether learning disability is a useful concept, it is well to differentiate between learning disability as a category for children with similar problems and "learning-disabled" as a label for a specific child.

To designate a category, "learning disability" is a useful term. It calls attention to the existence of a problem and, by facilitating communication among those who have a concern about and interest in this problem, it can contribute to an eventual solution. Unlike earlier terms—such as "minimal cerebral dyscunction"—"learning disability" is purely descriptive and carries no implication about a cause which, at this point, has not been established. Furthermore, by emphasizing that these children have trouble learning, the term places the responsibility for helping such children squarely in the realm of education and not, as do references to brain functions, into the field of medicine.

As a label for an individual child, the term "learning disability" is more equivocal. Like all other labels in use in the realm of psychological disorders, it is only a description and not an explanation of the problem one has observed. If a child has trouble learning and someone labels him or her learning-disabled, there is always the danger that, having found an impressive-sounding label for the child, efforts at providing help will cease because the label is viewed as an explanation for the problem. The statement "He has a learning disability, so of course he can't be expected to learn" all too often serves as an excuse for giving up on efforts to teach such a child. When used in this manner, the term "learning disability" is clearly objectionable.

On the other hand, if the child is in an educational system where specialized teaching efforts are undertaken for children who fall in the category "learning-disabled," the label, when correctly applied, can open learning opportunities that might otherwise remain unavailable. Still, the label itself will not lead directly to the specialized learning experience needed by any particular child. For that the category is still far too broad. Each child must be separately assessed so that educational planning can be relevant to his or her strengths and weaknesses.

Eventually, as Senf (1972) has pointed out, we should be able to identify subcategories within the area of learning disabilities. At that point, we should be able to make general statements about what educational approach is best for children in a given group. Until such time, "learning disability" as a label for an individual child can be deemed useful only if it serves as an administrative key that gives the child access to available resources. But as we shall see, even the assignment of as gross a label as "learning disability" is fraught with conceptual, semantic, and methodological problems that make its use anything but easy. Let us turn to the question how "learning disability" is to be defined.

TOWARD A DEFINITION

What Is Learning?

Before one can hope to define "learning disability"—that is, before one can talk about a condition where learning is not taking place—one must decide how one can tell when learning is taking place. In other words, to define "learning disability" one must define "learning." Yet "learning" is a curious concept. The word is a familiar term in everyday language and everybody presumably knows what it means, but a moment's reflection reveals that the word eludes ready definition. To say with the dictionary that learning is the acquisition of knowledge or skill does not go very far in helping us say what we mean by "learning."

The basis for this dilemma lies in the fact that learning is an abstraction, a concept, a construct; it is not a thing to which one can point, not an activity that can be defined in terms of observable behavior, like eating, for example. We can say that eating is the process of placing food in one's mouth and swallowing. One can point to a person who is engaged in this activity, and all observers will agree that this person is eating. Now substitute learning in this example. Is it learning when a child looks at a printed page in a book? What would one point to in order to show someone what we mean by learning?

Learning is presumably something that goes on inside a person's head, hence it is not something one can point to; it is a covert process, not an overt action. Furthermore, it is a process of change, and as such can be observed only through the observation of change. One must notice a given behavior that requires skill or knowledge and then record a positive change in that behavior. Under certain circumstances one can afterwards say that the change was due to learning. In other words, learning cannot be observed while it is going on, only after it has taken place.

Learning is not a behavior but a change in behavior; also, it is not a unitary event but a system of interrelated phases. These, as we shall see presently, in turn entail a complex process. When the entire system is subsumed under the label "learning," we are dealing with an abstraction known in science as a hypothetical construct. Hypothetical constructs are useful inventions because they help to organize many observations and facilitate discussion. Research aimed at discovering the relationship of the many variables involved in the construct often serves to advance knowledge.

Yet useful as they are, hypothetical constructs also have their disadvantages. Foremost among these is that careless usage can lead one to view the construct as an explanation. Take, for example, the observation that a boy who, unable to multiply 7 times 7 yesterday today gives the correct answer when presented with the same problem. One might ask why he is able to do today what he was unable to do yesterday and come up with the answer, "Because he has learned this fact." Clearly, nothing has been explained, since "learning" is but a label we use when we observe increase in skill or knowledge.

To explain the observation by the label we apply to it is circular; a pseudo-explanation. This circularity is immediately apparent if one asks the person who has "explained" the improved performance by invoking learning how he knows that learning has taken place. He will have to fall back on the very observation he had sought to explain in the first place.

Problem of Assessment

Learning, as we said earlier, can only be demonstrated by observing a change in behavior that reflects an increase in skill or knowledge "under certain circumstances." What are these circumstances? One is that there was indeed an increase in the ability to solve a given problem or handle a given task. The person must have changed from not knowing to knowing, from inability to ability. To demonstrate such change one must have measures of the person's behavior at two points in time: a record first of the state of inability, then of the state of ability; a pretest and a posttest. Like all measures, this one must be reliable and valid.

Let us assume that as a pretest a child is asked, "How much is 7 times 7?" and he replies with "I don't know." Are we justified in assuming that he does not have the knowledge needed to give the correct answer? Would he be able to give the correct answer if another person asked him at another time or if the question were presented in writing or in a different language? If, for a posttest, one were to ask this child the same question on the following day and he answered, "49," can we be sure that this reflects an increase in knowledge, or has someone, perhaps, just whispered the answer to him? Could it be that the apparent change is the result of an invalid pretest the day before—that the child knew the right answer all the time? For that matter, if this child should again reply that he doesn't know the answer, can one be really certain that he has failed to acquire the necessary knowledge; that no learning has taken place?

The second circumstance that must be present if one is to attribute a change in behavior to learning is that certain events to which one can attribute the increase in knowledge must have taken place between the two points of observation. These certain events are opportunities for the child to acquire the knowledge in question. This usually takes the form of someone engaging in behavior we define as teaching although, particularly in the realm of motor skills, opportunities for engaging in trial and error can also fill this requirement.

We need not here concern ourselves with the often spurious issue of whether a change in skill is due to maturation or to experience. A certain maturational level must have been reached if experience is to result in learning and for any but the most simple motor responses maturation and experience interact in bringing about increments in a child's behavioral repertoire. Not only must a child have reached a certain maturational level if he is to benefit from an effort to teach him something, but the teaching must also be relevant to his current skill level—attained through previous learning—and to his physical condition.

In order to be able to say that learning has or has not taken place, one must thus have a valid measure reflecting ignorance, an opportunity to acquire specific knowledge, and again a valid measure reflecting that knowledge. Since changes in performance may be spurious, such as the apparent changes that are due to unreliable measurements, and since they can be the result of events other than learning, such as changes in motivation, any statement about a person having learned something is an inference of unknown accuracy. What is more, the performance we observe in order to ascertain whether learning has taken place must be performance that is relevant to the skill or knowledge we are interested in.

In the case of motor skill, this does not present much of a problem. If we want to have a child learn to tie his shoelaces, the criterion of his having learned is that he can perform the shoelace-tying act. But if we want to have a child learn to read, what shall be the criterion? Is it enough if the child can look at a sentence and vocalize the words correctly? Is that *reading*? It is clearly possible to do a limited amount of this by simply memorizing the appropriate sounds while listening to someone else reading the words. Reading, after all, involves the ability to extract meaning from the written word; saying the word aloud is not reading. But how does one measure whether a person is able to derive meaning from what he reads?

It now becomes necessary to introduce the construct *comprehension* and to devise ways of making comprehension observable through some kind of performance. We do so by asking questions that can only be answered by a person who has understood the meaning of the written symbols he has decoded; thus we try to arrive at a valid test of comprehension with all the problems of semantics, double meaning, ambiguity, and irrelevance this brings with it.

An Issue in Logic It should be apparent from the above discussion that it is extremely difficult to ascertain whether someone has learned something, particularly where cognitive rather than motor skills are involved. Yet the difficulty is compounded when one seeks to demonstrate that someone has *not* learned after a teaching situation had been inserted between pretest and posttest. Failure to demonstrate a change does not prove that no change has taken place. This touches on a basic problem in logic: How does one demonstrate the non-occurrence of a phenomenon? Science can be used to prove that a phenomenon exists; one can never prove that a phenomenon does not exist.

This is why experimenters phrase their questions in terms of the null hypothesis. They test the proposition that there is no difference between two conditions. Then, when the results show that this is not the case—that the null hypothesis can be rejected—they can conclude that the phenomenon under investigation does indeed exist. In the context of learning, the null hypothesis would state that there is no difference in performance between pretest and posttest. When the difference is then demonstrated, one can conclude that learning has taken place; but when no difference emerges—when the null hypothesis cannot be rejected—the obverse conclusion, that no learning has taken place, is not justified.

Proving that something does not exist or that something did not happen requires that one exhaust all conceivable observations under all conceivable conditions, always leaving the possibility that there is one observation or one condition one has not thought of. In the case of learning, a different combination or type of pre- and posttest might have reflected change; the person may have learned but, for some reason, this is not demonstrable through changes in the performance we are trying to use as a criterion of learning.

We encounter a related problem in logic when we speak of learning disability, for this is presumably a condition where no learning is taking place. How is that to be demonstrated? A child apparently fails to learn under one teaching method. He might conceivably do very well under some other teaching method, possibly a method not yet invented. Is one justified in saying that he "has" a learning disability? The best one can ever do is to say that a child fails to reflect learning through changes in performance under the ordinary teaching methods which have been tried thus far.

We know that children who are presumed to have learning disabilities are able to learn when specialized teaching methods are introduced. Is a learning-disabled child who learns under specialized teaching still a learning-disabled child or simply a child in need of specialized teaching? It should by now be clear that there is no such *thing* as learning disability; that it is a label we apply to children who have special teaching needs, not an immutable entity that somehow exists in its own right. What must be demonstrated, then, is not that a child cannot learn but that he has difficulty learning under circumstances where learning would ordinarily be expected to take place. What are these circumstances?

Expectation and Performance

Circumstances where learning would ordinarily be expected to take place involve the appropriateness of the match between teaching or training efforts and the child's capacity to benefit from them. One must ask whether these efforts are relevant for this particular child in the current condition, taking into account his or her developmental and physical state, ability level, and past learning.

One obviously cannot speak of a learning difficulty if the child has a physical defect such as poor vision which, unknown to the teacher, makes it impossible for him clearly to see the material presented to him. Nor would one designate as a learning disability the problems faced by a child whose teacher expects him to learn a skill for the mastery of which he is several years too young. Again, it is not a learning disability if a mentally retarded child fails to benefit from instructions gauged for a child of average intelligence. Last, one should not speak of learning disability if mastery of material being taught presupposes prior learning which the child had no opportunity to acquire. The acquisition of reading, for example, presupposes that the child has been exposed to and has learned a spoken language; a child who has grown up in an environment that is largely nonverbal or where a different language is used would be expected to experience difficulty decoding written symbols into a language with which he has no familiarity.

In speaking of the appropriateness of the match between teaching efforts and the child's capacity to benefit from them, one places a tremendous responsibility on those who teach. There are great individual differences in the way children learn, and good teaching takes these differences into account. It is all too easy to seek vindication for a teacher's inability to teach a child by saying that the child has a learning difficulty when, in reality, the difficulty is not the child's but the teacher's. Only when a child fails to learn under conditions where other children of his or her age, intelligence, background, and capacity are able to learn should one raise the question of whether such a child might benefit from being called learning-disabled. Such a label would then give him or her access to specialized teaching methods that are not readily available in the regular classroom. As we said earlier, only where a label can benefit a child for administrative or statutory reasons is there any purpose in using a label such as "learning disability."

Expectation-Performance Discrepancy   We spoke of the match between teaching efforts and the child's capacity to benefit from them. It is admittedly difficult to ascertain whether a given mode of instruction is appropriate for a child; it is even more difficult to determine a child's capacity to learn. A learning difficulty represents a discrepancy between what we assume a child to be capable of learning (his or her potential) and what a child is actually learning (his or her achievement) under ordinary classroom conditions. This discrepancy between potential and achievement must be established by estimating what a child should be able to learn and comparing this with what he or she has actually learned.

What is "Learning Potential"? Remembering the problem we had in deciding on a valid measure of what someone has learned, we can now turn to a discussion of the problems involved in measuring a child's learning potential. Since learning can only be observed through changes in performance, potential is impossible to observe because it entails a prediction, testable only in the future. In speaking of learning potential, we are referring to the quality of a child's inherent endowment, of the "equipment" he or she brings to the task of learning. There is no way of measuring this quality at the present time. What we are left with is merely an estimate of a child's academic potential against which we compare the performance we can actually observe. If there is a discrepancy between the expected and the observed, we can speak of a learning disability, the label providing a convenient summary of what we have observed.

The usual mode of estimating a child's learning potential is to analyze his performance on a standard test of intelligence. Level of intelligence is assumed to relate to a child's learning potential. If he has test scores near the average or above average, he is assumed to be able to benefit from ordinary classroom instruction. If he can't, there is a potential-performance discrepancy, hence a learning disability. This would be a valid assumption if intelligence tests measured intellectual potential, but this no test can do. An intelligence test is no more than a measure of performance on tasks where prior learning materially affects how well or how poorly one does. If one has been able to learn many things in the past, one is able to do better on a test of intelligence than if one has learned only a few things. But doing well on such a test also means that one is able to put to use the things one has learned now that they are called for by the test.

In other words, what an intelligence test measures is how much of what a child has learned in the past he or she is able to display at the time of testing. This makes an intelligence test little more than a test of attainment or achievement. When children have learned little in the past, either because nobody taught them or because they had difficulty in learning for some reason, their test scores will reflect this fact. Both their intelligence levels and their achievement levels may be depressed, so that the looked-for discrepancy will not be apparent. If one then concluded that the poor school performance of such children is due to their low intelligence, possible learning disability would be overlooked. Such an unsophisticated use of an intelligence test would cause many children to be written off as "dull" when, in reality, they have a learning disability that might be overcome if appropriate teaching methods were instituted.

A somewhat more sophisticated approach to the use of intelligence tests in the assessment of intellectual potential is the analysis of consistencies and inconsistencies within the child's test performance. Tests of intelligence such as the WISC-R (Wechsler, 1974) call for a variety of performances, ranging from the recall of general information to the assembly of puzzles. Since some of these subtests are less dependent on prior learning than others, a psychologist can attempt to estimate the child's "true potential" by looking for evidence of good performance. Such an estimate, however, is only a guess, particularly since many subunits of the test have relatively low reliability and so-called profile analysis is of rather low validity (Ross, 1959).

In identifying a learning disability, one looks for a discrepancy between intellectual potential and academic achievement, between potential for learning and actual learning. Since there is no measure of learning potential, such identification is quite difficult. It is made even more complicated by the fact, alluded to earlier, that the assessment of learning is fraught with pitfalls. The measures we use to ascertain what a child has learned (achievement tests) are subject to various distortions related to the well-known psychometric problems of reliability and validity. Thus even when a discrepancy between estimated potential and measured achievement can be demonstrated, it does not necessarily mean that the child has a learning disability.

As in other areas of measurement, we must be aware of the existence of two kinds of errors, false positives and false negatives. A normal child might show a discrepancy between expectation and performance because our estimate of his potential is too high or because his performance on tests of achievement is spuriously low. We would be wrong if we called him learning-disabled. Conversely, a learning-disabled child might show no discrepancy between expectation and performance because our estimate of his potential is too low or because his achievement-test performance is spuriously high. We would be wrong if we decided that this child was not learning-disabled.

Another factor to be taken into consideration in a discussion of the assessment of learning disabilities is the general achievement level of the classroom or school in which a particular child is found. As Bateman and Schiefelbusch (1969) have pointed out, a child of average intelligence, placed in a class where the general achievement level and teachers' expectations are unusually high, may seem to be performing quite poorly. Conversely, a child's low performance due to a severe learning disability might go undetected if he has very high capacity but is placed in a low or low average classroom or school. These possible sources of bias must be kept in mind if one seeks to substitute teacher judgments or actual classroom performance for the more formal and standardized achievement tests.

To summarize, the facts that learning cannot be directly observed and learning potential is impossible to measure make an accurate identification of learning disabilities extremely difficult. Children may be identified as having learning disabilities when, in reality, their problem is a function of poor teaching. On the other hand, children with learning disabilities may be overlooked either because their problem is inappropriately ascribed to low intelligence or because, even with their difficulty, they manage to satisfy the low expectations of responsible adults.

Assessment for Intervention

The questions of the assessment and definition of learning disabilities are idle speculations unless their answers point to ways in which the children with whom one is concerned can be helped. One may know that a child encounters difficulty in learning—a fact most teachers can readily observe—and have ruled out such physical causes as impaired vision or hearing. Then the purpose of assessment is neither to find out how little the child has learned nor "why" she is not learning but rather what it takes to help her acquire additional skills and knowledge. Even the question of the child's intelligence-level is secondary, since the task is not to classify a child (and thus to establish an alibi for teaching failure) but to teach the child as much as possible without making assumptions about her ultimate capacity.

When the question is "how does this child learn and how can she best be taught?" the best way of answering it is by teaching her something under controlled conditions, using a variety of teaching formats and comparing their effectiveness. Severson (1972) refers to this as *diagnostic teaching* and reports that this is far more predictive of a child's later school achievement than any existing tests which are purported to identify learning-disabled children.

Diagnostic teaching (Severson, 1972) seeks to establish how much the child knows, how he or she learns new material, and how the varying of aspects of the learning-teaching situation change the effectiveness of learning. By determining the optimal conditions for adequate learning, one obtains important clues for remedial work for which the assessment is merely a means. That is the proper function of assessment for it should never be an end in itself. When a child is tested it should be of direct benefit to the child; all too often, testing has been used to find an excuse for teaching failure by seeking to discover what "is wrong" with the child.

LEARNING DISABILITY—A DEFINITION

So far we have avoided coming to grips with the question of what is meant by the term "learning disability," assuming, for the sake of discussion, that a demonstrable discrepancy between estimated academic potential and actual academic achievement could serve as a working definition. Yet, recognizing the measurement difficulties, we must move beyond that statement, because such a discrepancy can be brought about by many factors. If the problem is ever to be understood, a more circumscribed definition is needed: a definition that excludes problems in learning that are due to deficits in hearing or vision, basic intelligence, impaired psychological adjustment, or limited educational opportunities. We thus arrive at a definition by exclusion, to wit:

> A learning disability is present when a child does not manifest general mental subnormality, does not show an impairment of visual or auditory functions, is not prevented from pursuing educational tasks by unrelated psychological disorders, and is provided with adequate cultural and educational advantages but nonetheless manifests an impairment in academic achievement. . . .

Stripped of those clauses which specify what a learning disability is not, this definition is circular, for it states, in essence, that a learning disability is an inability to learn. It is a reflection on the rudimentary state of knowledge in this field that every definition in current use has its focus on what the condition is not, leaving what it is unspecified and thus ambiguous. Furthermore, when defined in this manner, "learning disability" is a heterogeneous category; progress in this field demands further refinement of the definition and an identification of subcategories.

In the course of the discussion to follow in later chapters, we shall arrive at a suggestion that may serve to narrow the definition of "learning disability." Available research begins to suggest that many learning disabled children share a developmental delay in the ability to sustain selective attention. We shall argue that the relatively slow pace with which these children develop this ability handicaps them in their early learning in school, so that a weakened educational base leads to later academic difficulties. Furthermore, we shall seek to show that other characteristics often attributed to learning-disabled children—such as hyperactivity, perseveration, distractibility, and impulsivity—are derivatives of this problem in selective attention. Anticipating the explication of these points, we can thus add to the definition presented above the clause " . . . that is associated with difficulties in sustaining selective attention."

We assume that this problem in selective attention represents a developmental lag, and it is possible that this is the cause of a great number of learning difficulties. These issues, however, require further research before they can be settled. In the meantime, the qualification we are adding to the definition of "learning disability" reduces the scope of that category to a more homogeneous group of children, and that should further both research and remedial efforts. At the same time, this qualification leaves open the possibility that there may be other children who manifest impaired academic achievement where the problem has its basis in some other phase of the information-processing function we call learning.

A LOOK BACK

At least part of the difficulty in having people agree on a definition of the problems encountered by children we now call learning disabled is due to the history of this area of educational research. A brief look at the historical background and development of this field can help our understanding of some of the controversies which even now are not resolved.

Our story begins in Frankfurt am Main, Germany, shortly after World War I, when Kurt Goldstein studied the aftereffects of brain injuries sustained by German soldiers (Goldstein, 1942). He found that these severely impaired individuals suffered from an inability to deal with abstract concepts, had difficulty in differentiating between a figure and its background, and tended toward a forced responsiveness to stimuli.

The scene now shifts to the early 1940s at Wayne County Training School in Michigan, an institution for the mentally retarded. There, Alfred A. Strauss and Heinz Werner applied Goldstein's ideas in research designed to differentiate between brain-injured and familial mentally retarded children (Werner & Strauss, 1941). One of the methods used in these studies was a marble board on which the child was to reproduce a design presented by the experimenter. Retarded children presumed to be brain-injured did less well on this task than retarded children thought to be without brain damage.

Strauss and Werner had set out to test figure-background problems. But the fact that their method required the child to look at or touch a stimulus (a perceptual act) and to respond with a motor movement soon led them and others to speak of perceptual-motor disturbances as characteristic of brain-injured children. It should be stressed that there was no independent evidence for the presence of brain damage in most of these cases. Perceptual-motor disturbances eventually became the focus of the work of two pioneers in the field we now know as learning disabilities—Newell C. Kephart and William C. Cruickshank—who had worked with Strauss in their earlier years (Hallahan & Cruickshank, 1973).

At first these perceptual-motor theorists concentrated on the study of brain-damaged children, such as those with cerebral palsy. While one needs a very elastic concept to stretch from adults with gunshot wounds to children with birth injuries, the idea that these two groups may have similar problems that are related to their impaired brain functions is at least tenable. It is when notions developed from work with injured soldiers come to be applied to children with no demonstrable brain disorder—groups which have nothing in common but trouble in learning—that things are likely to get a bit out of hand. This is what happened when Kephart turned his attention from the retarded to "the slow learner in the classroom," a phrase he used as the title of his influential book, which was first published in 1960 (Kephart, 1971).

On the assumption that motor skills are essential for perceptual development and that perceptual development precedes conceptual learning, followers of this orientation assert that motor and perceptual processes must be strengthened before one can hope to teach academic subject matter to a "slow learner." Kephart thus advocated various techniques designed to enhance a child's motor and perceptual-motor abilities. Although it has never been demonstrated that perceptual-motor training facilitates the learning of academic subject matter, this approach and variants of it, which have been championed by Ray H. Barsch (1967) and Marianne Frostig (Frostig & Maslow, 1973), continue to have many followers.

Probably because Werner and Strauss had worked with the mentally retarded, whose verbal skills are often quite limited, they paid little attention to the role of language. This important function is still relegated to a minor role in the theorizing of those who stress perceptual-motor development. An interest in language development and how it might relate to the problems of learning-disabled children was brought into the field by Katrina de Hirsch, who was interested in reading problems (de Hirsch, Jansky, & Langford, 1966), and Helmer Myklebust (Johnson & Myklebust, 1967), who had done research on the psychology of the deaf.

Another important contributor to this way of looking at learning-disabled children was Samuel A. Kirk (Kirk & Bateman, 1962), who came to this field after exploring communication problems in retarded children with cerebral palsy and in children whose language development had been impaired by culturally impoverished backgrounds. As we mentioned in the Preface, Kirk suggested the very term "learning disabilities" for the problem we are discussing, but he is probably best remembered as instrumental in the development of the widely used Illinois Test of Psycholinguistic Abilities (ITPA) (Kirk, McCarthy, & Kirk, 1968). This test, it should be noted, was originally developed to assess the communication skills of mentally retarded children. It is not primarily a test of learning disabilities, though that is how it is often applied.

As was pointed out earlier in this chapter, a learning disability is difficult to substantiate because there is no way of testing a child's learning potential. Frustrated by their inability to administer a specific test for learning disability, psychologists and others were quick to adopt instruments—such as the ITPA—whose title promised that it could assess the ability to use language. Though there remains much question as to whether this test does indeed test "psycholinguistic ability"—validity studies are contradictory and inconclusive—its popularity belies its weak psychometric foundation.

What is more, little is known about the relationship of the test scores to a child's learning ability. All too frequently, tests such as the ITPA or Frostig's Developmental Test of Visual Perception (Frostig et al., 1964) are adminstered to children who don't do well in school, and when deficiencies on some aspect of test performance are discovered, efforts are initiated to improve the test performance through various training methods. If and when the child then achieves higher test scores, the methods are viewed as effective, although the child may still be learning as little in the classroom as he or she did when first referred for testing.

The field of learning disabilities is long on theory and short on fact. One of the results of this state of affairs is the circularity involved when one uses the same test to diagnose a problem and validate a treatment method. Some call this "teaching to the test." Another result is the attribution of brain dysfunctions to children for whom there is no evidence to support this other than their difficulty in learning or their poor performance on a psychological test. The continued use of such terms as "minimal brain dysfunction" or "psychoneurological learning disability" is probably a heritage of the historical origins of this field. Yet another result is the indiscriminate assigning of culturally disadvantaged, language-handicapped, undermotivated, actually brain-damaged, or plain unruly children to the category of learning-disabled, which thus becomes so heterogeneous as to be meaningless.

Much of the difficulty with this field would seem to stem from the fact that those who have attempted to contribute to it have used an inductive approach, reasoning from the individual case to the entire group. People have worked with learning-disabled children and then, in their sincere desire to help them, have sat back and speculated about the problem. In so doing they have looked for analogies from the brain-damaged, the mentally retarded, the deaf, or the cerebral palsied, and the results of their efforts have been largely unproductive.

It would seem far more promising to take a deductive approach; to discover empirically based general principles that hold true for the group and to reason from these to the particular case. To know about learning-disabled children, one must study the processes of learning and the learning processes of the kinds of children about whom one is concerned. Nothing less will do.

SUMMARY

The term "learning disability" serves to identify children who experience difficulty in the acquisition of academic subject matter despite the fact that they are of at least normal intelligence and have no demonstrable physical, emotional, or social handicap. Learning-disabled children are not unable to learn, but they need special and individualized help if they are to benefit from the school experience. Because "learning" is a construct that cannot be observed directly and because it is difficult to ascertain how much a child should be capable of learning, the identification of a learning-disabled child is not easy. There is also a logical dilemma in that a learning disability represents an absence of learning, but the absence of something can never be proved. One of the best ways of establishing whether a child has difficulty in learning is to try to teach him or her something under carefully controlled conditions. Such diagnostic teaching not only tells us something about the child's learning ability but also indicates what special teaching methods are needed in order to help the child learn.

Available definitions of learning disability are usually circular—e. g., "a learning-disabled child is a child who is unable to learn"—and they cover a multitude of children with different problems. Anticipating elaboration in later chapters, we suggested that the use of the term "learning disability" be limited to those children whose learning problem is associated with difficulties in sustaining selective attention and we proposed that this difficulty represents a delay in a child's development. A learning disability is thus not an irreversible deficit but a form of intellectual immaturity that calls for a careful matching of teaching methods and academic expectations to the child's current developmental state.

A brief review of the history of the field that we now identify with the label "learning disabilities" revealed that its origins in the study of brain-damaged adults has colored the approach to learning-disabled children for many years. Inductive reasoning about these children—based largely on analogies from the problems of the retarded, the cerebral palsied, and the deaf—has contributed little to advancing the field. It seems time to turn to a deductive approach in which theorizing is based on empirical facts.

Learning Disabilities and Research on Learning

PHASES OF LEARNING

The phenomenon we call learning and to which we attribute observed changes in behavior is not a single event but a series of events, each of which must take place before one can infer that learning has taken place. If a child has difficulty at any one point in this series, this difficulty will manifest itself as a learning problem. Therefore, if we wish to help such a child, we must not only ascertain the point in the series where the trouble occurs but we must also be sure that the help we offer is relevant to his or her difficulty.

A useful analysis of the act of learning has been offered by Gagné (1970), who suggests that each act of learning can be broken down into distinct phases during which a specific process must take place if learning is to occur. The phases and the processes associated with them are shown in Figure 2-1. Their implications for a child with a learning problem are discussed below.

Motivation   Reinforcement theorists hold that learning takes place when a response is followed by a reward. But once an individual has had experience with such a contingency, they say, he or she probably comes to expect that if

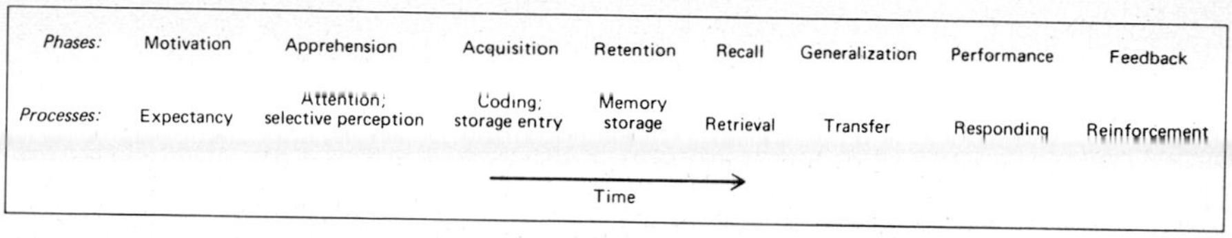

Phases:	Motivation	Apprehension	Acquisition	Retention	Recall	Generalization	Performance	Feedback
Processes:	Expectancy	Attention; selective perception	Coding; storage entry	Memory storage	Retrieval	Transfer	Responding	Reinforcement

Time ⟶

Figure 2-1 The phases and processes of learning. *(After Gagné, 1974.)*

a response is emitted, some desirable event will follow. This *expectancy* will then serve as an incentive that will motivate the learner to approach and stay with the learning task. For most school-age children, this motivation is rather subtle and difficult to identify. They probably work because they have discovered that learning results in greater competence which, in turn, permits mastery of new tasks. In reading, for example, the incentive may well stem from the recognition that knowing how to read permits one to find out interesting things about the world. In this fashion the child will eventually engage in reading "for its own sake," with the fun of reading providing the reward. Other motivations may play a role with other children. Praise from a significant adult, pleasure derived from success, winning in competition, or the satisfaction gained from achievement are among the many complex human motivations.

Because it seems present in one form or another in most children, we often take motivation to learn for granted. Some children, however, and especially those who have experienced repeated failure in school-related tasks, no longer expect that their efforts will lead to reward. It is for these children that anyone seeking to help must first establish motivation by instilling an expectancy of reward. This may have to take the form of offering very concrete reinforcers such as candy, trinkets, or money until such time as some minimal learning has been accomplished, so that ultimately more abstract reinforcements (such as satisfaction with a job well done) can take over.

In the early stages of such a program, the child may need to be rewarded for merely entering the classroom or opening a book, since these are prerequisites for the behavior we ultimately seek to establish. Such issues as behavior shaping, successive approximations of a goal response, token reinforcements, and other ways of helping a child whose difficulty lies in the motivation phase of learning will be discussed in greater detail in Chapter 7.

Apprehension Once a child has been motivated to do the work involved in learning, the next and most crucial phase is that he or she attend to the relevant stimuli of the learning situation. Having opened the book, the child must now selectively attend to the letter or word we hope to teach. There is considerable reason to believe that learning-disabled children have difficulty in maintaining the selective attention necessary for adequate learning—a point which will receive elaborate treatment in Chapter 3. Suffice it to say here that the remedial teacher can help such a child by varying the distinctiveness of the relevant stimuli, by careful instruction in what the child is to look at, by teaching selective attention as a response strategy, and by gradually extending the time during which the child is expected to maintain selective attention. What will not work are such general exhortations as "Pay attention!" or "Watch what you are doing."

Acquisition   Here we come to the core of the learning process, where material presented to the learner must enter his or her cognitive system for "storage" as memory so that it may later be recalled and used. The events in this phase are internal, and we can only draw inferences about them from subsequent observable events. Analogies from information processing by computers can help us conceptualize these inferred events, but—crucial as they are—we know relatively little about them. It is likely that some form of coding facilitates information storage. Therefore such mnemonic devices as attaching labels to pictures to be recalled, grouping lengthy series of digits, or forming associations to isolated or meaningless words seem helpful in many learning situations. A teacher can help a child at this phase by suggesting strategies for coding, but it is difficult to ascertain whether or not a child is having trouble with this phase. This is true partly because it is almost impossible to differentiate problems at the acquisition level from problems in the next two phases.

Retention and Recall   Once a learner has acquired a piece of information, he has to be able to retain this information and to recall it on the appropriate occasion. This is the area of memory, a topic that has been widely studied for many years but about which we still know relatively little. Although a child with a learning problem often appears not to be able to recall something she had presumably learned, it is likely that her problem lies in one of the earlier phases—such as motivation, selective attention, or coding—rather than in a true defect in memory storage or retrieval. This statement is based on the observation that learning-disabled children show no impairment in memory for other than school-related material and that, with help at the earlier phases, they usually have no trouble with later recall. There are, however, certain aids to retention and recall. Overlearning, many repetitions of the learning task beyond the point where immediate recall is achieved, can be shown to facilitate later recall; so can prompts or cues, as when a tutor vocalizes the first sound of a word a reading-disabled child has trouble recognizing.

Generalization   Once a certain piece of information has been acquired, the learner must be able to use it in a variety of different circumstances and situations. Having learned to read a word in the context of one sentence, the child must be able to read this word when it is encountered in a different sentence and in different places. This process of transfer should be a central goal of all teaching, for it is not enough to have a child learn to recall certain facts in the classroom; he must also be able to recall them away from school or in different classes and in different contexts.

Transfer is crucial not only in terms of material to be learned but also in terms of the learning process itself. That is to say that such processes as expectancy, selective attention, and coding, which in themselves are learned behaviors, must be available to the child not only in the structured learning situation but also under other conditions where something is to be learned. Transfer can be enhanced by having the child use a given piece of information or skill under a variety of different conditions during the initial teaching process. Thus a word should be shown in different contexts and written in different sizes and on different surfaces, but the teacher should never lose sight of the fact that the ultimate goal of the endeavor is to have the child read that word with maximum transfer.

Vellutino, Steger, Moyer, Harding, and Niles (1974) addressed themselves to this issue when they urged that remedial help for the learning-disabled child should aim for maximum transfer, pointing out that training in skills that are unrelated to the ultimate goal of what is being taught—such as giving training in discriminating geometric shapes to a child who has difficulty recognizing letters or words—contributes little or nothing to a remedial program. Similarly, if a child has to learn to maintain selective attention, it is better to teach this in the context of reading than to have him engage in exercises involving attention to parts of pictures or form-board puzzles. Educational strategies should directly relate to the skill to be learned, not to some presumed "underlying deficit."

Performance   This is, of course, the only proof we have that learning has taken place, for here the proces reemerges from the learner's internal operations and becomes observable. As was pointed out in the earlier discussion, whether a given act is or is not performed does not necessarily tell us whether learning has taken place; issues of motivation, relevance of the question, and comprehension of the requirement all call for consideration. Some children may have learned and yet be unable to perform, but this is usually related to such issues as fear of failure, anxiety about being evaluated, or the desire to spite a teacher or parent; this is not a matter of learning disability in the sense in which this term is here used.

Feedback   This is another important phase which is frequently overlooked by those who take learning for granted. After the response has been given, the learner must receive not only information as to the adequacy (correctness) of the response—so that future responses can be adapted accordingly—but also confirmation of the expectancy which was established at the beginning of the learning cycle. If this anticipation is not confirmed, the learner will not only not know whether the response was acceptable but also fail to develop an expectancy of reward on future learning trials, with the result that later learning will be impaired. It is very likely that reinforcement which follows a response not only serves a motivational function but also provides important informational feedback—in fact, the informational feedback may well be the more important of the two functions of a reinforcer.

   Assumptions about the learning processes of children with learning disabilities should never be based on observations of the approach used by a
person who has mastered a given task. For example, an accomplished reader
rapidly decodes whole words and series of words and requires neither extrinsic
incentive nor feedback as to accuracy. Reading for such a person is reinforcing "for its own sake," but this is not the case for either the child who is newly
acquiring that skill nor for the youngster who has failed to learn the adequate
use of the skill. The very fact that a child requires remedial help should tell us
that for him or her the usual teaching approach and the usual assumptions
have not worked and that we may have to resort to teaching methods that are
quite different from those which have been found to work for children who do
not have reading problems. Only a careful, individualized analysis of a learning-disabled child's learning process will permit one to decide on an appropriate remedial program. Generalizations from normal acquisition processes or
from the processes of the accomplished performer will usually lead one astray.
   Interest in the many aspects of learning has generated a substantial body
of research, much of which, though often guided by so-called basic research
concerns, has bearing on the applied problems faced by those who wish to
help learning-disabled children. In the following pages we shall review some
recent research on human learning and seek to relate it to the issue of learning
disability.

RESEARCH ON HUMAN LEARNING

In Chapter 1 we spoke of the many conditions which must be satisfied before
one can meaningfully speak of learning. These conditions inevitably pose a
challenge to those wishing to conduct research on human learning. The requirements that one must be certain that the skill to be taught is not already in
the subject's repertoire, that the subject be maturationally ready to learn the
skill, that it can be objectively measured, and that improvements in performance be indeed the result of the exposure to training had, for many decades,
led psychologists to limit their research on learning to work with animals. With
rats, pigeons, or monkeys, these conditions are relatively easy to control.
   When one knows the history of a colony of laboratory rats, one can be
sure that they have had no previous opportunity to learn pressing a bar upon
the appearance of a specified signal; if one deprives them of food and then
makes feeding contingent on the bar press, one can be reasonably certain that
they will emit the behavior once it has been learned. Rats don't pretend not to
know when they really know the answer to 7 times 7; they don't come into the
laboratory having already learned this fact from a previous subject; they don't
(we assume) think about baseball while the experimenter is trying to teach
them a new response. What is more, rats are always in their cages when the
experimenter wishes to use them; they don't stay home with chickenpox, don't
take important tests which prevent them from leaving the classroom, don't go

on vacations in the middle of an experiment. For all of these and other rea-sons, much of our early knowledge about learning came from studies of ani-mals under laboratory conditions.

As long as psychologists limited their studies of learning to work with lower animals, formulations of the results in terms of stimulus-response associ-ations provided a fairly satisfactory theory which gave rise to a great deal of research. In the mid-1940s, some students of learning began to substitute young children for lower animals as subjects in their experiments and the to be expected quickly became obvious: Children don't behave the way animals do in laboratory situations, and any effort to understand children's learning must invoke formulations more complex than the simple stimulus-response view-point.

As child psychologists turned their interest to the study of learning pro-cesses, studying children in their own right and not merely as stand-ins for rats, they began to invoke constructs—such as verbal mediation, selective at-tention, concept formation, rule learning, hypothesis sampling, expectations, and imagery—which seek to come to terms with the possibility that children think or, as the idiom of psychologists would have it, that cognitive processes play an important role in learning. Research on children's learning is thus a relative newcomer to the psychological laboratory and the conceptual tools being used are, in most instances, still in the process of being sharpened. As a result, most of the research deals with relatively simple, artificial, and circum-scribed problems. Answers to questions involving the learning of such com-plex behaviors as language, reading, or arithmetic and children's difficulties with these are therefore, at best, incomplete, tentative, and speculative.

At the conclusion of his thorough and authoritative review of children's learning, Stevenson (1972) comments that "concepts most relevant for educa-tion are the ones that are least explored and least understood" (p. 311). Those whose task it is to educate children and to help children who have difficulty in learning are thus placed in a dilemma. They cannot possibly wait until all answers are in and all problems solved. They must thus base their work either on hunch, tradition, and the pronouncements of self-styled authorities or at-tempt to make what use they can of the limited knowledge available from empirical research and fill in the blanks on the basis of pragmatic experience. As Stevenson put it, "Having partial answers does not mean that we are help-less, nor does it keep us from attempting to put what we do know into practi-cal application; it does mean that we must be aware of the limitations of our knowledge, of where facts leave off and beliefs begin" (1972, p. 1).

We shall, in the following, attempt to glean from the research of child psychologists those facts and principles which seem to have the greatest utility for students of learning disability. In so doing we shall use as a principal reference the excellent monograph by Stevenson (1972), who presents thorough documentation and references. (Many of these, for the sake of smoother exposition, will here be omitted.) A reader seeking a comprehensive discussion of children's learning, together with citations of original research, would be well advised to turn to Stevenson's text. What then can child psychologists tell us?

Developmental Changes and Individual Differences

It is, of course, a truism to state that children and their behavior change over time, that normal children learn more as they get older, and that the things they can learn become more complex. These often demonstrated facts become relevant to a discussion of learning disabilities if one adds to them the further fact that there are large individual differences in the rate at which these developmental changes take place. Normative statements about when "children" are able to use words as substitutes for actions, about when they are able to differentiate between the relevant and the irrelevant in a stimulus situation, or about when they can handle abstract concepts invariably obscure the fact that there are numerous children who are able to do these things earlier and others who will not be able to do them until later.

The existence of individual differences in rates of development is an incontrovertible fact, and this is probably the only phenomenon in psychology about which one can make such a categorical statement. Yet in its educational practices our society behaves as if this fact did not exist. It is a child's chronological age and not his or her developmental status which determines when school entrance is to take place. While allowances are made for the extremely "slow," the bulk of the school-age population is expected to progress at a more or less uniform rate. A child with a subtly different rate of development is likely to be handicapped in such a system. This will be discussed in greater detail as we turn to the development of selective attention, the retardation of which may well be a core problem in the development of learning disabilities.

Reinforcer Effectiveness Another unwarranted assumption which overlooks the fact of individual differences is that all children are reinforced by the same experiences. A teacher's smile or praise or attention, a certain score on a homework paper, or a given grade on a report card are supposed to mean to the child what they mean to the teacher. It has often been demonstrated that behavior that is reinforced will tend to be repeated, and it is true that behavior is (among other things) a function of its consequences; but research also tells us that what is a positive consequence to one may be a neutral or negative consequence to another. The effectiveness of a reinforcer is a function of the age, background, and condition of the child as well as of the nature of the task involved, the timing of the reinforcer, and the nature of the stimulus intended as a reinforcer. This is, of course, why the best definition of a reinforcer is the somewhat circular statement that a stimulus (event) is a reinforcer if it strengthens the behavior which it followed. That is to say, before one can assume that a presumed reward is indeed a reinforcer, one had better test its effectiveness.

Testing the effectiveness of a reinforcer is a relatively simple matter provided one is willing to maintain a record of a child's behavior over a period of time. First one identifies the response one wishes to strengthen, such as the act of completing a short and simple task, and the consequence one assumes to be reinforcing for the child, such as a smile and the words, "Good job!" It is important that both the response and the consequence be concretely and objectivly defined, because the next step is to make a note every time these do or do not take place. It is far easier to maintain an objective record of the number of tasks completed than of such inferred events as "making an effort" or "trying hard." Before long, a conscientiously kept record should permit one to make a statement about the proportion of times the child completed an assigned task and of the regularity with which the consequence was presented. If the proportion fails to reflect an improvement in performance or shows a decline despite the consistent use of the consequences, it is fairly safe to assume that the smile and the words "Good job!" do not operate as effective reinforcers.

One of the factors which influence the effectiveness of reinforcers appears to be the child's previous experience with a given class of potentially reinforcing events. These experiences seem to result in expectations about whether reinforcement will or will not be forthcoming. That is, a child who has repeatedly encountered nonreinforcement in the past is less likely to learn under conditions of reinforcement than the child who has been used to being regularly reinforced for behavior his or her environment deemed correct. Similarly, expectations of success or failure based on past experiences in similar situations will influence a child's performance—especially under conditions where reinforcement is irregular, that is, under a schedule of partial reinforcement. In most school situations reinforcement is delivered on a partial (and often very sparse) schedule. Therefore children with limited experience with reinforcement and low expectations of success are operating under a handicap compared to those whose environment has taught them that their responses are frequently correct and that correct responses are usually followed by reward. These differences in environments tend to be correlated with social class, and they may serve as a partial explanation for the higher frequency of academic difficulties among lower-class children compared to those from economically more favored families.

Some information on the effectiveness of the so-called social reinforcers, such as praise, is also becoming available from controlled laboratory research. Just as one can become satiated with food and therefore seek to avoid getting more to eat, so can one be satiated with social reinforcement. When praise is heaped on a child in a learning situation, its effectiveness may be reduced. This would suggest that praise statements should be varied and emitted frequently, but not on every occasion.

Research also confirms for us that an adult's effectiveness as agent of social reinforcement is heightened if he is enthusiastic, involved, and responsive to the child. If a child has had earlier positive experiences with an adult, she will later respond more readily to this person's reinforcements. On the other hand (and here research results are counterintuitive), the effectiveness of social reinforcement is increased if it is delivered by an unexpected source, such as an unpopular or disliked peer, a younger or an older child. Conceivably, praise coming from an unexpected source draws attention to itself and thus becomes more potent. For classroom application we might conclude that pairing children for peer tutoring should not necessarily be based on sociometric closeness.

Last, we find research results which tell us that between the ages of 4 and 7, reinforcer effectiveness is greater if adult and child are of opposite sex. Thus for kindergarten and first grade, we should have male teachers working with girls and female teachers working with boys if we want to maximize reinforcer effectiveness. This, of course, is but one of many reasons why we should have more male teachers in preschool and elementary classes.

Learning about Relationships

Much of what a child must learn can be viewed as a form of discrimination learning, that is, learning to tell things apart. Similar stimuli often demand different responses. Telling mother from father, edibles from nonedibles, own toy from playmate's toy, own house from neighbor's house, "b" from "d," and "pat" from "tap" all require discriminations. These examples involve only two stimuli; more complicated discriminations are required when three or more similar stimuli are presented. Telling the door to one's apartment from six similar doors on the same hallway or knowing one's coat when it hangs on a rack with twenty other coats are tasks most young children must master; usually they accomplish this with relative ease.

Discrimination Learning Psychologists have studied discrimination learning for many years and they have shown that lower animals can learn to make fairly complex discriminations under carefully arranged conditions. To investigate this with a simple two-choice discrimination (say between a circle and a triangle), one stimulus is defined as "correct" and the subject receives confirmation when it is picked. In the case of animals, this usually takes the form of a bit of food; with children, it may be a trinket or simply a verbal statement from the experimenter, such as "Right!" Learning is demonstrated when incorrect choices are replaced by more and more correct choices; the discrimination can be said to have been learned when the subject makes few if any errors.

The circle and triangle stimuli in this example will, of course, vary from presentation to presentation along such dimensions as position (right or left), size, brightness, color, or perspective; an adult in such a simple discrimination learning situation will quickly discover that one of the two objects, no matter how shown, is always the "correct" one. To do this, the person will probably say to himself something like, "It is the round one," if the circle has repeatedly been found to be correct. This use of words—or thoughts, if one prefers— helps the person make the discrimination. The words mediate between stimulus and response, and this is the process psychologists call *verbal mediation*.

There has been a great deal of research on various aspects of verbal mediation; from the standpoint of our interest in learning problems, a few of the results are highly suggestive of potential applications. One of these is that the production of labels for the objects to be discriminated will usually aid in making them more distinctive; discrimination learning thus becomes easier. Note the word "usually," for whether labeling will facilitate learning depends on the age of the child and on the complexity of the discrimination problem. It is apparently not sufficient that a child know the name of an object or has been taught a label for it; he or she must also develop the skill to use the label as a mediator.

On simple discrimination tasks, most children are able to use verbal mediation by about age 6; some will have reached that stage earlier, some will take longer. A child may be able to say, "My house is the one with the blue door" and yet not find his way home. Research in discrimination learning suggests such a child may be acquiring the ability to use verbal mediation a little later. Becoming exasperated with him, calling him stupid, or punishing him will do nothing to speed up this development. What may help, however, is to make the discrimination one of concrete relationships instead of abstract knowledge. Showing the child the two or more similar doors and having him walk to the correct one is a more productive learning experience than sitting down and asking him to tell the color of the right door.

There is, incidentally, another research result from child psychology laboratories that is relevant to the foregoing example. Given a choice between form and color, children until about age 4 tend to prefer color. Hence for young children, discriminations could be enhanced by using a distinctive color scheme, as on coat hooks, for example. After age 4, many begin to prefer form; but through kindergarten, some will retain the color preference. If one truly wished to individualize children's preprimary grade experience, one should find who prefers color and who prefers form and use teaching aids in terms of these individual differences.

Paired-Associate Learning   The role of words in assisting in coping with a task has also been studied in connection with paired-associate learning, that is, learning what goes with what. Basically, a paired-associate learning problem involves the presentation of a word or picture together with or immediately followed by a second word or picture. The person is required to learn to associate the two stimuli. Since the two stimuli have no logical relationship to one another, this is essentially a rote learning task, quite similar to much of the rote learning found in school and real-life situations. Learning to name letters or to read combinations of letters (CAT = "cat"), memorizing multiplication facts ($7 \times 7 = 49$), or even learning to associate names to faces of people can be construed as paired-associate learning. Indeed, the facility with which a child is able to learn paired associates in a laboratory experiment has been found to be a sensitive measure of learning ability and a good predictor of school achievement. Thus, Stevenson, Friedrichs, and Simpson (1970) found that the rate at which children learned paired associates at grade 4 correlated between 0.33 and 0.40 with achievement test scores when they were in grade 7.

The relationship between paired-associate learning and school achievement was also demonstrated in a study by Otto (1961), who compared paired-associate performance of good, average, and poor readers of average intelligence in grades 2, 4, and 6. His task required the association of geometric figures with three-letter nonsense syllables. For example, the children had to learn to say "wuc" when shown a triangle, "yad" when shown a star, and "gox" when shown a square. This means, essentially, that the children were to learn new names for familar shapes. The results showed that good readers learned more quickly than average and average more quickly than poor readers. Also the older children did better than the younger children. The performance of the poor readers can thus be viewed as immature in the sense that they performed in a manner similar to that of younger children. Another finding from this study touches on the question whether poor memory plays a role in poor reading. Otto reports that once the associations had been mastered, retention upon subsequent retesting was good for all children, regardless of reading level. The poor readers were slow in learning to associate the visual symbol to the right "word," but they did not have a poor memory for the verbal label once they had learned it.

Is there a way of improving paired-associate learning? Stevenson (1972) concluded from his review of several studies in this area that, after the age of 4 or 5, children seemed able to benefit in their paired-associate learning if they were given the opportunity to learn a verbal or pictorial mediating link between the original stimulus and the required response. Paired-associate learning, both in the laboratory and in the classroom, is often a task with little meaning—a task that requires rote learning. In the laboratory, the subject may have to learn to say "yad" when he sees a star; in the classroom the child has to learn to say the sound "a" when shown the shape of the letter "a." By providing the learner with a mediating link, we can add meaning to an otherwise rote task, thus making it easier.

This approach can be used in teaching letter-sound combinations. If a child has difficulty learning to associate the correct sound to the letter "a," one might first help him or her to associate "a" with "apple" by superimposing the letter on a picture of the fruit. The picture can later be made gradually less and less prominent and ultimately removed altogether; a process called "fading out." During the early acquisition phase, one would ask the child, "What goes with that letter?" Upon receiving the answer "Apple," one would inquire, "What sound does 'apple' start with?" "Apple" is thus used as the mediating link between the grapheme and the phoneme which, to a young child learning to read, are really no more than nonsense stimuli.

Research into paired-associate learning may thus provide us with valuable cues for teaching some aspects of reading more efficiently. This is not to say that reading is simply a matter of paired-associate learning for, as Gibson (1970) has persuasively pointed out, a stimulus-response approach may be quite incapable of elucidating not only the process of reading but much of behavioral development. Her suggestion for a perceptual approach to learning and development thus bears mention in this context.

Perceptual Learning

When an experimenter or a teacher presents a child with a stimulus and the child emits a response, two parts of this event are subject to observation: the stimulus and the response. This observability has led most students of learning to focus on the input and output ends of the learning process, and the so-called S-R approach to learning has become the dominant formulation among American psychologists. Reinforcement theorists, in particular, have concentrated their interest on the response and its consequences and—as we shall see—a highly productive and potent technology of behavior has resulted from the formulation that behavior is a function of its consequences. In all this, the stimulus end of the S-R sequence has generally been taken for granted. The experimenter or teacher can, after all, see or hear the stimulus presented to the child; therefore the stimulus, being observable, is a known and thus objective aspect of the learning situation. Or is it? The adult looks at a drawing of a stick figure and sees a man; he shows this to a preschool child and assumes that the child, looking at the drawing sees the same thing. But suppose the child looks only at the circle depicting the head or at the cross made by the intersection of body and arms; what is then the stimulus?

Gibson (1969) makes the point, supported by a great deal of research, that the perceptions of children differ markedly from the perceptions of adults. One of the most important aspects of development, she asserts, involves the child's gradual acquisition of the ability to see the world in terms of the distinctive and invariant features that permit adults to make "sense" of their environment. This is the essence of perceptual learning. In the course of explicating principles of perceptual learning, Gibson makes a number of statements which diverge rather drastically from S-R formulations of learning and which are important to consider if one seeks a comprehensive understaning of children's learning and learning difficulties.

Reduction of Uncertainty Reinforcement theorists maintain that learning takes place when a response is followed by an event in the environment that has or has acquired a positive quality from the learner's point of view. In the most primitive form, positive consequences (such as food) reduce tissue needs; events (such as a human smile) which are often associated with such "primary reinforcers" are said to acquire reinforcement potential. Ultimately the child can obtain reinforcement from such self-produced statements as"I have solved this problem correctly." This happens because doing things correctly has, in the past, been paired with smiles which, in turn, had originally occurred in connection with eating while hungry.

Gibson (1969) takes issue with this formulation. To her, motivation and reinforcement for cognitive learning do not have their origin in external events but are the result of the child's need for reduction of uncertainty. Behavior which reduces uncertainty is behavior that is learned; in Gibson's view, this behavior takes the form of perceptual strategies that discover structure in the environment and by so doing reduce the need for time-consuming information processing, thus increasing cognitive economy (Gibson, 1970, p. 143).

From this point of view, the environmental consequence which S-R theorists consider to be the reinforcing event that promotes learning derives its importance not from its archaic relation to food but from its information value. That is, the external reinforcer—be it a sound, a light, a candy, or the word "good"—tells the child that the response he has just made, hence the strategy he used in arriving at it, was correct. It is more an information feedback, more a confirmation than a reinforcement in the traditional sense of that term. It may well be that a material reinforcer has a dual function, particularly in situations—such as laboratory learning experiments—where the task is uninteresting and the work repetitious. Here the delivery of trinkets or food might constitute not only information feedback but also an incentive that makes continued effort worth the child's while. At any rate, Gibson's formulation does not require that the traditional formulation of reinforcement be totally discarded. In terms of the theory of perception developed by Gibson (1970), the need to get information from the environment is as strong and as necessary for survival as the need to get food. In obtaining needed information, the child or person is not passively receiving what the environment presents in the form of sensory stimulation but is engaged in an active process of search and exploration. Gibson views this search as being directed by the task and by intrinsic motives, that is by motives "built into" the organism as a safeguard of its survival. Once a search for information is initiated in a particular situation, it is terminated not by consequences provided by the environment that are either rewarding or punishing but by the internal reduction of uncertainty. In that sense, perception is a self-regulated, active, and adaptive process.

With the need to reduce uncertainty an intrinsic aspect of the child's makeup, what then is it that is learned in the course of development? To Gibson it is perceptual differentiation; an increasing specificity of what one responds to among the stimuli in the environment. Initially, what is perceived is relatively undifferentiated. In the course of development, however, as the result of both physical maturation and experience, the child learns to filter the sensory input and to abstract from it the information needed in order to make an adaptive response. Fine differences in stimulus dimensions come to be perceived, and invariant relations, structure, patterns, and relations will be recognized as distinctive features which furnish information about the environment.

Distinctive Features   The central notion of differentiation of critical features as the basis of learning can be illustrated by some examples. When one first meets identical twins, they "look alike," and if dressed alike, will be almost impossible to tell apart. Yet, as one gets to know the twins better, one soon finds that one can tell them apart. What has one learned? One has learned to detect subtle differences not previously noticed, such as a chipped tooth or a slight scar that differentiates one twin from the other. These are the distinctive features one has learned to recognize and on the basis of which one can now make the adaptive response of calling each by his or her name. Incidentally, the names, or labels, will not aid in the discrimination unless the label is one that calls attention to the distictive feature. That is, if one twin were to be called "She with the chipped tooth," telling them apart would be quickly learned. People will frequently resort to just such a private labeling, a verbal mediation which aids discrimination learning.

Sometimes parents of twins try to make it easier for people to tell the children apart, and they do this by having them wear a *distinctive* bow or other article of clothing. Learning is now facilitated by the addition of this distinctive feature (provided the twins don't make a sport of confusing their public by exchanging the bows in an unpredictable fashion). People's confusion will stem from the fact that they are unable to rely on invariant aspects of the stimulus situation, for the search for invariant aspects is one way of attaining perceptual structure.

Perceptual learning can thus be enhanced if those wishing to help the learner provide and highlight distinctive features, make sure that these features are consistent, and call the learner's attention to these features through informative verbal labels. Once a differentiation has been learned, further learning can be facilitated if new sets of stimuli to be discriminated have distinctive features with which the learner is already familiar. A new set of twins, to return to our example, would be more readily individualized if they too could be distinguished by an article of clothing.

These principles do, of course, have applicability in the academic realm. Gibson (1970), in a discussion of the development of reading, points out that instructional programs should seek to promote efficient strategies of perceptual search and detection of invariant order. Learning to read involves the differentiation of graphic symbols as a step that precedes the decoding of letter into sound and sound into word. From the child's point of view, the letters are all very similar; he or she must learn that each differs from all the others in one or more distinctive ways. The child must learn to focus attentively on the distinctive features; features the letters have in common with other letters are irrelevant and must be ignored or screened out if adaptive responses are to be produced with a minimum of effort. Gibson (1965) had earlier pointed out that a child learning to read learns how letters differ. She stressed that teaching should emphasize features which are distinctive for specific letters by presenting similar letters in contrast pairs and by giving the child repeated exposure to varied examples. The letters "b" and "d" should thus be presented together so as to emphasize their difference; this should be repeated many times with the letters appearing in different places, different sizes, and different colors.

Redundant Features   In differentiating between aspects of the environment, the distinctive feature is the most crucial. Stimuli have many features; some are relevant but redundant in that they merely repeat information already carried by the distinctive features. Others are irrelevant since they contribute nothing that would aid the discrimination. In the course of learning to cope with the world, we must learn to ignore irrelevant information. If each twin has freckles on the nose, attending to the freckles does not help us in telling them apart. Even relevant but redundant features may serve to delay the discrimination since, for maximum efficiency, it is necessary to notice only one distinctive feature. If, in addition to wearing distinctive hair ribbons, the twins also wore different necklaces, we would learn nothing extra by attending to both ribbons and jewelry. Once we have learned to look for the ribbon, the problem of telling the twins apart is solved; this learning is expedited if the ribbon is the only feature that distinguishes the pair.

In trying to help someone make a discrimination between two similar stimuli, it is better to highlight one distinctive feature than to add redundant features. There have been attempts to facilitate the acquisition of reading by presenting easily confused letters in different colors. The color is redundant information. The letters "p" and "q," for example, differ distinctively in the relative position of line to circle; making one blue and the other red adds no new information. In fact, since calling a splotch of red "q" would be maladaptive, this device may well be counterproductive. While the colors are relevant to the discrimination in the special situation of the classroom, they are irrelevant in the outside world. More helpful than coloring letters in hopes of aiding discrimination would be to add redundancy to the feature of shape, but to do this in an additional sense modality. One way of doing this is to present the letters in question as three-dimensional forms. The information about the relative position of line to circle is now repeated not only in another visual dimension but also through additional sensory input when the child is given the opportunity to handle the forms.

Another way of applying the notion of distinctive features in teaching discriminations between similar stimuli is to isolate the distinctive features and to present these alone until the discrimination is learned. The redundant features can then be added gradually so that, by the time the stimuli are presented in their complex totality, the discrimination is well established. Schreibman (1975) conducted a study in which she taught autistic children to discriminate between similar stimuli by using a gradual fading procedure. The task was to discriminate between two stimuli where one was the positive instance (S+) and the other the negative instance (S−). In such a situation, the child might be required to press a button upon the appearance of S+ and not to press to S−, to name S + by one label and S by another, or to press a button on the left to S+ and a button on the right to S−. Whatever the response mode chosen, the task is to tell the two stimuli apart and to respond differentially to them. The analogy to two similar letters is obvious.

As shown in Figure 2-2 Schreibman isolated the distinctive cue (the diag-

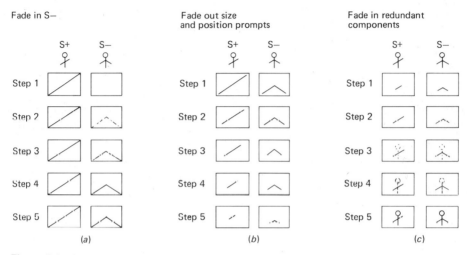

Figure 2-2 Fading sequence for visual discrimination. *(Redrawn from Schreibman, 1972.)*

onal versus the angle), first presented the diagonal (S+) alone, and gradually introduced the angle (S−). Note that the distinctive feature was exaggerated along the dimensions of position and size by having heavily drawn lines take up the entire display area. Once the discrimination was established, the exaggerated size and position features were gradually faded out. By the time Step 5 of this phase is reached, the child makes consistently correct responses. In fact, the procedure assures that there are very few errors in the course of the learning. Last, the redundant components of the total stimuli are faded in so that, by the time Step 5 of the third phase is reached, the child can make a discrimination he was unable to learn when the experimenter had merely pointed at the correct stimulus, hoping gradually to withdraw the pointing prompt.

The theory of perceptual learning developed by Gibson (1969) is an important contribution to the understanding of child development and the study of learning. In its stimulus-response approach to learning, American psychology has tended to overemphasize the response end of the sequence; Gibson contributes to a redressing of the balance by stressing that it may be more important to ask what a person perceives than how he responds. As we shall see, valuable advances have been made possible in the field of child psychology by a focus on the response and its environmental consequences; it is most likely that we shall see further advances if we now expand our interests and include in our considerations questions about the internal (perceptual) consequences of the stimulus. It is useful to know how to teach a child a certain response by manipulating the consequences; it is at least as useful to know how to teach a child to detect and attend to relevant cues, how to differentiate between the relevant and the irrelevant, how to use strategies for processing information, and how to generate, test, reject, and accept hypotheses about his environment.

Incidental Learning

Perception is an internal cognitive process that cannot be observed; its operation can only be studied by observing responses made in the presence of observable stimuli. In this manner it is possible to discover that a person is perceiving not only the most distinctive feature of a stimulus but also one or more incidental features. Assume that we are attempting to teach a young child to sort geometric shapes into separate piles and that each shape is presented on a background of a different color. The star is always on blue, the cross always on red, and so forth. The colors are redundant but irrelevant, and all we ask the child to do is sort the shapes into their respective places. After this has been accomplished, we put the cards away and ask, "What color went with the star?" By answering this question correctly, the child demonstrates incidental learning. We can then infer that the child perceived (attended to) not only the shape but also the color of the background. Studies devoted to incidental learning are thus essentially studies of perception or, as we shall see, of selective attention.

In laboratory studies of incidental learning, the number of redundant features can be systematically varied. One way of doing this is by using the method of discrimination-learning experiments. Here, the child is asked to discriminate between two or three stimuli, one of which the experimenter deems "correct," so that the child is reinforced when that stimulus is chosen. The stimuli can vary along several dimensions such as size, shape, color, or position. Usually one of these dimensions is relevant to the choice. For example, the triangular shape may always be correct regardless of its size, color, or position. Here, shape would be the relevant dimension and the others would be irrelevant. One or more of these irrelevant dimensions can be made relevant by arranging to lock it to (make it redundant with) the relevant dimension. If triangular shape was correct, one might decide to have the triangular shape always appear in the color red, with red never appearing in any other combination. Now the problem can still be solved by selecting the triangle and ignoring the red, but the selection of red would also lead to a correct response. In a test for incidental learning, the experimenter tries to find out whether a child has learned to respond only to the shape dimension or whether he or she has also (incidentally) learned that attending to color is another adaptive basis for responding.

Developmental Trends Using a variant of the method just described, Crane and Ross (1967) compared the incidental learning of second graders and sixth-graders in order to ascertain whether there are developmental trends in this mode of attending. The procedure used in this study required the children to discriminate between two colors and two forms in order to earn a reward. We shall not go into the number of refinements of this experiment but merely highlight the point most central to this discussion.

Let us trace the experience of one representative boy who participated in this study. He first learned to discriminate on the basis of color; blue was always correct and yellow always incorrect regardless of the shape in which these colors were presented. After the boy had learned that, the experimenter made shape redundant with color; the previously irrelevant dimension was now consistently presented with the relevant dimension. Thus the blue circle was the correct stimulus, the yellow cross the incorrect stimulus; and these shapes always appeared in these colors.

These pairs were now presented for 40 trials so as to make sure that the boy had really learned the discrimination. The experimenter refers to this as "overtraining." Now the crucial test is introduced. Without warning, a new series of trials is begun in which (for the boy in the example) color becomes irrelevant and only form serves as the basis for making correct discriminations. Circle is always correct regardless of its color; cross always incorrect even if it is blue. This "switching of signals" is called an "extradimensional shift" with respect to the original learning, and it serves as a test of whether the other dimension (shape in this case) had acquired relevance for the child during the second phase and whether he is able to use this learning after the shift in dimension.

The number of errors a child makes after the shift, before he "catches on" that the definition of what is correct has been switched, becomes the measure of incidental learning in a study of this sort. The results showed that the younger children had derived benefit from the incidental pairing of color and form, while the older children appeared to have concentrated on the aspect that had been relevant during original learning, managing to ignore the other dimension, and thus showing less incidental learning. From this and other studies which showed similar age differences for incidental learning, Crane and Ross (1967) concluded that once relevant aspects of a task have been identified, older children focus their attention on relevant stimuli to the exclusion of other material while younger children continue to attend to a wide range of stimuli in the situation even after relevant aspects have been detected. What does this mean?

Since the world is full of irrelevant stimuli, an individual would be flooded with useless information if he attended to everything. To be effective and efficient in the processing of information, the mature individual must be able to differentiate between the relevant and the irrelevant and learn to ignore the irrelevant. In that sense, the older, eleven-year-old children in the Crane and

Ross (1967) study were more efficient in the second phase, although the demands of the experiment were such that they were handicapped in the third phase. Sometimes, as when we are asked to testify as witnesses to an automobile accident, what had seemed irrelevant at first later becomes relevant, and the good observer is the one with a lot of incidental learning. On the whole, however, incidental learning does not pay off and may, in fact, be a handicap. In reading, for example, the task demands that many irrelevant aspects of the stimulus situation, such as brightness and size of letters, be ignored and attention concentrated on the shape, order, and spacing of the letter combinations. There is some evidence (Siegel, 1968) that, on a laboratory test of incidental learning, children who are better readers show less incidental learning than average readers. Advanced readers may thus be perceiving like somewhat older children; that is, they may be developmentally advanced with respect to that perceptual function. Could it be that poor readers are developmentally retarded and, like younger children, show more incidental learning? This question begs for investigation.

On the basis of a review of studies on incidental learning, Stevenson (1972) concludes that this phenomenon follows a developmental trend. Incidental learning increases from preschool age to about age 11 and then undergoes a decline. There thus seems to be a curvilinear relationship between incidental learning and age. The youngest children, with little experience in differentiating between relevant and irrelevant aspects of a situation, may be concentrating on one or the other, possibly based on the salience of the stimulus. Where both color and form are present, for example, children under age 4 will generally attend to color (whether or not it is relevant). After age 4, the preference tends to be for form. At any rate, a pronounced stimulus preference would result in low incidental learning. As the child gets older, he or she appears to attend to many aspects of a stimulus situation, as suggested by the increase in incidental learning. This increase continues and seems to reach a high point around age 10 or 11, after which it declines, ultimately falling to the level of the mature adult. Compared to the ten-year-old, the adult is far less observant when it comes to aspects of the situation the adult considers incidental.

Selective Attention

Objectively, the stimulus is the same for the ten-year-old child and his thirty-year-old father; they differ in the focus of their attention. Older children and adults select from the stimulus array those aspects which, for them, are relevant; that is, they select those which have, in the past, led most directly to the needed information or reinforcement. An older child or adult can attend to the incidental cue if the situation demands it, but incidental cues are disregarded when the task can be more efficiently handled without attending to them. (In ordinary reading we disregard defects in a type face; but when the task is structured as proofreading, such irrelevancies become the main focus of our attention.)

Developmental Trends   Developmental changes in incidental learning can be construed as reflecting developmental changes in the ability selectively to attend to relevant aspects of the environment; for the more refined one's selective attention, the less will be one's incidental learning, and vice versa. In a review entitled "The Development of Attention in Children," Hagen and Hale (1973) summarize a series of studies by Hagen and his associates. They conclude from these that the ability to attend selectively to the critical features of a stimulus and to ignore the unessential aspects is an integral part of the learning process (p. 117). They see children's ability to exercise selective attention as improving with age until early adolescence, by which time they are capable of using or not using selective attention depending on which strategy is likely to maximize their performance. Selective attention is thus an acquired skill which a person utilizes in situations where it increases efficiency of coping with a task. The likelihood that the development of this skill is, at least in part, dependent on environmental factors is suggested by findings from studies with retarded children and children in semiliterate rural settings whose selective attention develops more slowly and is less efficient than that of school children of normal intelligence.

Selective attention, as discussed by Hagen and Hale (1973), is assessed through incidental learning tasks. The experimenter designates certain features of the stimulus as relevant for task performance while others are defined as incidental. After a number of training trials, performance on the central task is assessed and compared with recall of information about the incidental stimuli. High selective attention is inferred if the subject has acquired little information about the incidental stimuli. On the other hand, if a lot of incidental learning has taken place, selective attention is thought to be low.

Between the ages of 7 and 13 (the age groups studied by Hale and his colleagues), central task performance improves while incidental learning remains relatively constant, so that the proportion of incidental learning declines. If selective attention were not operating, incidental learning should also improve with increasing age and improving learning capacity. It is not that there is less incidental learning at age 13 than at age 7 but that there is relatively less in relation to the improved central learning. If instructions or reinforcement contingencies are changed so as to put a premium on incidental learning, the older child is able to attend less selectively and gain improved performance on the incidental stimuli which have now been made relevant.

These findings suggest that selective attention involves a holding back, an inhibition of attention to the incidental cues. This inhibition is, however, subject to being lifted, for disinhibition can take place when this serves the purpose of effective task performance. If this formulation is correct, children with poor ability to apply selective attention would have to learn to inhibit attention to irrelevant stimulus dimensions. In trying to help such a child attend to that part of the stimulus we have identified as the distinctive feature, we must do more than give the admonition, "Pay attention." We should be specific and say, "Attend to this; ignore that."

SUMMARY

There are a number of phases in the phenomenon we call learning where difficulties can arise. Borrowing from an analysis offered by Gagné (1970), we discussed the following phases: motivation, apprehension, acquisition, retention, recall, generalization, performance, and feedback. This paved the way for a review of some recent research on human learning.

Psychologists have studied learning for many decades, but they have only recently turned their attention to the learning of children. As a result, their methods are still relatively primitive and the focus of their concern is often on rather circumscribed problems. Concepts of particular relevance to education remain among the least explored and least understood. Because those who are concerned with helping learning-disabled children can't wait until all the facts are established, we must do the best we can with the research-based knowledge that is now available.

Research studies tell us that there are vast individual differences, based partly on the child's age and background, in what will serve as an effective reinforcer. Not every child will respond favorably to praise, and too much praise can weaken its effectiveness. Learning to tell things apart (discrimination learning) can be made easier through the use of verbal labels, and children below age 4 seem to find it easier to discriminate objects by their color than by their shape. Learning what goes with what (paired-associate learning) is also facilitated through the use of verbal labels, so that a child who has trouble learning to attach the right sound to a given letter may be helped if he is first taught to associate a word with the letter.

We have learned from research that the perceptions of children differ markedly from the perceptions of adults. From this we conclude that the teaching of reading should not be based on the approach of a skilled adult reader. Students of perceptual development tell us that reduction of uncertainty is an important human motive that leads to the learning of perceptual differentiation. The child learns to differentiate among the many stimuli in the environment on the basis of distinctive features; those wishing to help a child with this learning would do well to enhance the distinctive features of such similar stimuli as the letters of the alphabet. One distinctive feature is sufficient for an initial discrimination. Features that are redundant may only confuse a child; these can be introduced later, after the discrimination has been learned.

Studies of incidental learning permit one to ascertain which aspect of a stimulus complex is the focus of the learner's attention. Incidental learning follows a developmental trend, increasing from preschool age to about age 11 and then declining. A large amount of incidental learning suggests that the child has been attending to many aspects of the stimulus complex, some central to the task at hand and some peripheral. Conversely, when incidental learning is limited, it suggests that selective attention has taken place—that the child has selectively attended to the central aspects of the situation. Studies on incidental learning thus show that selective attention follows a developmental course, that older children are more capable than younger children of using this perceptual mode. These considerations lead us to the more detailed exploration of attention and its relation to learning which will occupy us in the next chapter.

Attention and Learning

WHAT IS ATTENTION?

Words that are used in everyday language tend to cause confusion when they are also used in a technical sense by psychologists. "Attention" is such a word. Everybody presumes to know what attention is. But do they? When a teacher notices a student looking out of the window, the teacher may say, "Johnny, pay attention!" When the child then redirects his glance at teacher or chalkboard, the teacher may be satisfied that Johnny is now "paying attention"—but is he? How can the teacher know whether the child is paying attention? Certainly not from the direction of his glance. The only way of ascertaining whether the child is attending to the task is to ask a question which can be answered only by a child who has paid attention. If the child answers correctly, he has paid attention—or has he? Could it be that he answered the question correctly because he had learned the answer at an earlier time and was looking out the window, paying attention to something other than the teacher's words, because he was bored? Or if the child is unable to answer the teacher's probing question correctly, does this mean that he was not paying attention, or might it be that he had been paying attention (even though looking out the window) but failed to comprehend what was being said?

This dilemma is of course the result of the fact that attention is a covert event which cannot be monitored directly. As such, it is very much like the covert process of learning, which also has no direct referent and can be measured only by observing changes in performance. Unfortunately, attention is a prerequisite of learning; if both are measured by a change in performance, it is impossible to ascertain whether a lack of change in performance is due to defective attention, defective learning, or a combination of both. This problem of logical circularity has been discussed by Mostofsky (1970) but, as we shall see, there are ways out of this dilemma, and Mostofsky himself saw enough merit in the concept of attention to edit an entire book on the topic.

Before one can undertake a detailed discussion of attention and its relationship to learning and learning disabilities, one has to attempt to reduce some of the semantic confusion which besets this field. What we loosely call attention has a variety of aspects and may thus mean different things to different people. Berlyne (1970) made an important contribution to this field by helping differentiate the multiple meanings of "attention" and by suggesting that the technical use of the word be limited to only one aspect, that of selective attention.

Different Aspects of Attention

A person's environment is replete with potential stimuli, and another multitude of potential stimuli constantly emanate from within the body. They are *potential* stimuli because these events do not become functional stimuli until they become the occasion for a response. Whether a given event becomes the occasion for a response depends on the state of the person—whether he is awake or asleep, alert or listless, vigilant or oblivious. In other words, it depends on his state of attention. How much attention a person is giving to the stimulus field as a whole is what Berlyne (1970) identified as the *intensive* aspects of attention. Among these one can differentiate among *arousal, attentiveness,* and *degree of concentration.*

Arousal is generally associated with a psychophysiological dimension which can be construed along the continuum sleep to wakefulness. A variety of physiological changes have been shown to correlate with arousal and to coincide with responses to stimuli. Among these physiological changes are those in heart rate and in the electrical activity of the brain. Attentiveness, though closely related to arousal, identifies the person's momentary readiness to receive and process stimuli. Berlyne (1970) points out that attentiveness and arousal are not identical, since in extreme states of arousal (such as in high excitement) a person's attentiveness to minute variations in external stimuli is often very low. Degree of concentration, the third of the intensive aspects of attention, has to do with whether a person attends to a wide or a narrow range of incoming stimuli.

With what he calls intensive aspects, Berlyne (1970) thus identifies how much attention a person is giving to the stimulus field as a whole. How this amount of attention is distributed among the various elements of the stimulus field he would determine by studying the *selective* aspects of attention. Here he distinguishes three processes: *exploratory behavior, abstraction,* and *selective attention.*

"Exploratory behavior" is the term Berlyne (1970) assigns to the physical act of bringing a sense organ in contact with a source of stimulation. Moving the eyes in the direction of a visual event so that this event can be perceived as a stimulus is an example of exploratory behavior. That this act is not the same as attention is appreciated in the difference between looking and seeing or between hearing and listening. The teacher who assumes that the child who is looking at the chalkboard is attending to the lesson may be greatly mistaken!

Abstraction is another form of selecting from the stimulus field, and it is well to identify it separately. Here we are dealing with the process by which a person perceives (attends to) one dimension of a stimulus object while ignoring other dimensions of the same object. In differentiating between a blue and a white poker chip, we are ignoring the shape, size, weight, and texture— characteristics that are the same in these objects—responding only to the property of color. We abstract color out of a number of other, equally available but irrelevant stimulus properties.

Selective Attention

All the processes mentioned thus far have, at one time or another, been discussed under the heading of "attention," a term Berlyne (1970) urges us to reserve for the process he labels *selective attention.* At any given moment a person receives stimuli from a great many sources and through every sense receptor. Visual, auditory, tactual, kinesthetic, and proprioceptive nerve fibers are constantly carrying impulses which often demand conflicting, mutually incompatible responses. Behavioral chaos would result if the person were not equipped with the capacity to select among these impulses and to attend— hence to respond—to one or a limited number at a time. Selective attention is thus a highly adaptive capacity, and a defect in using this capacity can be readily seen as a considerable handicap.

Even within the concept of selective attention, Berlyne (1970) suggests that one consider three further processes. From the standpoint of an understanding of learning disabilities, these take on considerable importance. They are *attention in learning, attention in remembering,* and *attention in performance.* As discussed by Berlyne (1960, 1970) these three aspects of selective attention operate at temporally separated points.

Attention in learning addresses itself to the issue of stimulus selection at the point when a stimulus-response association is being established. In even the simplest learning situation, a person is receiving several stimuli simultaneously, but the response is learned to only one or a limited number of these.

Take, for example, a child who is supposed to learn to say the sound "bee" to the visual presentation of the letter "b" written on a chalkboard. Among the stimuli being received by this child at that moment is not solely the shape of the letter but also the teacher's pointing finger, the teacher's voice modeling the sound, extraneous noises in the room, other things written on the board, the color of the board, the color and size of the letter, a pinching shoe, a growling stomach, the pressures of the seat, and so forth. From among all these, the child must select the shape of the letter and the teacher's voice in order to learn the appropriate response. This remarkable feat requires selective attention; if selective attention is not functioning properly, the child will have trouble learning the lesson.

Such trouble can, of course, take many forms. Should the child overselectively attend only to the teacher's voice, excluding the written letter from attention, the teacher would hear the child say "bee" and assume that the child had learned. The error of this assumption will emerge only later when, in the absence of the auditory stimulus, the visual stimulus fails to control the appropriate response. It is also conceivable that a child attends to the teacher's pointing finger and the sound of her voice, thus learning to vocalize "bee" to the stimulus of a teacher's pointing finger. Then again, if the child were to overselect and attend only to the circular portion of the letter "b" he or she would, at later testing, emit the response "bee" when presented with the stimulus of the letter "d," thus manifesting the frequently encountered b-d reversal of beginning and retarded readers. The tendency to overselect a limited aspect of a stimulus complex has variously been referred to as stimulus overselectivity (Lovaas & Schreibman, 1971), overselective responding (Schreibman & Lovaas, 1973), overselective attention (Newsom & Lovaas, 1973), and selective responding (Lovaas, Schreibman, Koegel, & Rehm, 1971). Later in this chapter we shall suggest that the phenomenon might best be viewed as as instance of *overexclusive attention*.

To summarize Berlyne's (1970) notion of attention in learning, it addresses the problem posed by this question: When a child is receiving a number of stimuli under conditions conducive to learning, which stimuli will become most strongly associated with the response? *Attention in remembering* is very closely related to this issue, for Berlyne phrases this problem in the question: "When a human being is receiving a number of stimuli, which stimuli will he be able to remember on future occasions?" (1970, p. 31). Except for the fact that what we call learning usually takes place under explicitly structured conditions (while things we may later remember are sometimes encountered incidentally and not necessarily under conditions conducive to learning), there seems too little difference between attention in learning and attention in remembering to warrant more than passing mention of the latter.

The third process entailing selective attention does, however, represent a distinctly different issue and one that has a number of implications for the study of learning disabilities. Whether a child has learned something we have been trying to teach can only be ascertained by observing this child's later performance, as we have repeatedly pointed out. We have also said that if this later performance falls short of our expectations, this need not necessarily be an indication that learning had not taken place. Berlyne's (1970) issue of *attention in performance* is addressed to one aspect of this problem. A girl will have learned many responses to many stimuli by the time we place her in a situation where a specific performance is expected. In that situation, many stimuli will be present and competing for control over her behavior. Berlyne (1960) has used the term "conflict" to denote the situation where mutually incompatible responses are being instigated at the same time, and attention in performance is one of the means by which the individual copes with this conflict. She selectively directs attention to one or a limited number of stimuli and emits the response which she has learned.

To return to the simplistic example of the child learning to associate the correct sound to the letter "b," assume that learning has taken place and that the child "knows" the sound this letter symbolizes. Now the letter is presented with the question, "What sound does this make?" These are the stimuli to which the child is supposed to attend. But what if he attends instead to any of a dozen other stimuli that are also present at this moment and says "It's the siren of a fire engine" or "My stomach is growling" or "My uncle has a new puppy" or "My shoe is pinching me" or "Tomorrow is Friday"? Each of these is an appropriate response to current stimuli, some external, some internal, but he has failed to attend to the stimulus the teacher considers appropriate. This failure of attention in performance may well lead someone to say that this child is *distractible;* stimuli irrelevant from the teacher's point of view distract him from the stimulus he is expected to select as the focus of his attention. If the child should also be responding to various stimuli emanating from inside his body—the pinching shoe, the growling stomach, the pressure on his lower back—the observed motor responses may well lead someone to say that this child is *hyperactive.*

The frequently reported distractibility and hyperactivity of children with learning disabilities may thus be no more than another aspect of their problem with selective attention, a problem which, from the present point of view, may well be the source of the learning disability. If this formulation is correct, Berlyne's (1960) analysis of attention may offer hints as to how one might enhance the selective attention of a child who has difficulty in this area.

As Berlyne (1960) has pointed out, there are certain conditions under which the presentation of a stimulus will result in heightened attention. These conditions—Berlyne calls them "collative variables"—are novelty, complexity, uncertainty, surprisingness, conflict, and change. It can be demonstrated, for example, that the dimension of complexity relates to attention in a predictable manner. Using the length of time a subject directs his gaze at a visual stimulus as his measure of attention, Day (1966) has shown that a stimulus of low complexity, defined by the number of angles of a random geometric shape,

will hold attention for less long than a similar stimulus of higher complexity
provided complexity does not increase beyond a definable level. In other
words, a subject will show preference for a moderate level of complexity;
stimuli that are too complex and stimuli that are too simple appear to draw
reduced attention. Competent teachers of young children have long known
that their pupils can be kept interested (attentive) for a longer time if a task is
presented in novel, surprising, and changing ways. Those charged with teaching children with learning disabilities might well adopt a similar approach.
Words to be read or arithmetic problems to be solved can be presented in the
form of games, such as lotto, in order to introduce novelty. An element of
surprise can be brought about by hiding words in different parts of the classroom or by covering them with brown wrapping paper and sending the children on a scavenger hunt. Only the teacher's imagination limits the changes
which can be introduced in the presentation of tasks and material.

ATTENTION AND LEARNING DISABILITIES

Attention is a necessary but not a sufficient condition for learning. That is to
say that learning does not take place unless the individual is attending to the
material to be learned, but when learning takes place, processes other than
attention must also be involved. Thus, if a child is exposed to a situation that
is presumed to be conducive to learning and if, following this, he can perform
something he had not been able to do before, we can say with considerable
assurance that this child had been attending to the task. On the other hand, if
the child fails to acquire a new skill under these circumstances, it is impossible
to say whether this failure to learn was due to a failure to attend. This dilemma
makes it impossible to study attention in the context of a learning experiment,
for in such an experiment attention is confounded with such other variables as
aptitude, memory, and recall.

Measures of Attention

One way of resolving this problem is to use a task that does not require—
because it is already in the person's response repertoire—the acquisition of a
new skill. Such a task might be a simple motor response, like pushing a button,
to be made on the occasion of the appearance of a readily discriminable
stimulus. Once a person has been instructed to perform this task, a failure in
emitting the response to the appearance of the stimulus can be viewed with a
good deal of confidence as due to a failure to attend (provided one is dealing
with a cooperative, motivated subject). Such a simple stimulus-response arrangement permits a variety of modifications designed to study attention under different conditions. Thus, one can require one response to one stimulus
("push button on left when red light comes on") and a different response to
another stimulus ("push button at right when bell rings"). By the simultaneous
presentation of several stimuli, each controlling a different and mutually ex-
clusive response, it is possible to ascertain to which stimulus a person is selec-

tively attending. Vande Voort, Senf, and Benton (1972) used such a method in studying retarded readers and demonstrated a deficit which implicated attentional processes.

A variation of the above procedure is found in dichotic listening experiments where the participant hears two different auditory messages presented simultaneously, one to the left, the other to the right ear, by means of stereophonic headphones. Dichotic listening has been used in various experiments as a means of assessing a subject's attention (e. g., Broadbent & Gregory, 1964). Satz, Radin, and Ross (1971) employed this method with children who had reading difficulties and reported that these children had trouble recalling stimuli thus presented.

The use of simple motor responses, which require no skill in order to be emitted, or the presentation of stimuli in a fashion with which a subject could not have had any previous experience permits one to study attentional processes relatively unconfounded by learning. Furthermore, when one analyzes data from groups of subjects, one can use statistical methods of control for such artifacts as individual differences in fatigue, motivation, and response speed. Still, conclusions drawn about attention on the basis of observations of overt behavior remain no more than inferences about an unobservable process. A means of further reducing the hazards posed by such inferences is provided by the recording of physiological changes which accompany changes in external stimuli, and presumably reflect a subject's reactions to such stimuli.

It has been demonstrated, for example, that changes in the electrical potential of the brain coincide with psychologically induced states of expectancy and anticipation, in other words, with aspects of attention (e. g., Haider, 1970). Sroufe (1971) has shown that heart-rate deceleration occurs reliably with the presentation of such attention-related events as novel or surprising stimuli, changes in a stimulus, or a new stimulus. Cardiac slowing is also known to occur when a person anticipates the appearance of a stimulus, engages in visual fixation, or scans a stationary or moving object. Finally, slowing in heart rate has been found to correlate with reaction time and with accuracy of perceptual judgment. Inasmuch as all these situations involve attentional processes, deceleration of heart rate would seem to be an appropriate index of attention.

Because physiological measures, such as those of heart rate, require impressive equipment and reflect events taking place inside the body, there is a tendency to assume that these measures are more basic than such behavioral measures as reaction time of a motor response. This is not the case. If one interprets a line drawn by a pen on a moving paper tape as reflecting heart rate changes and attributes these changes to attention, one is still making inferences and not observing attention. Attention remains an inferred construct; it has not been made observable. However, if an investigator observes changes in reaction time and correlated changes in heart rate, both of which are attributable to changes in attention, he has reason to be more confident about the validity of his inference than when he uses only one such measure. Such correlations between independent measures that relate to the same construct permit one to assert the validity of the construct; it is a statement of construct validity.

Studies of Attention

A study which combined a behavioral measure (reaction time) and a physiological measure (heart rate) in an attempt to explore the relationship between attention, learning disability, and the effect of a stimulant drug was conducted by Sroufe, Sonies, West, and Wright (1973). In this experiment, a child was told to listen for a warning tone which would indicate that a light was to appear a short time later. When he saw the light, the child was to press a switch "as quickly as possible." Heart rate was monitored while the child was engaged in this task. In a fixed-foreperiod reaction-time situation such as this, a participant is set to attend to the anticipated stimulus during the interval between the warning sound and the appearance of the light. The more attentive the subject, the shorter should be the reaction time; long reaction times are attributed to a failure to attend, a deficit in attentiveness.

Sroufe, Sonies, West, and Wright (1973) studied the performance of 38 boys between the ages of 7 and 10. Twenty-one of these were children with normal intelligence who had been referred to a clinic because of attention and learning difficulties. The other 17 were boys who attended public school and who had no history of similar difficulties; they served as the control group. Both groups were individually tested on the reaction-time task; the learning-disabled (clinic) children were given a second testing session six weeks later. For this second session, 10 of the boys were given a stimulant drug (methylphenidate, or Ritalin) which is often prescribed for learning-disabled children; the other 11 were given a similar appearing but inert substance, called a placebo.

During the first session, the mean cardiac deceleration for the clinic children was significantly less than for the control children. When the clinic children were under the influence of the drug, their heart-rate deceleration increased significantly, both in comparison to the first session and vis-à-vis the placebo control group. In addition, the mean reaction time of the drug group was significantly faster than that of the placebo control group. It thus appears that there is a relationship between learning disability and aspects of attention and that the drug Ritalin (methylphenidate) modifies a child's ability to attend. That, of course, does not mean that the drug has an effect on the child's learning disability, a point we shall have occasion to elaborate in a later chapter.

In an earlier reaction-time experiment, Sroufe (1971) had demonstrated developmental changes in cardiac-rate deceleration from which he had concluded that the ability to maintain attention improves with age. The task used in this experiment also involved the presentation of a warning signal (tone), followed by a five-second fixed foreperiod and the appearance of a stimulus light. Sroufe (1971) reports a highly significant linear relationship between age and anticipatory heart-rate deceleration. Using six-, eight-, and ten-year old boys as subjects, he found that the older children showed greater and more reliable decelerations than the younger. The cardiac-deceleration scores correlated with median response latencies and there was a statistically significant relationship between age and response latency, that is, with the speed with which the children pressed the switch after onset of the stimulus light.

We have here highlighted only that aspect of the Sroufe (1971) study which resulted in clear-cut and significant findings. It should be pointed out that the results did not hold when the foreperiod was extended to 10 seconds or when the task was not a simple reaction-time task but a more complex problem involving the differentiation between three stimulus conditions which seemed to require the learning of a response strategy in addition to a focusing of attention. Nonetheless, the statistically significant results from this study do permit the important conclusion that "The obtained age differences in heart-rate deceleration suggest developmental improvement in [the ability to maintain attention]" (Sroufe, 1971, p. 342).

ATTENTION AS A DEVELOPMENTAL PHENOMENON

The studies just discussed (and others yet to be presented) point to a relationship between learning disability and problems in sustaining attention. The latter, in turn, appears to be an ability that improves in the course of a child's development. A child who develops the ability to sustain selective attention more slowly than others would thus be handicapped in learning and may well be identified as a learning-disabled child.

Developmental Studies

Further support for the formulation that the ability to apply selective attention develops with increasing age and is a major problem for learning-disabled children because they develop this ability more slowly than others comes from the work of Rourke and his associates (Rourke & Czudner, 1972; Czudner & Rourke, 1972). Their research method involves a simple reaction-time task with a warning signal before the onset of the stimulus.

The child is asked to depress a telegraph key, and this activates the warning signal. Following an experimenter-determined "preparatory interval" (foreperiod), the reaction-time stimulus appears; at that point the child is to lift the finger from the key as quickly as possible. The preparatory interval varied in length. In one procedure the interval remained the same for 15 trials before an interval of another length was introduced. In another procedure, the various intervals were presented in a random manner but with each appearing on 15 occasions. Under these conditions, a child's reaction time can be viewed as a measure of the ability to maintain a state of readiness to respond in the face of competing stimuli and hence to sustain selective attention. Only by focusing attention on the anticipated source of the stimulus can a child respond as quickly as possible when the stimulus appears. Slowing in reaction time would seem to reflect that the subject's attention was reduced in intensity or directed elsewhere.

The children studied by Rourke and Czudner (1972; Czudner & Rourke, 1972) were described as suffering from relatively mild, chronic cerebral dysfunction. While nothing is said about the learning ability of these children, their description is very similar to that of groups of children usually identified as having learning disabilities. The results of these studies can thus be deemed relevant to the present discussion.

There were two age groups. The *young group* had an average age of 7 years, 7 months, the *old group* had an average age of 11 years, 7 months. There were 10 boys and 2 girls in each of these clinic groups, and their performance was compared with that of children in a control group of 24 unimpaired children who had been matched with the experimental group on sex, mean age, and intelligence test scores.

These children participated in two studies, one (Rourke & Czudner, 1972) using the auditory modality, where warning signal and reaction-time stimulus were a high-pitched and a low-pitched sound respectively, and another (Czudner & Rourke, 1972) using the visual modality and relying on a white light and a red light in place of the sounds. Since the results of these two studies are virtually identical, they can be discussed together.

The children in the young clinic group displayed a significantly poorer performance than those in the other three groups. They had the longest mean reaction times and experienced particular difficulty in the procedure where the length of the preparatory interval varied in random fashion. In the visual study, all the young clinic children performed worse then any of the young normal controls; in the auditory study, the same was true for all but two subjects. While the clinic children in the young group thus displayed rather gross difficulties with attention, this was not the case for the older clinic group. Their performance did not differ from that of their normal controls.

Before we discuss the implications of these results, it is well to note the relationship between the length of the preparatory interval and reaction time. In the procedure where the interval remained the same for a series of consecutive trials, the investigators found a direct relationship between mean reaction time and length of interval; the longer the interval, the longer the reaction time. This was true for all groups—young and old, clinic and normal. As might be expected, it is more difficult to sustain attention the longer the period during which this is required. As Czudner and Rourke (1972) pointed out, environmental distractions and many other factors may have made it more difficult to maintain a state of readiness to respond as the length of the preparatory interval increased. This is consistent with the results of Sroufe (1971), who was unable to obtain consistent cardiac deceleration with a 10-second interval; although with a 5-second interval he had been able to show clear and age-related changes.

While it is a long way from a laboratory reaction-time experiment to classroom application, one might here risk a generalization. The finding that children perform better when preparatory intervals are brief and their length is predictable might tell us that a teacher working with young, learning-disabled children would do well to maintain a regular pace and to keep as short as possible the period between an alerting statement ("Now look at the blackboard") and the presentation of teaching material.

At this point we can return to the finding of the two Rourke studies which relates to developmental changes. The performance of the young clinic children was significantly less adequate than the performance of the young normal, old normal, and old clinic children. In other words, the slow reaction time manifests itself in young children with "relatively mild, chronic cerebral dysfunction" (Czudner & Rourke, 1971, p. 518) but not with such children when they are, on the average, four years older. Why should this be so? Rourke and Czudner (1972) offer the rather remarkable contention that such brain-damaged children as they had studied "may adapt to and/or recover from the deficit(s) involved in the inability to develop and maintain a state of readiness to respond" (p. 377). Instead of speculating about a highly unlikely "recovery from brain damage" or an adaptation to the deficit, it would seem to us far more parsimonious to propose that the capacity for selective attention is a developmental phenomenon that improves with age, especially during the childhood years.

Developmental trends toward greater selectivity of attention were also shown in a study by Pick, Christy, and Frankel (1972). They compared the performance of second-graders and sixth-graders on a task which required the child to indicate whether two objects were the same or different. The objects were colored wooden animals which varied in shape, color, and size. The relevant dimension on which comparisons were to be made was either shape or color. In one experimental condition, the child was told before the presentation of a pair whether the comparison was to be made on the basis of shape or on the basis of color; in the other condition, this information was not made available until after a pair of objects had been briefly exposed to the child's view.

The time it took a child to indicate (by pressing one or two buttons) whether or not the objects were the same was used as a measure of selective attention. This was based on the reasoning that the greater a child's capacity for selective attention, the more quickly he could focus on the relevant dimension of the stimulus. The two conditions of stimulus presentation (preinformed and postinformed) permitted an assessment of the degree to which selective attention contributed to the child's responses, since it would serve to facilitate responding more in the preinformed than in the postinformed condition. That is to say, being told what to look for before a stimulus is shown should help a child quickly to focus on (selectively attend to) the relevant dimension. When that information is not given until after the presentation of the stimuli, the relevant and irrelevant dimensions must be "sorted out" from memory, and this should take much longer.

From the standpoint of the developmental hypothesis investigated by Pick, Christy, and Frankel (1972), the relative difference in reaction times of the two age groups for the two conditions was of critical interest. As was to be expected, the reaction times of the older children were faster than those of the younger children in both conditions of the experiment, but the difference between reaction times in the two conditions was greater for the sixth-graders than for the second-graders. In other words, the older children were better able to take advantage of the prior knowledge about what aspects were relevant and irrelevant. The experimenters concluded from their findings that the ability to focus visual attention exclusively on relevant information improves with age and that the acquisition of this skill "may characterize developmental changes in selective attention" (p. 173).

Learning Disabilities as a Developmental Lag in Selective Attention

If the capacity for selective attention develops with age, as the studies we have cited suggest, there is no reason to assume that all children develop this capacity at the same time. In fact, there is every reason to assume that there are individual differences in the development of this capacity and that some children will develop it more slowly than others. When these children are then placed in a situation—be it a laboratory study of reaction time or a classroom setting requiring the acquisition of reading   where the ability to use and sustain selective attention is a requirement for success, these children can be expected to fail.

Developmental principles suggest that children who acquire a given skill more slowly than others will ultimately catch up, given time to let developmental processes take their course. As the work of Rourke and Czudner (1972) suggests, as children who had earlier failed a given task get older, they too develop the capacity for attention; if they are then examined, their performance is not discriminable from that of other children their age. Yet this is true only on the laboratory reaction-time tasks, not in the case of school performance, where the learning-disabled children continue to perform below grade level. Why should this be if earlier retardation in selective attention is no longer a problem?

The answer, of course, lies in the phrase "given time to let developmental processes take their course." As time passes, all sorts of events take place. Not only does a child's maturation run its course but the child is exposed to a multitude of experiences, some of which will enhance, some hinder development. Reaction time to simple laboratory perception tasks may well be relatively unaffected by these experiences, so that it can reflect the developmental "catching up" in selective attention. Academic performance is another matter. Here the child's problem persists, not because of continuing difficulties with selective attention but because successful performance in seventh grade presupposes learning in earlier grades, and this such a child did not acquire.

In addition, many years of failure in early years will have left their mark in terms of the child's perception of himself, his response to the school situation, his self-confidence, and the expectations of others regarding his potential. The fact that learning will continue to be a problem for such a child is not surprising, and this reasoning demands that he will need much help if he is to overcome the cumulative effects of his early developmental lag.

A series of studies conducted by Senf (1969) implicated the development of attention as the critical variable differentiating the performances of normal and learning-disabled children. The tasks involved the auditory presentation of three digits simultaneous with the visual presentation of a different set of three digits. Thus, for example, the written number 3 might appear in a display aperture at the same time as the word "seven" is heard from a loudspeaker. This would be followed by two more audiovisual pairs of digits. The child was then asked to repeat all six numbers. All subjects preferred to recall the digits in two modality sets, that is, repeating all auditory numbers before all visual numbers or vice versa. The 48 children with reading difficulties, who were the learning-disabled group, tended to repeat the auditory set before the visual set, while the normal readers showed no modality preference. When instructed to do so, the normal readers were able to repeat the digits in the audiovisual pairs in which they had been presented, but the retarded readers found this mixing of modalities very difficult. Their difficulty did not seem to be due to inadequate memory but to a problem in the "storing" process or in mixing modalities for recall.

Senf (1969) mentions some anecdotal data which suggest that the normal control children tried to translate the visual into auditory stimuli by saying the visual stimulus while listening to the auditory one. It may be that the retarded readers were unable to use this strategy. It should be pointed out that "saying" a visual stimulus is in fact the same as reading it, and the fact that retarded readers have difficulty with this is not too surprising. On the other hand, these children were able to perceive the visual stimuli; their recall of the visually presented series was unimpaired.

One of the most dramatic findings of the Senf (1969) research was that for the normal children, the ability to order both auditory and visual material into pairs *developed with age;* i. e., that this ability is a developmental phenomenon. This ability had apparently not developed in the learning-disabled children, suggesting again that theirs is a developmental retardation. Senf (1969) writes,

> . . . the ability to recode and reorganize may be critical. The ability to recode the information into comparable units to facilitate pairing, hypothesized not to occur in the learning-disordered group, suggests improvement within the memory system, specifically within its organizational capabilities. The possibility that reorga-

nization is increasingly occurring implies that the subject is gaining greater control over the organization of his perceptions and consequently over how he remembers things. The implication is that he is increasingly less dominated by the saliency of specific stimulus dimensions, for example, the modality dimension, but instead can exercise more control over his attention (p. 25).

In discussing why the learning-disabled children showed a marked preference for the auditory over the visual stimuli in the order in which the series were recalled, Senf (1969) speculates that these children might have developed negative reactions to visual stimuli as a result of their repeated failure experiences with reading material. This is a distinct possibility deserving further investigation, and it should remind us that any deficiency found in learning-disabled children may be the consequence and not the cause of their problem.

Many years of working with learning-disabled children in special class settings led Koppitz (1971) to suspect that many of these children had been developmentally immature when they had to enter school and that their difficulties were the result of academic demands for which they were not yet ready. She urged that allowance be made for individual differences in the rate of maturation, development, and progress and recommends early screening as a way of preventing many learning problems. While Koppitz (1971) emphasizes perceptual-motor integration as the capacity in which learning-disabled children seem retarded, her description of the behavior of many of the children in her study suggests that perceptual-motor integration and selective attention are closely related if not actually the same.

Follow-up Studies   Further support for the formulation that learning disabilities are related to a delayed development in the capacity for selective attention can be found in the relatively few follow-up studies conducted with learning-disabled children. Thus, Weiss, Minde, Douglas, Werry and Nemeth (1971) studied 64 severely handicapped children described as displaying the "minimal brain dysfunction syndrome." All these children were hyperactive. When they were restudied as adolescents five years later, the hyperactivity had diminished, although their social, personal, and learning problems persisted. If one perceives hyperactivity as an overresponding to task-irrelevant stimuli because of an inadequate capacity to maintain selective attention, these findings suggest that the reduction in hyperactivity reflects the eventual development of this capacity. As pointed out earlier, the social, personal, and academic problems children acquire in their earlier years (while their delayed development of attention is a handicap for them) will continue to persist unless they receive specific psychological and scholastic help.

The acceptability of the argument just offered hinges on the validity of the connection between hyperactivity and selective attention, inasmuch as Weiss et al. (1971) did not study selective attention as such. A related study conducted by the same research group (Sykes, Douglas, Weiss, & Minde, 1971) must thus be cited in order to strengthen this argument. Again working with children described as hyperactive, these investigators used a task which required the detection of significant stimuli and hence maintenance of attention. Compared with a matched normal control group, the performance of the hyperactive children was impaired; they detected fewer of the significant stimuli and made more incorrect responses to nonsignificant stimuli. It would therefore appear that children described as hyperactive do indeed have problems in maintaining attention to relevant stimuli. This relationship is usually explained in terms of hyperactivity causing an inability to attend. What is here proposed is that the causal relationship might be the reverse: The inability to attend results in hyperactive behavior, because attention to extraneous (task-irrelevant) stimuli leads to extraneous responses.

The study by Sykes et al. (1971) had been designed to assess the effect of the drug methylphenidate (Ritalin), and it revealed that the performance of hyperactive children who were given this drug showed significant improvement. The effect of this drug has often been viewed as "paradoxical" in that it is a psychic energizer that "slows down" hyperactive children. This apparent paradox disappears if one views the drug as increasing ("energizing") the child's capacity to maintain selective attention, for with that his responses to extraneous stimuli (i. e., his hyperactivity) should diminish. We shall return to the topic of drugs and their effect on learning in a later chapter. Meanwhile, it is worth pointing out that the use of chemicals is not the only way by which attention can be increased. As Martin and Powers (1967) and Wagner and Guyer (1971), among others, have pointed out, it is possible to increase the attention of children by the systematic use of operant conditioning methods.

Another follow-up study which offers some suggestive support for the formulation of learning disabilities as delayed development of selective attention is the work of Rourke, Orr, and Ridgley (1973). Unlike the investigators cited thus far, this research group defines the target population as retarded readers who were given a large battery of neuropsychological tests on two separate occasions three years apart. While the focus was thus on learning disability and not on hyperactivity, there was no explicit effort to study attention. Instead, the measure of particular relevance to the present discussion was what Rourke et al. (1973) have elsewhere called a complex psychomotor task. This involved the Grooved Pegboard Test, where the child is given the task of fitting keyhole-shaped pegs into similarly shaped holes as quickly as possible. This obviously calls for a number of skills and functions, but an important one among these would seem to be the ability to sustain attention. At any rate, performance on this test was associated with reading ability for the retarded readers *at the younger age levels* but not later on. As Rourke, Orr, and Ridgley (1973) conclude, whatever functions are measured by this test, they seem to become less important as a factor in reading ability with advancing years.

Future research, aimed specifically at the hypothesis here advanced, will have to determine its adequacy in explaining learning disabilities and particularly those involving reading. However, the limited data currently available can be interpreted as supporting the notion that delayed development in the capacity to sustain selective attention creates a handicap for children who are required to learn such academic subject matter as reading. The difficulties they encounter have effects on these children's personal and social adjustment so that, when their capacity for selective attention finally develops, they are not only significantly retarded in reading but also markedly impaired in terms of these psychosocial attributes. An early matching of attention capacity to academic method and demands would thus go a long way in preventing problems and helping children learn.

DEVELOPMENT OF SELECTIVE ATTENTION

A discussion of incidental learning (Chapter 2) had shown that this phenomenon undergoes developmental changes. That is, very young children display little incidental learning, children around age 10 display a lot, and older children, beginning around age 12 or 13, again display little. We suggested that selective attention is, in some respects, the obverse of incidental learning. Where selective attention is high, incidental learning would be low, and vice versa. In the present chapter we examined selective attention in greater detail and concluded that it also undergoes developmental changes, just as its proposed relationship to incidental learning would demand. At this point we shall attempt a formulation of the development of selective attention and its relationship to learning disabilities, prefaced with the caveat that this represents a speculation and that it should not be assumed to be based on established fact.

Overexclusive Attention The very young child is "captured" by one aspect of the stimulus and attends to it to the relative exclusion of all others. Even in infancy, however, one can find individual differences, with some infants consistently orienting toward a single feature while others alternate their gaze between single and multiple features (Salapatek & Kessen, 1973). One would need a long-term follow-up study in order to determine whether these individual differences can predict later visual behavior. At any rate, we know from eye-movement studies that until about age 6, children generally restrict their scanning of a stimulus to a limited area (Vurpillot, 1968). Incidental learning would be low during these early years and one might categorize the child's behavior as showing *overexclusive attention.*

If a child were to continue to function in this manner after an age when most other children develop beyond this perceptual mode, he or she would be handicapped in any task where adaptive behavior demands more thorough exploration of the stimulus complex. It may be that one finds an extreme of this developmental retardation in children with early infantile autism and a milder form in certain reading disabilities. This might have been the case with the poor readers studied by Senf (1969), who had difficulty responding to simultaneously presented visual and auditory stimuli. These children, it will be recalled, attended primarily to the auditory portion of this complex stimulus.

What we here call overexclusive attention has been variously referred to as overselective attention, stimulus overselectivity, or overselective responding in the writings of Lovaas and his colleagues who study autistic children (Lovaas, Schreibman, Koegel, & Rehm, 1971; Newsom & Lovaas, 1973). None of these terms seems to convey the fact that the responses are much more a function of the stimulus characteristics which "capture" the child's attention than of any (voluntary) selection on the part of the child. At any rate, the autistic child appears to continue to function like a very much younger child with respect to his response to a stimulus complex.

When presented with a stimulus composed of several dimensions, the autistic child appears to respond to only one of these dimensions, showing no incidental learning (Lovaas, Schreibman, Koegel, & Rehm, 1971). Since incidental learning is an important aspect of social development (mannerisms, gait, voice level, and other response modes are probably acquired incidentally from observing others), the impoverished social repertoire of autistic children, as well as their atypical mannerisms and movements, might well be explained by their low incidental learning, or, conversely, by their stimulus-bound, overexclusive attention. It is likely, as Newsom and Lovaas (1973) have stressed, that attention is a learnable skill which autistic children have, for some reason, failed to acquire. If one could discover techniques to teach these children the skill of attending to all relevant aspects of a stimulus in a learning situation, one would contribute significantly to their education.

Overinclusive Attention   Some children with reading difficulties may be having trouble because their way of attending to a stimulus is immature and resembles the overexclusive attention of the much younger child. With their development thus retarded, they should also experience difficulty in the next phase, the period in childhood when incidental learning normally reaches its apex. Here the normal child seems to attend to many aspects of a stimulus situation, many more, in fact, than the minimum essential for efficient detection of the distinctive features. We might call this *overinclusive attention*. We may also note that a child who attends to many irrelevant stimuli will progress in learning more slowly than the one who, having developmentally progressed to the following phase, is capable of selective attention.

Stevenson (1972) points out that in reading, a child must attend to the relevant aspects of letter combinations and disregard their irrelevant features, such as color or size. Siegel (1968) found that good readers show less incidental learning than normal readers. This may reflect that good readers are less overinclusive in their attention or that they have already moved on to the next developmental phase. While we have no data to support this, it is plausible to speculate that some poor readers are such because, arriving at the overinclusive phase late, their attention to irrelevant stimuli handicaps their reading acquisition.

Selective Attention   Available research suggests that incidental learning shows a decline after about age 12. This decline is probably the obverse of the individual's increasing ability to engage in *selective attention*, that is, to focus on those aspects of a stimulus complex which carry the distinctive feature. This would involve the suppression or inhibition of responses to the irrelevant and incidental features. It may be that the learning-disabled child, and particularly the disabled reader, is again slow in acquiring this skill. Such a child might still be using the overinclusive mode of attention when his or her peers are already functioning at the level of selective attention. Such children would respond to all manner of irrelevant stimuli, making them appear impulsive, distractible, and hyperactive.

The hypothesized differential development traced in the above is shown in graphic form in Figure 3-1. This figure is based on the assumption that the developmental rate for selective attention may be slow *(dotted line)*, average *(dashed line)*, or fast *(solid line)*, and that this development moves from the overexclusive, through the overinclusive, to the selective mode. Changes from one mode to the next are not abrupt steps but occur gradually during periods where the modes overlap.

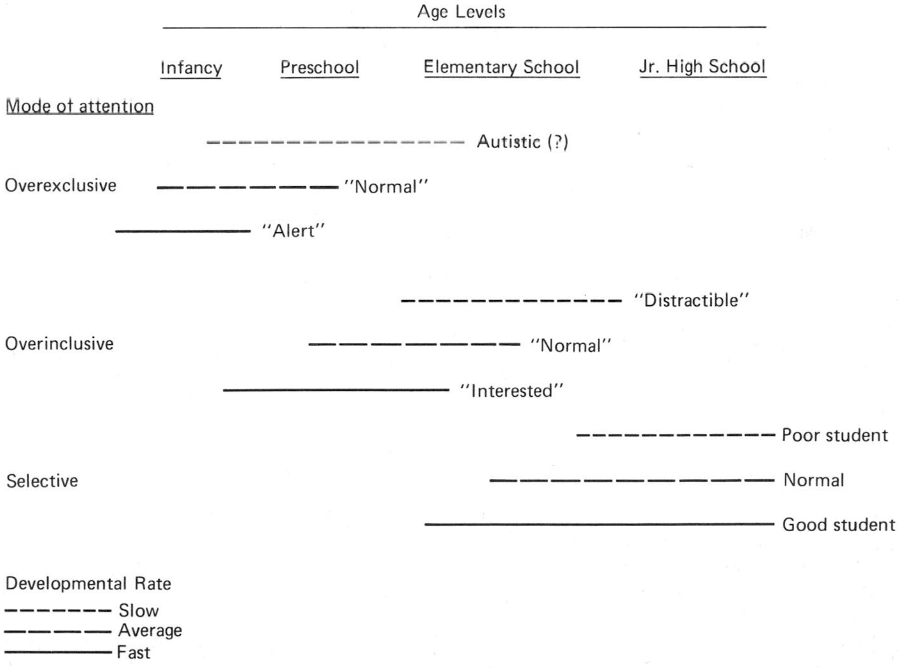

Figure 3-1 The effect of individual differences in the development of selective attention at various age levels.

A girl whose developmental rate is fast might be seen as alert during infancy when she maintains focus on a given object with apparent interest. Moving early into the next phase, this child's overinclusive attention would have her "notice everything," and people might describe her as interested in the world around her. Her early development of the ability to sustain selective attention would then stand her in good stead upon entering school, and one might expect her to be considered a good student.

A child, on the other hand, whose developmental rate is slow would still be functioning in the overexclusive mode when others have moved beyond that. This would handicap learning in the preschool years. Were this mode to be retained beyond that, all learning would be so profoundly impaired that the label "early infantile autism" might apply. Fortunately, only very few children fall in this category. Others, whose development is not that extremely slow, might move late into the overinclusive stage and remain in it longer than others. Finding it difficult to attend to school-related material in a selective manner, they would have difficulty learning, and they might be described as distractible because they attend to stimuli deemed irrelevant by their teachers. When these children finally arrive at the level of selective attention, they would be viewed as poor students, largely because they have by then fallen behind their peers in their academic achievement.

The so-called normal child, represented in the figure by the dashed line, would be moving through the phases of development in an unremarkable fashion because his or her mode of attention at each age level fits the expectations of society. With capacities that match the environment's demands for achievement, such a child should experience no difficulties in school.

The lines in Figure 3-1 are intended to reflect the assumption that differences in selective attention represent individual differences in the relative rates of development and that they are not due to an absolute failure in development. Some children may reach a given level earlier, some later than others; but eventually all should arrive at relatively similar levels *provided* they are given appropriate and in some instances highly specialized learning environments and that the pressures brought to bear on the more slowly developing child are not such that they create secondary problems and deflect the child's progress from its normal course.

Enhancing Selective Attention

Inasmuch as the ability to attend selectively to the relevant critical feature of a stimulus complex is highly adaptive in learning and problem solving, research has been directed at the question whether and how this ability can be taught and strengthened. Because selective attention is critical to performance when a task requires one to differentiate between two or more stimuli or when a discrimination learned under one set of conditions must be applied under a different set of conditions, most of this research has used the paradigms of discrimination-learning experiments.

One way of enhancing selective attention is by modifying stimulus aspects. This can take the form of exaggerating the differences between the stimuli, thus making the critical features more obvious. This can be accomplished by using a series of graded steps where the critical features are at first presented in isolation and irrelevant features are added gradually (faded in). This was the approach used by Schreibman (1972), whose work was discussed in Chapter 2.

The fading-in technique was also used by Caron (1968), who thereby succeeded in teaching three-year-old children to differentiate between roundness and angularity, concepts that children of this age group are usually unable to handle. During early trials, the corners of the angular figures and analogous portions of the rounded figures were emphasized; the rest of the outlines were barely visible. As trials progressed, the outlines were made more and more pronounced until the full figures appeared on the final trials. This and similar studies have demonstrated that even very young children can learn to make difficult discriminations if they are provided with opportunities to learn to attend to the relevant aspects of the stimuli.

Preschool children, particularly those under 5 years of age, manifest great difficulty discriminating between visual stimuli that differ only in orientation. It does not matter whether these stimuli are arrows, horseshoes, parentheses, or the letters "p," "q," "b," and "d." As the child gets older, the ability to differentiate between up and down improves, but the difference between left and right continues to be a source of confusion. Thus, children will acquire the ability to discriminate "b" from "p" based on the direction of the stem, while "b" and "d" as well as "p" and "q" continue to be confused. Eventually, approximately by age 6, the child learns to attend to both the up-down and left-right dimensions of difference. In the case of the letters, the position of the stem and the position of the circle relative to the stem are now observed and the letters correctly identified. Some children, however, lag behind in this development and continue with letter reversal, a phenomenon not unusual with disabled readers.

Koenigsberg (1973) worked with 120 children between the ages of 4 and 6 who had not yet acquired the ability to discriminate "b" from "d," seeking to identify the conditions under which such children can be aided to learn the discrimination between mirror-image stimuli. Studies by other investigators had demonstrated that it is possible to teach the discrimination to such children by having them engage in a motor response relative to the stimuli, such as tracing them or aligning a stencil over the letters. Success with these training procedures was usually explained in terms of Piagetian sensorimotor development. As Koenigsberg points out, all these methods of training have in common that they help focus the child's attention on the visual stimulus, so that the sensorimotor aspect of the experience might not be an essential part of the procedure.

The method Koenigsberg (1973) devised for her study involved matching stimuli which differed in orientation, the child being asked whether these were the same or different. Training involved the placement of a transparent copy of the stimulus over both the standard and the comparison. In one group this was done by the experimenter, in another group by the child. In every case, the experimenter verbalized the correct answer (same or different) and explained the relationship in terms of the fit of the overlay. Control groups received various modifications of this procedure, such as the inclusion of hand contact with the stimuli or of a motor response toward the stimuli.

This design permitted Koenigsberg to assess the relative effectiveness of sensorimotor activity and mere observation on the part of the child. The results indicated "that the principal factor responsible for improvement in performance was the demonstrations. Training using some form of sensorimotor activity appeared to add little to the benefits of demonstrations" (p. 768). Koenigsberg (1973) concludes that it is possible to teach preschool children to discriminate orientation and that their "performance depends to a large degree on the manner in which the task is presented" (p. 768), particularly "when the child's interest is adequately aroused and his attention is properly focused" (p. 769).

It stands to reason, and research has confirmed, that the presence of irrelevant dimensions will retard learning, particularly with young children who have difficulty in making the discrimination between the relevant and the irrelevant. However, if the relevant dimension is presented in a variety of exemplars or in several forms as, for example, in a third dimension, learning can be enhanced. While the presentation of a given stimulus in a variety of forms will aid the child's discrimination, it has been found that the repeated presentation of the same form tends to reduce the effectiveness of the stimulus. If one wishes to teach a child to differentiate between "b" and "d," for example, it is preferable to present these letter pairs in a variety of sizes and degrees of brightness as well as in different parts of the writing surface than to repeat the presentation of the same pair over and over again. This principle seems to follow from research findings which indicate that children are more likely to attend to new rather than familiar stimuli; novelty, as Berlyne (1960) has pointed out, is a feature that increases attention.

There is, of course, a limit to the amount of novelty which can be introduced into a learning task; there are many routine and repetitious situations in which learning is nonetheless required. When this is the case, children can not only be kept at the task but their attention can also be maintained at a high level if correct responses are followed by a reinforcing consequence. For older children this need be no more than knowledge of results; but for younger children a more concrete reward appears to be necessary. The function of a reward in such a situation may be both motivational (keeping the child at a dull task) and informational (providing feedback as to response accuracy).

For a child who has difficulty in reading, a situation involving reading is often one of repeated presentation of the same familiar stimuli. Unable to obtain information from the symbols in front of him, the child has little if any interest in the task, accumulated failures may, in fact, have made the situation aversive for him. Under these circumstances, the introduction of extrinsic and, from the point of view of reading, artificial reinforcers may serve to enhance selective attention to the relevant aspects of the reading material and account for the success of remedial programs which apply reinforcement principles to the teaching of reading (Heiman, Fischer, & Ross, 1973; Staats & Butterfield, 1965). With young children and with learning-disabled children who may be functioning at an immature level in terms of selective attention, it appears best if one seeks to enhance their attention by modifying the stimuli. Older children may benefit more from being provided with a response strategy involving the labeling of stimuli.

Such a strategy involves the issue of verbal mediation, which has been the focus of an earlier discussion (Chapter 2). It appears that children who are able to label relevant aspects of a stimulus but are not yet of an age where such labels are spontaneously used in arriving at a discrimination can benefit if one teaches them to use the label by demonstrating to them that this is a more effective way to achieve success. On the other hand, children who have already acquired a fairly efficient use of selective attention seem to be distracted when they are forced to verbalize labels since they may be using a more effective strategy in their problem solving, one that does not involve overt verbalization.

A study by Wheeler and Dusek (1973) speaks to this point. These investigators compared the performance of children in kindergarten, third grade, and fifth grade on an incidental learning task. The children were shown cards with drawings of animals and household objects on them and half of the subjects were instructed to say aloud the name of the animal on each card. The criterion task was to recall the positions of the various cards which, after display, had been placed on a panel with the picture covered. The results showed (among other effects) that labeling had facilitated recall for the young children while it made no difference or was detrimental in the performance of the older children.

A developmental effect of this nature raises two related points that are often overlooked in planning teaching methods. A technique that is of value when used with a young child who is acquiring a given skill at a certain age is not necessarily helpful and may, in fact, be detrimental if applied with an older child who failed to learn the skill when younger and is in need of remedial or compensatory training. One has to develop teaching methods that are appropriate for the age and condition of the prospective student. What works in teaching reading to a child in first grade will probably not work if used without modification in teaching reading to a ten-year-old with a reading disability or to a semiliterate adult. Any assumption to the contrary ignores what we know about human development.

The second point to be made in this connection is essentially the reverse of the above. A strategy that is effectively used by a skilled adult in solving a given problem is not necessarily the ideal strategy to be used by a child who is in the process of acquiring that skill, nor need that strategy be helpful to someone who failed to learn the skill as a child and has to acquire it at a later age.

Reading skill provides an obvious example to illustrate this point. The proficient adult reader decodes whole words or even word groups and does not attend to the individual letters in the process. That is clearly the ultimate goal for any program of reading acquisition; but it is unwarranted to assume that the beginning reader had best not attend to the individual letters but attend to the whole word instead. The strategy used in the process of acquiring a skill is not the same as the strategy used once proficiency in the skill has been acquired. The same is probably true for problem readers who may have to unlearn inefficient or faulty strategies before they can proceed to work toward the acquisition of mature reading skills. For them, neither the decoding strategy of the beginning reader in first grade nor that of the proficient adult may be the appropriate approach.

These issues will receive further discussion in Chapter 8 and in the chapters that deal with the teaching of the learning-disabled child (Chapters 6 and 7). Before turning to these issues, however, we must examine two topics which have come to be closely associated with most discussions of learning-disabled children; the topic of brain functions and the topic of hyperactivity as it relates to the effects of medications.

SUMMARY

There are many different aspects of attention. In order to discuss the relationship between attention and learning, one must first decide what one means when one uses the word "attention." In line with a recommendation made by Berlyne in 1970, we restricted the use of the word to the process that is usually called selective attention. Selective attention helps us limit the number of stimuli that we process at any one time. Without that capacity, man would be overwhelmed by stimulation and unable to produce an adaptive response. Selective attention is crucial in learning, remembering, and performance. A child who attends and responds not only to stimuli the teacher considers important but to many other stimuli as well or instead may well appear to an observer as hyperactive and distractible.

For the purpose of laboratory experiments, attention can be measured by requiring the child to make a simple motor response upon the appearance of a stimulus for which he or she had been instructed to wait. Other measures involve the monitoring of heart-rate changes and the presentation of simultaneous auditory messages. Studies of this nature demonstrate that the ability to employ selective attention improves with age in the course of childhood. A child whose development of that capacity is slow would thus be at a disadvantage in comparison to peers who develop at a more rapid pace. Learning disabilities may thus be viewed as the result of delayed development in the capacity to employ and sustain selective attention. A number of studies conducted with learning-disabled children bear out this formulation.

The developmental course of selective attention may begin in infancy, where the dominant mode of attention can be described as overexclusive. This is followed by an increasing attention to a great variety of stimuli, a mode one might term overinclusive. As the child gets older and nears adolescence, the capacity to focus on a limited number of stimuli, as demanded by the situation, seems to reach the mature level we designate by the term "selective attention." Given the expected individual differences in rate of development, one can expect some children to be retarded and some advanced in attaining selective attention. Unless the school's expectations take account of these differences, the slower children will encounter academic difficulties. Careful attention to the nature of the teaching material that is presented to such children, so as to make it easier for them to attend to the critical features, is one method of helping the learning-disabled child.

Chapter 4

Learning Disabilities and the Brain-Dysfunction Hypothesis

Learning and the Brain

Learning involves the brain. That is a statement one can make with a great deal of assurance. This generally accepted statement has a corollary which seems attractively logical. It is this: If learning fails to occur, there must be something wrong in the brain. We have previously discussed the difficulties one encounters in trying to establish whether or not learning has taken place, so we won't reopen that issue. For the moment, we shall assume it to be possible to demonstrate unequivocally that under optimal conditions of teaching, a given child fails to learn. Is one then justified in making the statement, "There must be something wrong in the child's brain"? The answer to this question depends on what one means by "something wrong." Obviously, in the example we are using, "something" is not working right, not functioning correctly. On this vague and general level, it is difficult to take issue with the statement. Learning is a function of the brain, so if there is something wrong with this function, it reflects a malfunctioning of the brain or, as some would have it, a *brain dysfunction.*

In a moment we shall return to the notion of brain dysfunction and examine its implications and status as an established fact. First, however, it might we well to look at the word "function" in terms of its definition. One meaning of "function" is the normal and special action of an organ or part of a living person. In that sense, we can say that learning is a function of the brain, just as we say that digestion is a function of the gastrointestinal system. There is, however, another meaning of the word "function." It is a relationship between two events which are dependent upon and vary with each other. We are familiar with that idea from mathematics where we say that x is a function of y; when the value of x changes, the value of y also changes.

The reason for this lexicographic digression is that the two definitions of "function" are often confounded when people speak of brain functions. They say, "Learning is a function of the brain," meaning that learning is something the brain does; but at the same time they expect some sort of fixed relationship between learning and brain activity, as if the two were known to vary with each other in terms of the second definition.

Having observed a deficiency in learning and attributing this to a brain dysfunction, many assume that this means that there is a physical abnormality, damage to or a lesion in the child's brain. From this, it is all too easy to conclude that children who have difficulty learning are brain-damaged, thus introducing notions of traumatic causation, irreversibility, limited potential, and need for special classes. As we shall see, there is no support for the assumption that learning-disabled children have structural abnormalities in their brains. Recognition of this fact eventually led proponents of the structural impairment point of view to add the word "minimal" to brain damage as if to say, "even though we can't demonstrate the damage, we know it is there, but minimally." Eventually, the word "damage," even with the modifier, could no longer be defended and the term "minimal brain dysfunction" was introduced and given currency (Clements, 1966).

The trouble with the term "minimal brain dysfunction" is that it continues to place the emphasis on the brain despite the fact that the involvement of the brain in learning disabilities is based on nothing more than the assertion we stated at the opening of this chapter: learning takes place in the brain. Given this tenuous basis, it would seem far preferable to focus on the one characteristic all these children have in common, their problem with learning. The function of learning is impaired, so we prefer to speak of "learning dysfunctions" (Ross, 1967) or to use the more commonly accepted expression "learning disabilities."

The Methodological Dilemma   It is a requirement of a good theory that it be susceptible to disproof and thus to modification or rejection. The assertion that there is a causal relationship between learning disabilities and brain abnormality is very difficult to disprove. Put in terms of the null hypothesis used by scientists, this assertion states that there is no difference between children with learning disabilities and children with known brain abnormalities. In order to test this, one needs a sample of brain-damaged children, a sample of learning-disabled children, and a relevant measure of their performance. If one found a difference between the two groups, the null hypothesis could be rejected and one could conclude that learning-disabled and brain-damaged children represent two different populations. Studies leading to this conclusion have indeed been conducted, yet the theory has shown remarkable durability. Why should this be?

> To upset the conclusion that all crows are black. there is no need to seek demonstration that no crow is black; it is sufficient to produce one white crow.

By this logic (attributed to William James) we have sufficient proof to conclude that learning-disabled and brain-damaged children are not the same—a white crow has been produced. Yet it is easy to agree on the definition of a crow, of black and of white. It is far more difficult to define "brain damage," "learning disability," and appropriate performance measure. Hence the continuing controversy. No matter how many studies refute the brain-damage–learning-disability assertion, its proponent can always claim that one did not study the right children, examine the right variables, or apply the right measures; a different study, he might allege, would prove him correct. It is a major weakness of this formulation that it cannot be put to conclusive test.

Another problem with the brain-damage hypothesis is that it asserts a causality; that the learning disability is caused by the brain disorder. This too is difficult to prove. Here, however, the dilemma is not in the logic of scientific method but in the ethics of conducting research. Proof of this causal relationship would require that one take a normally learning child, introduce a specific abnormality in the child's brain, and then observe whether a learning disability develops. None would perform such an experiment, nor do we know at this point just what kind of brain abnormality one would have to produce in order to test the vaguely stated hypothesis. Those gross and often non-specific damages to the brain which stem from illness or injury cannot be used as a substitute for the impossible experiment because they are usually accompanied by many features, such as lengthy hospitalization, that might be responsible for the psychological changes often observed in the victims. Incidentally, these changes rarely take the form of the kind of learning disability with which we are here concerned.

When the definitive experiment involving direct manipulation of the independent variable is impossible, one is limited to observing correlations. One might demonstrate that children with known brain abnormalities exhibit learning disabilities, but the fact that these two variables go together (correlate) cannot be used as proof that the first variable caused the second. By the logic of a correlation, one can just as legitimately argue that the causal chain functioned in the opposite direction.

The brain-abnormality hypothesis thus suffers from its vague formulation and the impossibility of conducting a definitive experiment. Still a third problem has to do with its formulation in terms of unobservables. There is no way in which one can directly observe an abnormality of a living, functioning brain. All available measures of brain functions are indirect, such as the electroencephalograph (EEG), requiring inferences for their interpretation. Indirect measures which require interpretation can be misinterpreted, may be the wrong kind of measures, or might be measuring something other than what they are supposed to measure. They are, in other words, not necessarily valid or reliable, and any conclusions based on the use of these measures must be viewed with wariness.

All in all, a statement that asserts that learning disabilities are the result of brain abnormalities reflects a theory that is not susceptible of disproof because it defies a definitive experiment and depends on measures of unknown validity. These are not the attributes for a good theory.

LEARNING DISABILITIES AND BRAIN ABNORMALITIES

At the beginning of this chapter we anticipated a discussion of relevant studies by stating that there is no support for the assumption that children with learning disabilities have demonstrable structural abnormalities of the brain. Let us look at some of the more recent evidence for this statement.

The Assumption of a Syndrome

The usual formulation assumes that a child's difficulty in learning is one among several interrelated symptoms of brain abnormality which, together, form a syndrome that is said to be diagnostic of the underlying organic problem. In many circles it is thus customary to speak of a "minimal brain dysfunction syndrome." An authoritative definition of this syndrome was proposed by a group of experts who worked on a project sponsored by the National Institute of Neurological Diseases and Blindness (Clements, 1966). This definition speaks of

> children of near average, average, or above average general intelligence with certain learning or behavioral disabilities ranging from mild to severe, which are associated with deviations of function of the central nervous system. These deviations may manifest themselves by various combinations of impairment in perception, conceptualization, language, memory, and control of attention, impulse, or motor function (pp. 9–10).

A careful look at this definition reveals that it takes children with "certain learning disabilities" who manifest an impairment in various forms of behavior (some of which, like conceptualization and language, involve learning) and attributes their learning problem to "brain dysfunctions" without requiring any external evidence. In its basic components, this definition says no more than "children who have learning disabilities and who manifest learning disabilities have something wrong with their brains." It is obvious that this circu-larity has added nothing to our knowledge and less to our ability to make constructive plans for the learning-disabled child.

Clements (1966) is among those who speak of minimal brain dysfunction syndrome, thus suggesting an analogy between learning disability and a medi-cal illness. In medical diagnosis, a syndrome is a cluster of symptoms, com-plaints, or difficulties which usually go together and as such a cluster identify the disease. Not all symptoms need necessarily be present in every instance, but they should coincide sufficiently often to present a consistent picture. A review of the literature on children with minimal brain dysfunctions led Clements (1966) to list no fewer than 99 symptoms and prompted the admis-sion that this indicates that there is a "variety of syndromes contained within the primary diagnosis of minimal brain dysfunctioning" (p. 11). He then listed 10 characteristics of the children in question which are most often cited by various authors. In order of frequency, these are:

1 Hyperactivity
2 Perceptual-motor impairments
3 Emotional lability
4 General coordination deficits
5 Disorders of attention (short attention span, distractibility, persever-ation)
6 Impulsivity
7 Disorders of memory and thinking
8 Specific learning disabilities
  a Reading
  b Arithmetic
  c Writing
  d Spelling
9 Disorders of speech and hearing
10 Equivocal neurological signs and electroencephalographic irregulari-ties

These difficulties then, are presumably at the core of the "minimal brain dys-function syndrome." If there is such an entity, children who are to be labeled under this rubric should manifest a consistent combination of most of these problems.

Testing the Assumption   This prediction was put to test by Routh and Roberts (1972). They carefully examined 73 boys and 16 girls between the ages of 6 years 5 months and 13 years 8 months who had been seen at a university clinic to which most of them had been referred for evaluation of poor school performance. All had IQ scores above 85 and none had severe visual or audi-tory problems, cerebral palsy, or epilepsy. A multidisciplinary team examined each child and obtained 16 measures and ratings relevant to the most frequently cited symptoms of minimal brain dysfunction as listed by Clements (1966). The only problems not specifically evaluated were distractibility, perseveration, thinking disorder, handwriting disability, and EEG irregularities. (There were 16 measures because some of the symptoms were assessed in several ways; thus general coordination deficits were tested in three different ways and disorders of attention were checked by two tests.)

The measures thus obtained were intercorrelated in order to discover significant relationships between and among the symptoms, for if they represent a syndrome, many or most of them should occur together in individual children. As one might expect, there were significant relationships for measures addressed to the same symptom. The three tests designed to assess general coordination deficits, for example, yielded significant intercorrelations; a fact that is even less surprising if one recalls that all three of these tests were administered by the same individual who based his rating on a subjective judgment. When the effects of age and intelligence test score were taken into account, the only relationships between symptoms which yielded significant correlations were those between fine motor skill deficits and impulsivity and between disorders of attention (inattentiveness and difficulty in concentration) and memory disorder.

Their failure to find the kind of relationships between symptoms that would be demanded if they did indeed form a syndrome led Routh and Roberts (1972) to the conservative conclusion that this "is somewhat damaging to the idea of such a syndrome" (p. 313). This careful statement takes cognizance of the fact that their study has certain limitations, primarily in the fact that many of the assessments had to be based on unstandardized methods of examination and clinical judgments. Nevertheless, the fact that the scores from the objective learning-relevant tests (reading, arithmetic, and spelling) *failed to correlate with any* of the most frequently cited "symptoms" of minimal brain dysfunction should give one pause for thought as to the validity of this formulation regarding learning disabilities.

Before leaving the Routh and Roberts (1972) study, it is well to take a closer look at the reported correlation between disorders of attention and disorder of memory. Since the rating of attention was based on the teachers' judgments, the authors suggest that the correlation might be spurious in that teachers could be reacting to children with poor memories by seeing them as inattentive and as failing to concentrate. This overlooks the fact that their measure of memory was the Digit Span subtest on the Wechsler Intelligence Scale for Children (WISC). For this subtest the child is asked to repeat series of numbers that are called out by the examiner. This is usually viewed as testing immediate memory span, but a failure to do well on this subtest can also be interpreted as reflecting an inability or failure to attend when the numbers are first presented. This is the dilemma created when one tries to draw inferences about covert processes (i. e., memory) when only input and output can be observed. At any rate, the correlation reported by Routh and Roberts (1972) may reflect a problem in attention, lending further support to our suggestion (see Chapter 3) that there is a relationship between learning disabilities and the development of selective attention.

As we pointed out, the concept of minimal brain dysfunction implies that children so labeled share characteristics that are similar to or the same as the characteristics of children with known brain damage and that, furthermore, their characteristics differ from those of normal children and of children who have difficulties with learning but who are not to be classified under the rubric "minimal brain dysfunction." A study conducted by Crinella (1973) bears on some of these issues. He administered an extensive battery of neuropsychological tests to 90 children. Of these, 19 had known brain damage, 34 had been independently diagnosed as having minimal brain dysfunction (MBD), and 37 were a control group of children functioning at an above-average level. The children ranged in age from 7 through 12 years, but the mean age of the MBD group was significantly below that of the other two groups.

The data obtained from this study were subjected to a rather complicated series of statistical analyses. These permitted not only an identification of characteristics which clusters of the 90 test variables had in common (factors) but also facilitated a comparison of the three groups on these factors. Crinella (1973) not only failed to find a unitary MBD syndrome but also discovered "that MBD children as a group were in some ways unlike children with known brain lesions" (p. 43).

From this one might conclude that the so-called syndrome is not a syndrome and that the so-called MBD children do not have a *brain* dysfunction. This, however, is not the conclusion Crinella chose to draw from his study. Having noted that *some* MBD children have damage or defects within similar neuroanatomic systems (as inferred from a factor analysis of behavioral tests) and acknowledging that other children sharing the MBD diagnosis had little behavioral communality with actually brain-damaged children, he suggests that "alternative forms of MBD exist as independent diagnostic entities . . . and/or that MBD is similar to types of known neuropathology not sampled in this study" (p. 43). This is an example of the never-say-die posture made possible by a theory which does not lend itself to disproof. Instead of modifying or relinquishing the theory in the face of evidence which fails to confirm its prediction, advocates of such a theory maintain that researchers haven't looked long enough or hard enough or in the right places because, ultimately, the theory must prevail.

Assessing Brain Damage   It is not too surprising that attempts to demonstrate the presence of organic brain damage in learning-disabled children by means of psychological tests are fraught with difficulties. Even when one is dealing with children who are known to be brain-damaged, psychological tests do not provide unequivocal indexes to that effect. This was demonstrated by McIntosh (1973), who asked a highly skilled and experienced clinical psychologist to judge the presence or absence of deficit due to organic brain damage on the basis of the protocols of three psychological tests. These tests were the Wechsler Intelligence Scale for Children (Wechsler, 1949), the Benton Visual Retention Test (Benton, 1963), and the Minnesota Percepto-Diagnostic Test (Fuller, 1969). They had been administered to 34 children with brain damage and an equal number of normal controls. Brain damage had been independently diagnosed by two medical specialists on the basis of clinical and laboratory neurological methods, using highly objective and demanding criteria.

Each of the psychological tests used in this study has established norms and cutoff scores or ratios which presumably identify brain damage. For example, on the Wechsler Intelligence Scale for Children, a difference of 25 points or more of verbal over performance IQ has been reported to be diagnostic of brain damage (Holroyd & Wright, 1965). Clinical judgments of the psychologists could thus be compared with so-called actuarial predictions based on such scores.

The research design used by McIntosh (1973) permitted him to assess the accuracy not only of the clinical judge, using any one or a combination of the three psychological tests, but also of the test-cutoff scores based on the actuarial norms. The results showed that neither of the methods used, clinical judgments or actuarial norms, was able to classify the children significantly better than chance. In other words, with the tests and clinician used in this study, the children involved could not be differentiated in terms of presence or absence of brain damage. If this is the case with grossly impaired children who have seizures, abnormal EEGs, or a history of known brain trauma, how much less likely is it to substantiate something as vague as "minimal brain dysfunction"?

Studies of Brain Functions

Any test of the hypothesis that children with learning disabilities have a central nervous system impairment must include a careful neurological examination. It is not sufficient to administer psychological instruments such as the Bender Gestalt test (Koppitz, 1963) which assesses visual-motor coordination and presumably permits inferences as to brain functions. The test requires the child to copy nine geometric designs. Inadequate performance is said to reflect "organicity," that is, an impairment of brain functions. In using the test with children, however, performance must be evaluated in terms of the child's chronological age, so that inadequate performance could just as easily be interpreted as reflecting visual-motor immaturity, a failure to have acquired the age-appropriate skills needed for adequate performance. Poor performance on this test might thus reflect no more than another aspect of the child's learning disability. To break out of this circularity, assessment of a child's brain functions should be based on tests that are minimally dependent on learning. A good neurological examination satisfies this requirement.

A neurological examination was included in a study on learning disorders reported by Owen, Adams, Forrest, Stolz, and Fisher (1971).

> It included a classical examination of cranial nerves, motor power and tone, reflexes, cerebellar and sensory functioning, posture and motility, right-left discrimination, laterality, extinction to simultaneous tactile stimulation, ability to reproduce tapped patterns, and examination of selected physical characteristics such as variations of size, form, and symmetry of the external ears (p. 27).

The subjects of this study were 76 children who were 1½ to 2 years below grade level in spelling and/or reading and had a full scale WISC IQ of 90 or above. The authors refer to these as "educationally handicapped children." They were compared with a matched group of academically successful controls, the siblings of these controls, and their own same-sex siblings. The neurological examination revealed that only 3 of the 76 educationally handicapped children showed definite medical signs of damage to the central nervous system. The authors are thus justified in concluding that "organic damage per se could not be considered a major causative factor in the learning problems" of the educationally handicapped children in this population (Owen et al., 1971, p. 64).

It is also worth noting that electroencephalographic (EEG) studies conducted on a subsample of these children "did not prove to be significantly associated with degree of learning problem" (p. 65) so that the authors concluded "that the EEG is not a useful tool in diagnosing or planning for the remediation of learning disorders at this time" (ibid.).

The research group working with Owen (1971) was thus unable to relate learning disabilities to organic damage when they applied strictly neurological tests which do not require the child's active participation. On the other hand, on performance tests which require that the child attend to the examiner, they found "convincing evidence" that the educationally handicapped children "suffered from immaturies or inadequacies in performing tasks which have to do with ordering and sequencing auditory stimuli" (p. 35). Here the examiner would tap a pattern on the table while the child watched, hence attended, before being asked to reproduce the pattern. Other tests that differentiated between the learning-disabled and the control children can also be viewed as requiring the child to sustain attention, for they involved performing rapid, directed motor movements such as touching the hand to the face, and alternating finger or hand movements. On all these tests, the children with learning problems performed in a manner appropriate for younger children; in other words, they performed at an immature level.

In the absence of clear-cut signs of neurological damage, the work of Owen et al. (1971) would seem to suggest that the learning-disabled child is principally an immature child, a child whose central nervous system (or a crucial part thereof) has lagged in the development of functions that are essential for learning under the conditions and expectations encountered in the ordinary environment. We thus find another instance where research results point in the direction of a relationship between learning disabilities and a lag in the development of the ability to sustain selective attention.

Thus far the Owen, Adams, Forrest, Stolz, and Fisher (1971) study has been discussed only from the standpoint of the neurological findings. These, however, represent only one aspect of this important work. The study is also of considerable interest because of the light it throws on possible familial aspects of learning disability which have been investigated only rarely. As was pointed out, the authors compared the learning-disabled children not only with normal controls but also with their own same-sex siblings and with the siblings of the controls. All together, 304 children were examined, and most of their parents were interviewed. As usual, there was a preponderance of males among the children with learning disabilities, so that the sample was composed of 244 boys and 60 girls.

Although the siblings of the educationally handicapped children did not have severe learning disabilities, the study revealed that they and their impaired sibling had many problems in common. Compared to the academically successful children and their siblings, the learning-disabled and their brothers or sisters did significantly less well on some aspects of the intelligence test, the Bender Gestalt test, a drawing test, and the previously mentioned performance tests. Inasmuch as the parents of the educationally handicapped children often reported histories of poor school performance, a familial factor may well be involved in the development of some learning problems; but it is impossible to say whether this is genetic or environmental in nature or to what extent one is dealing with an interaction of these two factors.

Sequencing One of the most striking differences between the learning-disabled children and the normal controls reported by Owen et al. (1971) was on tasks calling for the ordering and sequencing of auditory and visual stimuli. The children with educational problems "gave evidence over and over again that they were severely impaired in temporal order and in the ability to sequence events and objects appropriately" (p. 26). In the auditory realm, this impairment was revealed on the tapping task described earlier; in the visual realm, it was reflected in the confused order in which the children reproduced the designs of the Bender Gestalt test.

Difficulties in sequencing have been found in a variety of studies of children with learning disabilities. These difficulties emerge, for example, when reading-disabled children are asked to match an auditory configuration with an analogous visual configuration, as was done by Birch and Belmont (1964). These investigators presented elementary school children with auditory rhythm patterns of pencil taps, with short and long intervals between taps. They then asked the subjects to choose from among three patterns of typed dots the one that represented the visual equivalent of the auditory pattern. This skill not only increased with age but also had a positive correlation with reading proficiency (Belmont & Birch, 1965). The investigators attributed their finding to an inadequacy in intersensory integrative functions; that is, in the ability to recognize and relate two or more stimulus patterns received from different sense modalities. Since younger children had more difficulty with such a task than older children, Birch and Belmont (1964) considered intersensory integration a development skill.

Intersensory Integration   Later research (Vande Voort, Senf, & Benton, 1972) has thrown doubt on the postulated defect in intersensory integrative function of children with reading difficulties. When a child fails to select from a pattern of visually presented dots the one that (from the examiner's point of view) represents an auditory rhythm pattern to which he or she had previously been asked to listen, the failure might be due to several problems other than inferred intersensory integration. Since the two patterns are presented in a temporal sequence, first the auditory than the visual, the child must be able to recognize the visual on the basis of memory of the auditory pattern. Hence, the failure may be due to the child's not having attended to the auditory, not having stored it in short-term memory, not attending to the visual, or not being able to recall the auditory so as to be able to recognize its equivalence in the visual. Obviously, any combination of these failures and/or a failure to understand the nature of the task can also lead to inadequate performance.

Vande Voort, Senf, and Benton (1972) conducted a study designed to test whether a defect in immediate memory rather than a defect in intersensory integration might explain the difficulty of retarded readers on auditory-visual matching tasks. Their subjects were 48 boys ranging in age from 8 to 13 years who were of at least normal intelligence but deficient in reading. They were matched with a control group of normal readers.

The children were required to identify as "same" or "different" two sets of temporally distributed (auditory) or spatially distributed (visual) stimuli. These were presented in one of three combinations: auditory-auditory (A-A); visual-visual (V-V); and auditory-visual (A-V). An unfortunate omission in this design was a visual-auditory sequence, since this may be the most crucial from the standpoint of learning to read where the child first looks at the word and then hears it pronounced (Beery, 1967). It should also be pointed out that a "same-different" matching task is a somewhat different (and more difficult) test of memory than the multiple-choice recognition task used by Birch and Belmont (1964).

The study by Vande Voort et al. (1972) had a number of different aspects. We shall here focus only on the part that dealt with the question of whether retarded readers have a memory problem that might account for their poor performance on intersensory matching tasks. The analysis of their results led these investigators to conclude that "processes involved with the accurate encoding of the initial stimulus are more important in this context than memory" (Vande Voort et al., 1972, pp. 1266 f.). Memory thus does not seem to be the key skill in which retarded readers are deficient. What is? Vande Voort, Senf, and Benton (1972) draw from their study "the obvious implication . . . that retarded readers are deficient in and do not develop some skills that are developing in control Ss; likely possibilities are defects in attention or in the perceptual processes required to assimilate accurately the two stimuli for subsequent matching" (p. 1270). They suggest that retarded readers might be unable to encode all the relationships in a complex stimulus configuration.

While this formulation is attractive, it fails to explain why the retarded readers had less trouble on the V-V matching than on both the A-V and A-A tasks. The complexity of dots on paper does not seem to be much less than the complexity of tones from a loudspeaker. On the other hand, it is much easier for an experimenter to monitor the attention of a child on a visual than on an auditory task. One can see whether a child is looking at the stimulus, one cannot tell whether he or she is listening. Conversely, it may be easier for a child not to attend to an auditory than to a visual stimulus. The alternate explanation offered by Vande Voort et al. (1972) which points to defects in attention would seem to be more plausible. Certainly attention is a prerequisite for any encoding or assimilation of stimuli, and if attention were defective, increasing complexity of stimuli would result in increasing difficulties in performance.

We have previously (Chapter 3) pointed to a certain similarity between the difficulties autistic children and children with learning disabilities experience when they are asked to respond to complex stimuli. The results of Vande Voort et al. (1972) again suggest the possibility that the problems of learning-disabled children are a very mild form of the profound and pervasive learning problems of children with early infantile autism. As demonstrated by Lovaas, Schreibman, Koegel, and Rehm (1971), autistic children taught to respond to a stimulus complex composed of simultaneously presented auditory, visual, and tactile cues seem to attend exclusively to only one of these aspects, ignoring the rest. In the study by Vande Voort, Senf, and Benton (1972), who used simultaneously presented auditory and visual cues, learning-disabled children (retarded readers) experienced difficulty in making the required comparison. It is a question to be answered by future research whether this difficulty is due to overexclusive attention to one part of a stimulus complex and is thus similar to the attention problem of autistic children.

Selective Attention   Learning-related functions of the brain can only be investigated by presenting a child with stimulus material and observing his or her responses to that material. Investigators pursuing the brain dysfunction hypothesis of learning disabilities thus invariably measure performances which require that the child has attended to the stimuli they presented. It often seems that observed performance deficits are most conservatively interpreted as deficits in the area of attention. When simultaneously presented stimuli must be attended to before an adaptive response can be emitted, as was the case in the sequencing studies by Birch and Belmont (1964, Belmont & Birch, 1965), it seems gratuitous to speculate about intersensory integration in order to explain the poor performance of learning-disabled children. Difficulties in selective attention would seem to explain such results at least as well.

Attentional processes of learning-disabled children were studied in a series of investigations conducted by Dykman, Ackerman, Clements, and Peters (1971). In one of their studies, these investigators assessed 82 boys with learning disabilities whom they compared with 34 academically adequate controls. The learning-disabled children ranged in age from 8 years to 11 years 11 months and were failing in school despite at least average intelligence-test scores. A detailed neurological examination revealed that the older learning-disabled children (aged 10 and 11) had far fewer neurological problems than those who were younger (aged 8 and 9). The authors view this as a sign of developmental lag, a hypothesis that is in line with many clinical reports which suggest that learning-disabled children cease manifesting certain motor problems, such as hyperactivity, as they get older. We shall return to the issue of developmental lag later in this chapter.

In order to study the attentional processes of the learning-disabled children, Dykman et al. (1971) used a reaction-time task in which the child has to respond to a signal under a variety of distracting conditions. Compared to the normal controls, the learning-disabled children made significantly more errors and had slower reaction times. In a related study which had also included an operant conditioning procedure, a tone discrimination task, and three psychophysiological measures, Dykman's colleagues had subjected their data to a statistical procedure (factor analysis) which revealed that "focus of attention," the primary factor, differentiated between learning-disabled children (here labeled as having "minimal brain dysfunctions") and controls. Taken together, these results led the authors to the following conclusion:

> The neurological results suggest that the main cause of learning disabilities is a developmental lag. Neurological immaturity could well explain the attentional deficits of learning-disability children. . . . One of the most outstanding characteristics of the neurologically immature child is his poor coordination, both gross and fine actions. Motor incoordination can be related to and correlated with faulty attention, we believe, in at least two ways. First, it can be argued that attention is perfected through one's early mechanical manipulation of self and environment. Success and exploration sustain attention. Second, it can be argued that motor incoordination as well as short attention span and distractibility are

usually seen and considered normal in very young (preschool) children. But, the school age child who retains these immature behaviors often wears the label "learning disabled" (pp. 88—89).

Dykman and his colleagues (1971) stress that postulating neurological immaturity as the major factor in learning disabilities does not imply that the problem is essentially medical or genetic. Aspects of the child's nervous system can be immature; but immaturity, unlike the hypothesis of a permanently impaired brain mechanism, implies the potential for continuing development and a reaching of maturity. Neural maturation depends in part on one's life experiences, and among these formal education plays an important part.

> The significant task is to develop educational programs that will help the presumably neurologically immature child develop to his full capacity with a minimum of frustration-induced anxiety. It is unlikely that this can be accomplished in a fixed age-grade system or indeed by any one technique of special education. More importantly, many of our present educational efforts may be misplaced if the most critical defect of learning-disability children is faulty attention (Dykman, Ackerman, Clements, & Peters, 1971, p. 89).

A study based on a developmental theory of reading disabilities was conducted by Satz, Rardin, and Ross (1971). They postulated that what they call "developmental dyslexia" reflects a lag in the maturation of the central nervous system which delays the acquisition of those skills which are in ascendancy at different developmental ages. Following a Piagetian view of development, these authors state that visual-motor skills develop before language skills; they therefore predict that younger children with reading disabilities (ages 7 to 8) should manifest visual-motor problems, while older children with reading disabilities (ages 11 to 12) should manifest language problems. Conversely, they hypothesize that the younger children would not display language difficulties while the older children should not display visual-motor problems.

Satz, Rardin, and Ross (1971) tested their hypotheses by comparing disabled readers with normal readers at each of the two age levels. The predicted difference emerged on only one of three nonlanguage measures: the younger disabled readers performed significantly less well than the controls on the Bender Gestalt test, which requires the copying of geometric designs. No such difference was found for the older children. On the other hand, the older disabled readers had significantly lower scores than the controls on four of five measures testing language skills. These were the verbal scale of the WISC, a test of verbal fluency, and a dichotic listening test on which the child had to recall numbers simultaneously delivered in disparate pairs over stereo headphones. The fourth test was the absolute difference between the scores on WISC verbal and performance scales. On the language measures, the younger disabled readers differed from their controls only on the verbal scale of the WISC. The authors interpret their results as generally confirming their hypotheses and supporting their theoretical formulations, although they recognize that their data do not provide a direct verification of their speculation about a maturational lag of central brain mechanisms.

A critical reading of this study reveals a number of points that militate against ready acceptance of the authors' conclusion that they have demonstrated support for their interpretation of reading disabilities. Even if one chooses not to cavil over the reliability of the Bender Gestalt scores—which were based on three-point ratings (poor, medium, good) of four judges—the results show only that the young disabled readers also have visual-motor problems while the older disabled readers do not manifest these but show language and attention problems instead. The apparent, relative improvement on the visual-motor integration test might be viewed as in keeping with a developmental model, but this model would also predict that the younger children should display language difficulties as well.

Intellectual development, according to Piaget (Piaget & Inhelder, 1969), is not only sequential (sensorimotor integration preceding symbolic language function) but also hierarchical, so that successful later development is viewed as presuming the establishment of earlier skills. Since, contrary to the theoretical expectation, the younger children did not display a language deficit on any of the measures Satz and his colleagues (1971) considered valid, a different formulation might have to be introduced to explain the results.

This formulation would point out that children who have problems in learning to read also have problems in learning to copy geometric designs in an accurate fashion, and that a failure to acquire adequate reading skills will, at a later age, be reflected in low scores on verbal intelligence test scales and in a deficit in quickly naming words beginning with certain letters (verbal fluency test). By age 12, ability to read may well be contributing to verbal facility. In other words, the observed correlation between low reading scores and low language scores can be interpreted as readily in one as in the opposite causal direction.

What remains to be explained among the findings of Satz et al. (1971) is the difference in scores on the dichotic listening tests where the control group did significantly better than the group of older disabled readers. Satz et al. chose to view this test as reflecting differences in the relative dominance of the two cerebral hemispheres and referred to it as "a fairly valid behavioral measure of cerebral lateralization of speech in children" (p. 2015). There is, however, no independent support for this formulation. In a more parsimonious interpretation, the task would seem to require close and sustained attention. This would leave one once again with the observation that reading-disabled children manifest a disorder of attention.

Perceptual-Motor Functions   Inferences in support of the assertion that learning disabilities have their cause (etiology) in some form of damage to the brain are often based on presumably observed similarities between the performance of children with learning disabilities and adults known to be brain-damaged. Such adults usually manifest severe impairments, including hemiplegias and hemipareses, often due to recently sustained injuries such as gunshot wounds. They have had careful and detailed neurological examinations and, occasionally, neurosurgery, so that the diagnosis of brain damage can be viewed with confidence.

The learning-disabled children, on the other hand, do not manifest such gross and obvious signs of brain damage. For this reason, as we have pointed out, the proponents of the brain-damage etiology have introduced such terms as "minimal brain dysfunction." Investigators who hold this point of view believe that they find support for their etiological speculation when they can demonstrate that learning-disabled children and brain-damaged adults perform in a similar manner on given tests. A study by Rourke, Yanni, Mac-Donald, and Young (1973b) is an example of this approach.

This study (Rourke et al., 1973b) was designed as a test of the appropriateness of the cerebral dysfunction approach to the explanation of learning disabilities in older (ten- to fourteen-year-old) children. The authors point out that studies of brain-damaged adults have shown that when such individuals are given tasks requiring perceptual-motor performance, those with lesions of the left cerebral hemisphere experience more difficulty when using their right hand than their left hand. Conversely, those with lesion of the right cerebral hemisphere show deficits in using the left hand. When the Wechsler-Bellevue intelligence test is administered to such individuals, studies cited by Rourke et al. (1973b) show that those with left-sided motor deficits tend to excel on the verbal scale while those with right-sided motor deficits tend to do better on the performance scale.

Rourke, Yanni, MacDonald, and Young (1973b) administered the Grooved Pegboard Test to a large number of children who had been referred for assessment because of "a 'learning' and/or a 'perceptual' problem to which it was thought that cerebral dysfunction might be a contributing factor" (Rourke et al., 1973b, p. 130). It should be noted that the nature or degree of the "learning disability" was not otherwise defined. From this pool of children, the investigators selected 46 individuals between the ages of 10 and 15 who were grouped on the basis of the pegboard test performance.

The pegboard test is a measure of speed and accuracy of hand-eye coordination in that it requires the child to fit 25 keyhole-shaped pegs into similarly shaped holes, first with the right hand and then with the left hand. On the basis of their performance, the children were assigned to four groups, those whose pegboard score was normal with either hand; those whose score was impaired with either hand; those whose score was normal with the right but impaired with the left hand; and vice versa. Because of their interest in lateralized impairment, the latter two groups were crucial to Rourke et al. (1973b), who had reasoned

> If the performance of these groups of children with learning disabilities were shown to be similar to those of adults with known brain lesions, this would constitute supporting evidence for the view that learning disabilities in such children are due, at least in part, to dysfunction at the level of the cerebral hemispheres (p. 129).

The children, grouped as indicated, were compared on a series of tests selected to assess language functions and nonverbal problem solving. In order to adduce the "supporting evidence" sought by these investigators, the left-hand impaired children and the right-hand impaired children should have shown diametrically opposite performances on tests of language and of perceptual-motor functions. For the language group of tests, the authors' expectations "received some support" (p. 133), but the hypotheses relating to differences between these groups on perceptual-motor tasks "were not confirmed" (p. 133).

The children with left-hand impairment had an above-average WISC verbal IQ and a below-average WISC performance IQ. Those with right-hand impairment, however, had below-average scores on both parts of this intelligence scale, although their scores on the verbal scale were slightly lower than those on the performance scale. While the difference between these group averages did not reach the conventionally accepted level of statistical significance (the p- value is reported as less than 0.10) and only a first-order interaction between verbal IQ and performance IQ for the two groups proved significant, the authors found sufficient justification in their data to state

> What is abundantly clear about the results of the present study, with respect to the patterns of Verbal IQ–Performance IQ discrepancies exhibited by [the two groups], is that they are strikingly similar to those seen in adult patients with well-documented lateralized cerebral lesions (Rourke, Yanni, MacDonald, and Young, 1973b, p. 133).

They further conclude, "The comparisons yielded many striking similarities, thus lending support to the view that learning disabilities in such children are due, at least in part, to dysfunction at the level of the cerebral hemispheres" (ibid., p. 128). Read by one not committed to the cerebral dysfunction hypothesis, the "striking similarities" are not that readily apparent and the results make nothing "abundantly clear."

We have devoted considerable space to this inconclusive study because it is fairly typical of the research that is often cited in support of the brain-injury etiology of learning disabilities. A critical reading of such studies usually reveals that the conclusions go considerably beyond the data and that analogies between the performance of brain-injured adults and learning-disabled children are, at best, tenuous.

A different aspect of the work of Rourke and his co-workers does, however, merit further attention. In the article cited above (Rourke et al., 1973b), the authors repeatedly stressed that they were drawing conclusions only with re-spect to "older children with learning disabilities." Younger children, they point out, have a different pattern of psychological test performance. This observation derives from two earlier studies (Rourke & Telegdy, 1971; Rourke, Dietrich, & Young, 1973a).

In the earlier of these two studies, 45 learning-disabled nine- to fourteen-year-old boys were given the Wechsler Intelligence Scale for Children (WISC) and, on the basis of their scores, were divided into a high-performance–low-verbal; a verbal equal to performance; and a high-verbal–low-performance group. They were then given a series of tests measuring complex motor and perceptual-motor abilities. The results showed the high-performance–low-verbal group to be superior to the high-verbal–low-performance group on the tasks involving complex visual-motor coordination regardless of the hand em-ployed (!). In other words, high scores on the performance portion of the WISC correlate positively with scores on other performance tests. Rourke's gratuitous inferences about the differential integrity of the two cerebral hemi-spheres need not concern us here.

In the 1973 study by Rourke, Dietrich, and Young, the research method sketched above was applied to a group of 82 boys in the age range of 5 to 8 years who "had been referred for neuropsychological assessment because cere-bral dysfunction was suspected to be a factor contributing to their difficulties in academic learning" (p. 277). Unlike the group of older children mentioned above, this younger group was described as "probably" including a high per-centage of brain-damaged children, because many showed borderline or ab-normal electroencephalographic (EEG) records. The results of this study re-vealed few significant differences between the three WISC-score groups. While relatively higher verbal scores tended to predict above-average performance on tests for reading, spelling, and arithmetic, relatively high performance scores did not correlate with scores on visual-motor tests. The data for the younger children were thus markedly different from the data for the older children. The authors conclude that the results "would not support the view that such discrepancies reflect the differential integrity of the two cerebral hemispheres in younger children with learning disabilities" (p. 282).

The different results for younger and for older children may be simply a reflection of the fact that the WISC is not a particularly reliable test when used with children as young as 5 and 6. At the same time, a failure to find "evi-dence" for cerebral dysfunction in younger children, many of whom were probably brain-damaged, when finding such "evidence" in older learning-dis-abled children, who seemed to have no independent diagnosis of brain pathol-ogy, would seem to be inconsistent with a cerebral dysfunction explanation.

If learning disability is related to (caused by) cerebral dysfunction, such a dysfunction should be present in younger children if it can be found in older children—that is, unless the older children were not learning-disabled when younger and only became so around age 9. But that assumption runs counter to the histories of most learning-disabled children, who seem to have manifested learning problems from an early age. If anything, one might expect to find evidence of brain dysfunction at an early age while, at a later time, with increasing maturation and compensatory learning, these signs might become obliterated (Dykman et al., 1971). A different interpretation would seem to be necessary.

Developmental Lag   A difference between younger and older learning-disabled children such as reported by Rourke and his co-workers (1971, 1973a), if it indeed exists, might be explained by a developmental hypothesis. According to this, learning-disabled children have an impaired ability to learn from early in life, possibly from birth. As a result, they lag behind their peers and siblings in the acquisition of academic skills. Given the typical response of their parents and teachers, which increases the stress for the children and makes them feel inadequate, insecure, and anxious in any learning and testing situation, these children become more and more disorganized. Thus the older they get (without receiving appropriate help), the more they appear like the disorganized, anxious, inadequate-feeling adults who have sustained injury to the brain. This formulation leads one to conclude that learning-disabled children should receive specialized instruction and help from the earliest possible moment before their problem has become complicated by a complex of untoward psychological reactions.

Learning Disabilities as a Developmental Lag

Improvement in the performance of a skill is the only way by which learning can be demonstrated. Learning disabilities are therefore demonstrable only when performance fails to show expected improvement. In the case of children, one bases this expectation on the child's chronological age and the opportunities for learning provided by the environment (teaching). Chronological age is taken into consideration because we do not expect a child to be able to learn certain skills (such as writing) until physical maturation has reached the required level. This physical maturation includes not only such obvious aspects as muscular strength and motor coordination but also more subtle capacities such as visual-motor coordination, memory span, symbolization, sequential ordering of stimuli, and sustaining selective attention.

Some of these capacities are easily observed and no one would expect a child to benefit from writing instruction unless he or she had developed the capacity to hold a crayon and control its movement on a flat surface. The more subtle, less readily observed capacities are usually assumed to be present if the child has reached a given chronological age, but this assumption may not be valid for quite a number of children. The existence of individual differences in rate of maturation is an established fact, but many educational systems operate as if this were not the case. For most children, entry into school is determined not by maturational readiness but by date of birth.

The issue is complicated by the fact that there are not only individual differences in maturation but also intra-individual differences in the rate at which the various learning-relevant capacities mature. Just as there is no reason to assume that all six-year-olds have reached the same level of visual-motor coordination, so there is no reason to believe that a given six-year-old has reached the same maturational level in visual-motor coordination, memory span, and ability to sustain selective attention. If a child were to develop the ability to sustain selective attention somewhat more slowly than other abilities essential for academic learning, this child would be handicapped in school, where it is assumed that he or she is "old enough" to benefit from instruction aimed at the average child of that age. This handicap may then find expression in a failure to learn a specific skill, such as reading, and the child might then be identified as having a learning disability. This is the reasoning which underlies the assumption of those who view learning disabilities as due to a developmental lag or developmental imbalance, an assumption that requires no speculations about the integrity of the brain.

Gallagher (1966) has been among those who view learning disabilities as an expression of developmental imbalances. Finding that etiological speculations regarding brain functions are logically deficient, epistemologically inadequate, and educationally irrelevant, Gallagher proposed the following "psychoeducational definition" of learning disabilities, a definition which focuses on ability patterns.

> Children with Developmental Imbalances are those who reveal a developmental disparity in psychological processes related to education of such a degree (often four years or more) as to require the instructional programming of developmental tasks appropriate to the nature and level of the deviant developmental process (p. 28).

Gallagher points out that this definition places the emphasis not on assumptions about neurological etiology but on behavior and patterns of development. It thus highlights necessary remedial steps which should focus on areas where the child's development shows disparities. The large intra-individual differences in academic skills that are manifested by children with learning disabilities are their identifying characteristics. Unlike the mentally retarded child, whose performance level is generally deficient in all areas, the child with learning disabilities shows imbalances, as Gallagher's definition makes clear. The implication of Gallagher's definition for an educational program is that such a program must allow for individual attention and tutoring. Educational planning must not blindly follow a pattern that may have been successful with such other groups as the mentally retarded or the brain-injured.

Perceptual-Motor Training   As we pointed out in the brief historical review in Chapter 1, the fact that many of the early pioneers in the field of learning disabilities had first worked with brain-injured children may have led to an emphasis on an aspect of behavior with which brain-injured people often experience difficulty: perceptual-motor coordination. Since the children who carry the label "learning-disabled" are a very heterogeneous group, it is not surprising that some of them do poorly on tests of perceptual-motor coordination. In fact, delayed development of selective attention may be reflected in such test performance.

There now exist several remedial programs for learning-disabled children which focus on exercises designed to enhance perceptual-motor functions (e.g., Kephart, 1971; Frostig & Maslow, 1973). These programs are usually built around special tests. After having received training designed to improve functions on which they have been found wanting on the tests, children often show improved test performance. Two important points are often overlooked in the discussion of such programs. One is that not all children whom one identifies as learning-disabled have perceptual-motor problems; thus they don't need such training. The other point is that, ultimately, the problem of the learning-disabled child is that he or she has difficulty in learning to read, to write, or to do arithmetic. The test of the efficacy of a particular remedial program of perceptual-motor training is therefore not whether the child can do a better job matching or copying geometric figures but whether he is successful in the acquisition of reading, writing, or arithmetic. The answer to this is singularly difficult to obtain from available research.

Methodologically sound studies on the efficacy of perceptual-motor training programs in helping learning-disabled children achieve in their academic work are exceedingly rare. To provide meaningful answers to the question of efficacy, investigators must use a relevant population and valid tests of academic achievement. They must control for the effect of contact with teachers who have a high investment in the method yet use it in the manner in which its proponents advocate it. They must further assess the effect not only immediately upon termination of the intervention but also after a period of time has elapsed, because the effect may be a subtle modification of developmental processes which show an influence only some months after the intervention. We did not find a single study in the literature which satisfied all of these requirements, the last, of course, being the most difficult to meet because of the time constraints under which most research is conducted. Two studies which come close to the ideal fail to support the efficacy of perceptual-motor training.

O'Donnell (1969) studied the effect of the highly publicized Doman-Delacato technique (Delacato, 1963), about which there has been extensive controversy (Freeman, 1967). Sixty disabled readers between the ages of 7 and 10 were randomly divided into three groups, two of which received various Doman-Delacato procedures while one was given an equal amount of physical education activities to control for attention and teacher contact. After 20 weeks, during which the children had received exercises for 30 minutes each day from teachers who rotated in order to control for teacher effect, the three groups did not differ significantly in their mean difference scores on standardized reading tests. The Frostig program (Frostig & Maslow, 1973) did not fare much better in a study conducted by Anderson (1972). Here, 33 second-graders with "visual-perceptual difficulties" and reading problems received 16 weeks of daily treatment by teachers who had been trained in the use of the method. Compared with a control group which had received the same amount of teacher attention, the treatment group failed to show significant improvement. What improvement there was seemed more a function of personal attention than of the specifics of either the Frostig program or of remedial reading.

It may well be that these disappointing results are a function of inappropriate selection of the children treated. As long as one groups children simply in terms of learning or reading disabilities and fails to ask just what the nature of their particular difficulty is, one will apply and test remedial programs with such a heterogeneous population that potential improvements in a few children for whom the method is appropriate will be obscured by the lack of change or by deterioration among those children for whom the method is irrelevant. It is not likely that much progress will be made in this field until the category "learning disabilities" is broken down into component units based on children's specific disabilities.

In a later chapter (Chapter 7), we shall have occasion to comment on the need for relevancy of training methods. Suffice it here to point out that it is naïve to assume that a child who has trouble learning how to read will magically learn reading as a result of a program solely aimed at improving visual-motor coordination. A child will learn reading only when one provides the opportunity to learn reading, by teaching him or her to read. No amount of perceptual-motor training can take the place of carefully individualized tutoring that takes the child's maturational level and prior learning into account.

SUMMARY

In searching for an explanation for children's learning disabilities, people have looked for disorders in the brains of such children. The hypothesis that learning disabilities are due to a malfunction in the brain has never been proved, and the vagueness of the formulation makes it impossible to disprove. Observations that learning-disabled children are sometimes hyperactive and distractible and that some of them manifest difficulties in perceptual-motor coordination have been used in support of the assumption that there exists a minimal brain dysfunction syndrome. Research on this issue has failed to substantiate that the observed behavioral phenomena cluster as the concept of a syndrome would demand.

Studies aimed at the brain functions of learning-disabled children have failed to find evidence for brain damage. The studies do tend to reveal devel-

opmental immaturities and problems on tests of sequencing, intersensory integration, and similar tasks requiring attention to complex stimuli. These results
were interpreted as offering further support for the assumption that learning-
disabled children are children with a developmental delay in acquiring the
ability to sustain selective attention.

The observation that some learning-disabled children have trouble on
tests requiring visual-motor coordination has led to the development of many
programs which aim to enhance this coordination. Perceptual-motor training
is often recommended for learning-disabled children regardless of whether this
is indeed an area of weakness for them and in the absence of proof that such
training helps children improve their academic performance.

Chapter 5

Hyperactivity and the Effects of Medication

HYPERACTIVITY

In discussions of learning-disabled children, frequent mention is made of their activity level, which is said to be greater than that of the so-called normal child. In fact, when Clements (1966) listed the order of frequency in which the various characteristics of learning-disabled children were cited in the literature, hyperactivity led all the rest. For some writers (e. g., Werry, Weiss, & Douglas, 1964), the term "hyperactivity" is synonymous with "learning disability," yet the high frequency with which hyperactivity is found among learning-disabled children may well be an artifact due to selection bias.

Hyperactivity and Learning Disability

As was pointed out in Chapter 1, a disability in learning is difficult to detect, since it can only be identified by comparing a child's actual performance with his or her presumed potential. As a result, very bright children with learning disabilities may well elude detection because they can function at an average level, thus not necessarily arousing anyone's suspicion that they could do much better.

   Imagine two such learning-disabled children in the same class, neither of whom is suspected of having a problem. One of the two, however, fails to sit still, is constantly on the move, fidgets, speaks out of turn, and occasionally hits other children. It will be the latter who will be singled out for study and thus likely to be identified as learning-disabled, while the former continues to sit in class, learning less than his or her capacity might permit and maybe being considered "slow." Even where a teacher suspects that a given child might conceivably do better—that is, might be learning-disabled—referral for assessment is more likely if that child is hyperactive and thus disrupts classroom routine than if he or she sits quietly and is no trouble for the teacher.

   If one multiplied these examples sufficiently, one could arrive at the observation that all learning-disabled children are hyperactive—not because this is in fact the case but because it is the hyperactive learning-disabled child who attracts attention and thus comes to the notice of the people who write journal articles and textbooks. Whether the hyperactivity these children display is no more than high but normal motility, whether it is their reaction to repeated failure experiences, whether it is an aspect of their difficulty in sustaining selective attention, or whether it is in some or all cases indeed a reflection of neurological problems (minimal brain dysfunction) remain questions calling for research.

   In this connection it is of considerable interest to note the results of a survey conducted by Tuddenham, Brooks, and Milkovich (1974), who administered a 100-item behavior inventory to more than 3,000 mothers of ten-year-old children who represented a sample of the normal population. One of the items on this inventory read, "Hates to sit still, restless." Mothers of boys checked this as true for their child in 42 percent of the cases; mothers of girls, 30 percent of the time. There was a significant difference between white and black children for both sexes. For boys from black families, this item was checked by their mothers as descriptive 52 percent of the time; for girls, 44 percent of the time.

   With such a high prevalence of this behavior among presumably normal children, one must be extremely circumspect in drawing conclusions about the presence of the same behavior among some learning-disabled children. Werry has speculated (Werry, Minde, Guzman, Weiss, Dogan, & Hoy, 1972) that hyperactivity may represent a "biological variant" on the dimension of activity level—that it constitutes the upper end of the normal distribution of this behavior. He suggests that this level of activity manifests itself as a problem as a result of the society's insistence on universal literacy, which is to be acquired in a sedentary position. In other words, the problem of the hyperactive child is a problem only because our society places a premium on controlled activity and lengthy periods of sitting still.

   Before we can examine some of the research that has been carried out on the topic of hyperactivity in children, it is well to remind ourselves that hyperactivity, though a noun, is not an entity but only a descriptive term that implies a judgment. Some influential person in the child's environment must have decided that his or her activity level is beyond the ordinary, beyond tolerable limits, beyond the accepted norm. The Greek prefix of that linguistically hybrid term should not lead one to forget that all hyperactivity says is that somebody thinks that the child moves around "too much."

Yet what is "too much" for one person or group of persons may be quite acceptable to others, so that hyperactivity is essentially a relative, descriptive label which reflects other people's reactions to the child's behavior. There is no norm for what the appropriate level of a child's motor activity is other than that residing in the expectations of the social environment. As has been the case with other behaviors that fail to conform to the expectations of society, physicians have given it a quasi-Greek label with connotations of abnormality. They thus speak of a "hyperkinetic behavior syndrome" (Laufer & Denhoff, 1957) or a "hyperactive child syndrome" (Stewart, Pitts, Craig, & Dieruf, 1966). It was not long before the children who thus had been labeled as if they had a disease were treated with such drugs as methylphenidate (Ritalin) which, with some of these children, reduces motor activity.

No doubt, a child who engages in a great deal of vigorous motor activity can be difficult to have around the house and annoying in a classroom. Such a child causes problems, but that does not necessarily mean that they are his or her problems. In some instances at least, the problems may lie in the low tolerance level of the people in the child's environment. At times it might be worth considering whether intervention should be aimed at raising the tolerance level of significant adults instead of lowering the activity level of the child.

At any rate, in focusing on a child's easily observed activity level, one should not lose sight of his less readily observed problem of learning disability, for our task is not so much to reduce the activity level as it is to help the child learn. Where learning disability is accompanied by hyperactivity, there is often the risk that intervention is aimed solely at the motor behavior on the untenable assumption that the learning problem will take care of itself once the child "settles down."

Hyperactivity and Cerebral Damage

The observation that many learning-disabled children are also hyperactive has been cited in support of their contention, by those who seek a cause for learning disability in the malfunctioning of the child's brain. The illogical basis of this argument is that children with known brain damage (often) display hyperactivity; hence, learning-disabled children who display hyperactivity must be brain-damaged. By extension of this logical fallacy, it is then concluded that all learning-disabled children are brain-damaged and that the brain damage caused their learning disability. Since the original observation that many learning-disabled children are also hyperactive is no more than a correlation, any conclusion regarding causality is, of course, unwarranted. A number of investigations, in fact, have failed to find a link between brain damage and the hyperactivity of learning-disabled children (Minde, Webb, & Sykes, 1968).

Werry (1972) reviewed the research literature dealing with hyperactive children from the standpoint of the role of brain damage. His carefully worded summary, replete with qualifiers, bespeaks the current state of ignorance in this field. He states that the majority of studies he reviewed suggest that

> the hyperkinetic syndrome is associated to a varying extent with certain paranatal, neurological, EEG, and cognitive abnormalities. The relationship between these variables and indeed their very significance is obscure, but they seem to be weakly suggestive of some kind of cerebral dysfunction, the nature of which is unclear but which may reflect a variety of causes ranging from frank brain damage through normal variation to adverse socio-familial experience (p. 106).

Werry believes that in the majority of cases it is impossible to determine which of the several potential causative factors was responsible for a child's hyperactivity. He writes further,

> A significant number of children who exhibit some of the behavioral components of the hyperkinetic syndrome probably have no abnormalities in any other areas of function or, in short, have no signs of cerebral dysfunction. In no sense, then, can these behavioral symptoms be taken in themselves as diagnostic of cerebral damage of [sic] dysfunction (pp. 106–107).

Characteristics of the Hyperactive Child   It has been estimated that about one in 25 children in first grade displays hyperactivity; that is to say, there is, on the average, one hyperactive child in every first-grade class. Stewart, Pitts, Craig, and Dieruf (1966), who offered this estimate, conducted a controlled study which demonstrated that hyperactivity can be found in the absence of clear indications of brain damage. These investigators studied 37 children (32 boys and 5 girls) who were attending a clinic chiefly concerned with behavior disorders. These children were between the ages of 5 and 11 and their problem behaviors included overactivity and short attention span. For comparison, the authors selected 36 children who were attending first grade and came from a socioeconomic background similar to that of the clinic cases. In order to obtain this comparison group, the investigators had interviewed the mothers of 47 children. Among these they found 3 who met their criterion for hyperactivity, and this formed the basis of their estimate of the frequency of this problem.

The interviews conducted in the course of the study by Stewart et al. (1966) revealed that hyperactivity, "fidgeting," distractibility, and short attention span differentiated the clinic children from those in the comparison group. Unlike the latter, the clinic children frequently were also described as unpredictable, wearing out furniture and toys, impatient, unresponsive to discipline and correction, defiant, reckless, and frequently getting into fights. Of the 37 clinic children, 22 had a history of discipline problems and 15 a history of repeated fights in school.

Although the initial selection of the clinic children studied by Stewart, Pitts, Craig, and Dieruf (1966) was based on hyperactivity and short attention span, most of them also had learning problems. Thus, 15 of the 37 clinic children had repeated one or more grades in school, and delayed speech development was reported for 20 of the hyperactive but for only 9 of the comparison children. Other reflections that the clinic children had difficulty in learning new skills might be seen in the maladaptive social behavior (frequent fighting) and in the poor coordination which was found with far greater frequency among the clinic than among the comparison children.

The descriptive term "poor coordination" obscures the behavior to which it refers. Children such as those studied by Stewart et al. (1966) are often reported to have had inordinate trouble learning to ride a bicycle, learning to hit a ball with a bat, or learning similar gross motor skills. With this observation one can inquire what in the child's learning strategy makes it so difficult for him to acquire new skills, or one can ask why these children have these problems. Stewart et al. (1966) chose to ask this etiological question, and although only four of their clinic children "had a history which suggested probable brain injury" (p. 866), they interpreted the speech problems and the poor coordination as suggesting that "brain dysfunction" (ibid.) is often the basis of hyperactivity or, as they put it, of the "hyperactive child syndrome."

The delay in language development, defined as not using words until after age 2 or not speaking in sentences until after the age 3, was not the only difference in early development which Stewart et al. (1966) found between the hyperactive and the normal children in their study. The mothers of the hyperactive children also reported with a significantly higher frequency than did the mothers of the comparison children such early problems as feeding and sleep difficulties and "poor health" in the child's first year of life.

The composite picture of the infancy and early childhood of the hyperactive children in this sample is of children who are difficult to feed, have trouble sleeping, are often in ill health, and do not learn to speak or speak adequately until age 3 or later. It is noteworthy that these children were not described as hyperactive when they were little, although their mothers tended to place the onset of the problem in infancy. The problem, however, appears to be that such an infant is generally a "difficult child" (Thomas, Chess, & Birch, 1968) who only later comes to be identified as "hyperactive."

We don't know why some children are "difficult" children, they seem to be born that way; they may have a constitutionally determined behavioral style, a temperament, that sets them apart from other children who are reported to be "easy" to raise. Nothing in their history suggests that these "difficult children" are neurologically damaged children. In the Stewart, Pitts, Craig, and Dieruf (1966) study, there were no differences between the hyperactive and the comparison groups in incidence of reproductive complications such as difficult pregnancy or delivery; head injury requiring medical attention was found in five of the normal and only one of the hyperactive children.

The Hyperactive Child and the Environment

A child with a behavioral style that makes for difficulty in his or her development does not grow up in a vacuum. It is well to remember that such a child, or any child for that matter, represents a stimulus complex for the parents initially and for others later on—a stimulus complex to which these people respond. The child, in turn, reacts to these responses, and we thus have a transactional system of interpersonal behaviors which ultimately culminates in the child's behavior pattern, which some like to call personality.

We have pointed out elsewhere (Ross, 1974) that such a transactional point of view of human development makes it quite pointless to ask whether the parents or the child are to blame if the child's condition turns out to be problematic. The same child with different parents or the same parents with a different child would, in all likelihood, have led to a different outcome. If we are to look for a cause, we must look at the interaction between child and parents; if we are to attempt to prevent the development of particular problems, we should probably address ourselves to modifying this interaction.

This point was discerningly made by Sameroff and Chandler (1974), who reviewed the literature on the relationship between pregnancy and delivery complications and later intellectual performance. When one identifies a group of children of low intelligence and high academic difficulties and traces back to their early development, one finds a very great frequency of reproductive complications. This strongly suggests that these children suffered some damage to their brains around the time of birth. (Note that we are here not speaking of children with learning disabilities.) Such retrospective data had long led behavioral scientists to assume that perinatal difficulties are an important cause of many cases of intellectual inadequacy.

More recent work, however, has followed large groups of children from before birth to the early years of school, and from this we learn that children who suffered a reproductive complication may or may not develop later difficulties *depending on the caretaking environment in which they are reared.* Specifically, children with poor reproductive histories who are raised in economically deprived families, or whose mothers have had poor educations or psychological disorders, tend to be intellectually retarded when they are tested at school age. On the other hand, children with similar reproductive complications who are raised in an advantaged environment appear to overcome whatever difficulties may be associated with their birth history, so that by school age they appear little different from children whose perinatal experience was uneventful.

It would seem that difficulties around birth do not necessarily lead to later problems, but that it depends on who suffers these difficulties and what experiences he or she has during infancy and childhood. If these experiences are favorable, reproductive complications may have no later consequences. It is not so much the nature of a child but the interaction this child has with the environment that determines the child's later status. Sameroff and Chandler (1974) point out that children with poor reproductive histories tend to have more disrupting temperaments than those with good histories. They tend to elicit poor caretaking responses from their parents, and it is this transaction which places the child "at risk" and contributes to developmental disorders. Early attempts to help the caretaking environment adjust to the special needs of an infant who may be temperamentally deviant should permit one to prevent the development of a whole range of psychological disorders.

Similar conclusions were reached by Battle and Lacey (1972), who pointed out that

> High levels of motor activity in children may not, in themselves, be detrimental; rather the effects of high activity levels on the child's interactions with his environment may sometimes be damaging. The reactions and reinforcements he receives from peers, parents, and other adults may result in the kind of negative behaviors (aggression, defiance, discipline problems) which have been observed in clinical samples (p. 758).

These investigators present data which lend strong support to the assumption that many of the behaviors that form a part of the hyperactivity "syndrome" are the result of the child's reinforcement history and not an inherent characteristic of a disease, as the medical word "syndrome" implies.

The data used by Battle and Lacey (1972) had been gathered in the course of the Fels Longitudinal Study, in which individuals had been followed from birth to young adulthood. It should be noted that the participants were a nonclinical sample; unlike those usually studied, they had not been referred to a clinician because of learning difficulties or other behavior problems. At the time these data were collected, during the period 1939–1957, the "hyperkinetic syndrome" had not yet been named (discovered?), so that the observations and ratings were not influenced by attitudes which might lead one to view an unusually active child as abnormal.

Battle and Lacey (1972) defined hyperactivity for the purpose of their study as the degree to which the child's motor behavior had been recorded as "impulsive, uninhibited, and uncontrolled, as well as the total amount of vigorous motor activity" (p. 761). They found that over three childhood periods (birth to 3, 3 to 6, and 6 to 10), motor hyperactivity was relatively stable. They found further that the hyperactive males showed less evidence of general achievement striving and, during the first two age periods, "a particular lack of approach toward intellectual tasks" (p. 767). There was no significant relationship between IQ scores and hyperactivity, nor was there a significant association with grades attained in high school or college (data regarding performance in elementary school were unfortunately not available). In spite of this, hyperactive three- to six-year-olds had been rated by their mothers as possessing lower levels of intelligence during elementary school years, and boys who were hyperactive in infancy estimated their own intelligence to be low during adolescence. The same group also expressed anxiety about their intellectual competence in adulthood.

The reaction of people to hyperactive boys—that is, the reaction which may affect the development of their behavior—is highlighted by the report that the mothers of these boys were "critical, disapproving, and severe in their imposition of penalties for disobedience; lacking in affection, protectiveness, and babying; and characterized by a low intensity of interaction with their sons" (ibid.). The boys, on the other hand, demonstrated a lack of compliance toward adults; seeking rather to gain the adults' attention and to dominate them during the childhood years. They also showed physical aggression toward their peers and attempted to seek their attention and to dominate them.

All this stands in marked contrast to the observations recorded for the hyperactive girls. Negative maternal reactions were not significantly correlated with hyperactivity; and while girls too were physically bold and socially aggressive during the ages of 3 through 6, they, in contrast to the boys, "demonstrated significantly *greater* achievement approach efforts in childhood and a high estimate of their own intelligence in adolescence" (p. 771). In adulthood, on the other hand, these females held lower values and standards for academic achievement, as if the negative reactions of their teachers to female assertiveness and vigor had the same stifling effect that had been observed for males, only at a much earlier period.

In summary, Battle and Lacey (1972) point out that the hyperactive behavior of boys is received negatively by their mothers from the earliest years, and that this disapproval is particularly associated with the intellectual-academic aspects of their behavior. The mother erroneously evaluates her son as having low intelligence and finds him to be both low in achievement striving and nonpersistent at intellectual tasks. When these boys become adolescents and adults, they manifest doubt and anxiety toward intellectual competence and academic achievement.

The authors suggest that their data reveal the contribution of parental and environmental forces in the exacerbation of the problem and the particular focus on intellectual-academic aspects of it. From this they conclude that "it would seem wise to consider the possibility of changing the social context surrounding motor hyperactivity for young boys and for elementary school-age girls" (p. 772) instead of relying on drugs to "manage" troublesome youngsters. One may question to what extent correlational data based on information gathered without a specific focus on the problem under investigation permit one to draw this conclusion. But the overreliance on drugs for the "treatment" of children whose excessive motor behavior disrupts the class room rests, as we shall see, on even weaker data than those on which this objection is based.

Studies of the relationship between hyperactivity and other variables usually begin with a group of children who have been identified as hyperactive and referred to a clinical facility because of this or related problems. These children are then studied in some detail, but whatever conclusions are drawn from such a study apply only to that clinic population and not to any of the children, either with or without problems, who were not included in the original sample.

A rare exception to this approach is found in a study by Wolff and Hurwitz (1973), who gave a neurological screening examination to an unselected population of 1,300 presumably normal ten- to twelve-year-old children attending a public school. The examination was designed to detect *choreiform movements*. These are small jerks of brief duration which occur irregularly in different muscle groups over the entire body. For the examination, the child is asked to place the feet together and to stand for 30 seconds with head centered, arms extended, fingers spread as wide apart as possible, and eyes closed. Choreiform movements are most easily noticed when one observes the child's fingers, wrist joints, arms, and shoulders (Wolff & Hurwitz, 1973). The presence of these movements is usually taken to suggest the presence of neurological dysfunction, and they have been reported to be associated with a history of complications during pregnancy and delivery. In view of this, it is of interest that Wolff and Hurwitz, in their survey conducted in a public school, found choreiform movements in 11.4 percent of the children.

From among the children with choreiform movements identified in their survey, Wolff and Hurwitz (1973) selected 103 boys and 25 girls for a more detailed study and comparison with an unimpaired control group. (The boy-girl ratio reflects the skewed incidence of the phenomenon in the original sample.) Independently obtained teacher reports, school records, and intelligence test data were examined. The results revealed that boys with choreiform movements had significantly more reading and spelling difficulties than boys without these tremors. This relationship was not found for girls. On the other hand, while there was no relationship between intelligence test scores and tremors for boys, these scores showed a marked difference between choreiform and nonchoreiform girls, with—surprisingly—the former having significantly higher IQ scores.

For both boys and girls, however, choreiform movements were strongly associated with teachers' unfavorable comments about the children's behavior. Boys with the tremors were reported to be less motivated, more immature, less cooperative, less well coordinated, and to have poorer work habits than the boys in the control group. Speech and hearing difficulties were also more frequent among the boys with choreiform movements than among the controls. On the other hand, neither hyperactivity nor poor attention span differentiated the two groups. This is of particular interest in view of the frequent assumption that these problems are related to "minimal brain damage," of which choreiform movements are sometimes presumed to be an indication.

To turn to the results for the girls, here too those with choreiform movements received significantly more unfavorable comments from their teachers than did the control group. These girls were reported to be less mature, to have shorter attention spans (unlike the boys!), and to be less cooperative. None of the other behavioral items revealed a difference between the two groups. As far as intelligence test scores and reports from teachers are concerned, it appears that boys and girls with choreiform movements present a somewhat different picture, and this should serve to warn us against generalizations about "children" when only boys or only girls are studied.

Wolff and Hurwitz (1973) are suitably conservative in interpreting their results. They stress that their findings may hold true for only the one school they studied and conclude that in this school choreiform movements can identify individuals whose classroom behavior differs significantly from that of other children. Since one obviously does not need a neurological test to make that particular identification, what does the relationship between muscle jerks and unfavorable teacher reports tell us?

> Choreiform movements are obviously not pathognomonic [diagnostic signs] of minimal brain damage, minor cerebral dysfunction, or minimal brain dysfunction; nor do choreiform movements *cause* sever psychopathology, juvenile delinquency or learning disabilities (with which they are also associated). It is possible, however, that the behavioral correlates of choreiform movements such as clumsiness, distractibility, and emotional lability make the child a prime target of parental disapproval even before the school years, or that they interfere with the child's schoolwork. The interaction between behavior disturbances commonly associated with choreiform movements and an intolerant social environment may, therefore, predispose the child to one of several well-defined childhood disorders (pp. 112–113).

The conclusion reached by Wolff and Hurwitz (1973) is thus very similar to the thinking of Sameroff and Chandler (1974), who speak of a continuum of caretaking casualty whereby a child with a given characteristic which may be present from birth develops behavioral problems as a result of the interaction between the characteristic and the reactions of the social environment. The term "intolerant" used by Wolff and Hurwitz implies that the child's problems might be prevented if the social environment could be helped to be more tolerant of the child's individual characteristic.

Conclusions

What can one conclude on the basis of studies on hyperactive children? We can say that learning-disabled children are often described as hyperactive and that hyperactive children frequently have academic difficulties. Such a correlation tells us nothing about the direction of the relationship; whether hyperactivity causes learning disabilities, whether learning disabilities make children hyperactive, or whether both phenomena have a factor in common that causes both remains unknown. Certainly the correlation between hyperactivity and learning disability is not high enough to permit one to speak of a "syndrome," and there is no evidence to support the contention that either learning disability or hyperactivity are caused by identifiable abnormalities in the brain.

The most appealing hypothesis is the one advanced by Werry (Werry et al., 1972). According to this, activity level is seen as a normal dimension of behavior along which all children are distributed, and those at the high end of the continuum encounter difficulty because of the expectations and reactions of the social environment. The repeated criticism and negative evaluation encountered by such children might lead some of them to develop academic difficulties. However, it is likely that true learning disabilities, as we defined them in Chapter 1, are only related to hyperactivity by virtue of the fact that the learning-disabled child who is also hyperactive is more likely to be referred for study than will be the child who, though learning-disabled, sits quietly in his seat.

None of the above should be read as implying that there are not some children whose excess motility represents a genuine state of abnormality. We must, after all, remind ourselves of the fact that any group of children who have no more in common than that someone thinks that they are more than normally active ("hyperactive") must contain a great variety of individuals. Such a group, no doubt, represents a quite heterogeneous population. Some may move around a lot because that is their individual characteristic, some may be extraordinarily active because their environment has repeatedly reinforced them for that behavior, and some may be hyperactive because they do indeed have a neurological or biochemical disorder of which hyperactivity or hyperkinesis, as it is sometimes called, is a genuine symptom.

As we pointed out at the beginning of this chapter, hyperactivity is not an entity but merely a word that describes observed behavior. As such, it tells us only that the child so labeled moves around a lot; the observation cannot tell us more. It is well to keep this in mind as we move to a discussion of the use of drugs with children identified as hyperactive.

USE OF DRUGS

It frequently happens that when a phenomenon has aspects that place it at the border of two related disciplines, the study of the phenomenon will suffer, particularly if it is of a puzzling nature. This is the case because in their puzzlement the members of each discipline assume that the explanation lies in the other discipline. Physicians who are puzzled by a given disorder may thus be tempted to say, "It must be psychological"; while psychologists, at a loss to explain the same problem through their formulations, will suggest, "It must be organic," that is, something belonging in the realm of medicine. Both parties will then be satisfied that they have explained the problem and neither bothers to investigate it further, much to the loss of those who are afflicted with the disorder.

Matters are not helped when, as has at times happened, the members of one or the other discipline eagerly accept the attribution of responsibility for a given problem regardless of the suitability of their methods or their genuine interest in the topic. When the assignment of responsibility is then written into the laws, it may be decades before any meaningful work on the problem can be accomplished. This was the sequence of events that befell the area of mental subnormality, where educators and psychologists, puzzled by the phenomenon of people who could not learn, decided that the problem must be in the brains of these people, hence a problem for medicine. Medicine, partly by default, assumed responsibility for "oligophrenia," the word then used for mental deficiency.

Eventually the statutes required that the heads of the state institutions housing the mentally subnormal had to be licensed physicians—even though the name of such an institution might continue to include the word "school." This practice has only recently begun to be reversed, with the growing recognition that failure to learn, even when profound, is at least as much an educational as a medical problem. One hopes that educators, physicians, and others can work together on such problems. Thus, where none can know everything, each may well be able to contribute a part to the solution.

The purpose of this digression was to set the stage for the argument that the educator should guard against assigning total responsibility for understanding the problem of the hyperactive child to members of any other profession. No matter what may ultimately be discovered about the (probably) multiple causes of hyperactivity, these children's education is the problem of the school. They need to learn to participate in class, to attend to relevant material, and to remain task-oriented. They need to learn, and learning falls squarely into the psychoeducational realm.

But what about the use of medication? It is widely known that certain kinds of behavior problems can be reduced by the administration—clearly a medical function—of certain stimulant drugs such as amphetamines. Before examining the matter of medication, we need to be clear that the effectiveness of a drug or drugs, even where clearly proved, tells us nothing whatsoever about the cause of the problem which the medication alleviates. To think otherwise is to entertain the logical fallacy of *post hoc, ergo propter hoc*. Aspirin alleviates headaches; this does not prove that headaches thus successfully treated were caused by a deficient supply of acetanilide in the neurons of the brain. By extension, the apparent effectiveness of methylephenidate with certain learning-disabled or hyperactive children does not prove that their problem had an organic cause.

Methodological Issues

The effectiveness of a pharmacological agent is very difficult to prove, and this is particularly true in the case of a disorder as poorly defined as the problem that is variously labeled "learning disability," "hyperactivity," "hyperkinetic syndrome," "hyperactive child syndrome," "minor cerebral dysfunction," or "minimal brain damage." We know that the children thus labeled are often characterized by motor restlessness, impulsivity, attentional problems, distractibility, learning difficulties in one or more academic areas, and low tolerance for criticism, frustration, and interpersonal stress. We also know that not every child whom someone considers as belonging in this category will exhibit every one of these characteristics nor that each will be found at the same magnitude. It thus becomes a matter of judgment for the individual clinician whether a particular child should or should not be labeled according to that clinician's personal preference as to nomenclature.

The first decision which must be made by an investigator wishing to study the effectiveness of a drug used with hyperactive children must thus be what children to include in the hyperactive category. Unfortunately, no two investigators use the same definition, so that comparisons between studies or generalizations on the basis of several studies are impossible. Satterfield (1973), for example, wishing to study "children with minimal brain dysfunction," used criteria which require clear evidence of hyperactivity and distractibility and the presence of "any 6 of the 28 symptoms found to be most characteristic of the syndrome" (p. 36). The heterogeneity of a sample defined in this manner will make it difficult to interpret and generalize from the results of a study.

The source of the children in such studies is almost invariably a clinic to which they have been referred for help. Hyperactive children who have not been referred are thus not included in the research, and this introduces a sampling basis of unknown proportions which is difficult to overcome because of the ethical issues involved in administering drugs to children whose parents have not sought professional help.

Having decided on the definition and sampling criteria, the investigator must next settle on a research design. Here too drug research with children encounters complications. It has been established that there are psychological effects related to the knowledge that one is taking what one believes to be an effective medication. Such effects are often observed even in people who are ingesting an inert substance with no known chemical potency, a pseudo-medication called a *placebo*. In order to ascertain whether a particular drug derives its effectiveness from its chemical or its psychological attributes, an investigator must be able to control for this so-called placebo effect. One must therefore compare a condition where the child is given the drug to be tested with a double-blind placebo condition where he or she is given a pseudo-drug in such a fashion that the child, the parents, the teacher, and the dispensing physician believe that the child is receiving the real drug. Each child in the study should be evaluated under both the placebo and the drug condition, some receiving first the placebo and later the drug, others experiencing these conditions in reverse order. This order must, of course, be based on a carefully randomized design.

The children in the study would have to be given relevant behavioral tests before the administration of any substance and under each experimental condition. Since many such tests are affected by repeated administration, alternate forms of the tests are required, and the sequence in which these are used must also be counterbalanced. All these procedures (and the laboratory tests necessary to check on physical side effects) require many clinic visits and child-physician contacts. A well controlled study would want to assess the effect of these contacts by including a condition where the children receive neither medication nor placebo but merely the personal attention involved in the research procedures. In practice, of course, many of these methodological refinements are sacrificed for various reality considerations, leaving us with a host of inconclusive drug studies, as an extensive review by Sroufe (1975) has so clearly shown.

Because as elusive an entity as "minimal brain dysfunction" is difficult to diagnose, it has become customary in some circles (Wender, 1971) to place hyperactive children on a trial regimen of a drug like methylphenidate (Ritalin) in order to observe its effect. If the child's activity level then shows some reduction, this is used as the basis for the diagnosis of minimal brain dysfunction, usually in the absence of other supporting evidence and in clear disregard of rudimentary rules of logic. This deplorable practice being the case, studies on the effect of drugs should include yet another control group; a sample of normal children. This is necessary for, unless one knows how normal children would respond to the drug, one cannot possibly draw conclusions as to the etiology of hyperactivity from the responses of some hyperactive children.

Were normal children also to display a reduction in activity level upon ingesting methylphenidate, the conclusion about minimal brain dysfunction in hyperactive children would have to be called into question, though the pragmatic effect of the drug need not be challenged. A normal control group for a drug study would be difficult to obtain, and most investigators choose not to include such a group in their studies. This, therefore, is yet another strategy decision, and while one cannot quarrel with it, we should be aware that it limits the conclusions that might be drawn from such research.

Calling for a control group of normal children who would be given a medication raises an interesting ethical dilemma that highlights the ethical issue involved in the use of drugs with learning-disabled and/or hyperactive children. Administering an amphetamine-like drug to a group of normal children is something few if any experimenters are willing to do and no school authority would countenance. At the same time school authorities and experimenters have, at times, selected children for drug studies merely on the basis of teacher referral and without independent diagnostic assessment. Clearly, an unknown percentage of children thus selected are essentially normal youngsters whose only problem is that they are more restless or learn less readily than their teacher or parents would like.

Thus far we have discussed the methodological issues surrounding sample selection and research design. All these involve decisions an investigator has to make before a study on the effects of medication on hyperactivity can be launched. Still other strategy decisions involve such questions as which of several available drugs to study, what dosage to use, and how to assure that the children receive and actually ingest the pills they are supposed to be taking. This last point is next to impossible to monitor when, as in the case of hyperactive children, the participants in a drug study are not hospitalized but living at home and attending school.

The Criterion Problem Even assuming that all the questions of research method, design, and strategy could be satisfactorily resolved, there remains the biggest question of all: by what criterion and with what measure to assess effectiveness. By whatever name they are called, the children in whom we are interested have difficulty learning academic subject matter, move around a lot, and have trouble attending to a task. To demonstrate effectiveness any treatment would have to show improvement in these three areas. How is one to measure this improvement?

There are many standardized tests which reflect knowledge of academic material; tests of reading achievement, for example. These, unfortunately, do not reflect the gradual and subtle changes which a drug might bring about from week to week. Nor, for that matter, are they designed to measure changes in *learning capacity*, which is what a truly effective chemical agent should enhance. As O'Malley and Eisenberg (1973) have pointed out, drugs do not produce learning; they make it possible to learn to the extent that they are effective in suppressing overactivity or impulsivity and thus in increasing a child's ability to attend. In order to assess changes in learning capacity, one would need an instrument specifically designed to measure just that. Unfortunately, no good test of this nature is in existence. Drawing of pictures, copying of designs, tests of intelligence, or other tests of achievement simply do not provide the necessary index. Most investigators, however, use just such measures, or they fall back on global judgments of teachers and parents and report "improvement" on a three-point scale.

The picture is not much brighter when it comes to measuring changes in motor activity and attention. A few investigators use laboratory measures of attention and distractibility, and some have devised seat cushions or activity watches to monitor body movement; these, however, provide an index of behavior only while the child is in the laboratory and give no information of what goes on in classroom or home. For that one would need a time-sampling observational approach as was used by Sprague, Barnes, and Werry (1970) but by few other investigators.

Having reviewed the obstacles that stand in the way of conclusive research on drug effects, we can now understand why the studies which have been reported leave the question of the effectiveness of drugs in cases of hyperactivity and learning disabilities essentially unanswered.

Drugs and Learning

The drugs most frequently used with hyperactive, learning-disabled children are the stimulants dextroamphetamine (Dexedrine) and methylphenidate (Ritalin). Dexedrine appears to be the more potent of the two; it is thought necessary to administer roughly twice the amount of Ritalin in order to obtain the behavioral change produced by a given milligram dosage of Dexedrine. Unfortunately, even this statement about the comparative effectiveness of the two most widely used drugs is not based on established fact but on inferences drawn from unrelated studies (Omenn, 1973). In order to establish the relative effectiveness of two drugs, it is necessary to conduct a study in which the same individuals receive each of the treatments and a placebo in systematically arranged blocks of time, blocks that are carefully counterbalanced so as to control for a potential sequence effect. Such a study has never been conducted. This is unfortunate, since it is conceivable that some children may respond better to one drug than to the other.

If we resign ourselves to the fact that a methodologically ideal study may never be done and that powerful drugs will continue to be given to children on the basis of less-than-certain knowledge, we can summarize existing research by quoting the impression recorded by Omenn (1973), who felt "that prompt and dramatic improvement occurs in only a small proportion of cases, that the majority have some or considerable improvement, due at least in part to environmental structuring and placebo-effect, and that some have no response or even become worse" (p. 10). Regarding the last possibility, that children become worse under medication, Omenn (1973) cites a report by Safer, Allen, and Barr (1972), who found a suppression of growth in weight and height of a small group of hyperactive children being treated with stimulant drugs.

In cases where they are effective, stimulant drugs appear to decrease hyperactivity, impulsivity, and accompanying aggressivity and destructiveness. Performance on routinized, repetitive tasks requiring sustained attention and selective control over motor responses tends to improve (Campbell et al., 1971; Sykes et al., 1971), especially in structured situations (Ellis, Witt, Reynolds, & Sprague, 1974). Improvement is often reflected in scores on those tests of intelligence (such as WISC performance items and the Porteus Maze Test) where poor motor control, impulsivity, and limited attention interfere with adequate performance. It should be obvious that this improvement in intelligence test scores does not mean that drugs improve intelligence; they merely permit a child's intellectual capacity to be expressed in a scorable fashion. Reasoning, problem solving, and learning do not seem to be affected (Rioute & Stewart, 1973).

This relates to a point made earlier to the effect that drugs do not produce learning; they can only make learning more possible. That they do this is, of course, no mean achievement, particularly since the drug-induced changes in the child's behavior elicit changes in the attitudes others (peers, parents, and teachers) hold about the child. Such children, in fact, tend to perceive themselves in a more favorable light. It is these changes in attitudes held by significant people in the child's environment which are reflected in the ratings of "improvement" that are so often used to assess the effectiveness of drugs.

Risks and Benefits   The school-related behavior of some children definitely improves when they are given a stimulant drug; many other children do not improve, and some get worse. At this point it is not possible to predict which of these three possible outcomes is to be expected with any given child. This means that there are many children who are given medications that will either not help them or that will make them worse; medications whose long-range effect is not known and the taking of which has, as we shall see, a number of negative implications. In balancing the possible risks against the possible benefits, personal bias inevitably enters.

Wender (1971) examined what he calls the "pay-off matrix" and chooses "a trial of stimulant (amphetamine or methylphenidate) therapy in all children in whom the diagnosis of MBD [minimal brain dysfunction] is suspected" (p. 130). In other words, he recommends that drugs be tried on the mere suspicion of "minimal" brain damage. If, in the course of this trial, the child's behavior undergoes a change, Wender would draw the conclusion that the diagnosis was correct. We have previously pointed out that this is fallacious reasoning, particularly in the absence of data regarding the reaction of normal children to these stimulant drugs. Yet Wender (1971) goes so far as to suggest that *not* using stimulant drugs may amount to medical malpractice—that is, to constitute harmful withholding of a useful treatment.

The problem with Wender's (1971) reasoning is that he has set up a straw man by comparing the effectiveness of medication with the results of doing nothing or giving a child traditional psychotherapy (which he correctly views as the equivalent of doing nothing). Doing nothing or engaging in demonstrably ineffective efforts would indeed be unethical, but these are not the alternatives to drug treatment. The effective alternative to medication is behavior therapy. The changes in hyperactivity, attention, and motor control which can sometimes be brought about by drugs can also be produced without the use of drugs by the application of psychological principles in classroom management programs (O'Leary & O'Leary, 1972) or individualized treatment (Patterson, Jones, Whittier, & Wright, 1965).

This being the case, we are faced with a choice between a behavioral and a pharmacological approach to treatment or with a decision to use a combination of the two. Ideally, such a choice should be an empirical question. We should be able to refer to research that answers the question of relative effectiveness in clearly defined situations. In the absence of such research and with the pressing need to make decisions nonetheless, one must base one's decisions on less objective grounds. The prescribing of a drug to induce behavior change is obviously the quicker and (for the therapist) easier of the two methods; but despite this apparent advantage, there would seem to be several reasons for preferring a drug-free approach to the problem. These reasons have to do with the psychological implications of managing behavior with drugs and involve issues of locus of control, attribution, and abuse potential.

Drugs and Attitudes

A person who experiences a change either in physical sensations or in overt behavior will usually attempt to attribute this change to some cause. As the classical study by Schachter and Singer (1962) demonstrated, this attribution is not necessarily accurate and it can be influenced by a variety of factors, including the situation in which the person finds himself at the time. Thus, when physiological arousal is induced by chemical means, the person might say, in one situation, "I feel this way because I am angry," or, in another, "I feel this way because I am afraid." Similarly, when a person stops smoking after taking a pill that is advertised as a "cure" for smoking he or she may attribute the change in behavior to the pill even though it was a totally inert substance. It is likely that this same person would attribute the success to "self-control" if the cessation of smoking followed participation in a program explicitly labeled as teaching control over one's own behavior with respect to smoking. Research on the modification of smoking behavior strongly suggests that a person who attributes his or her cessation of smoking to a pill will desist from smoking for a shorter period of time than the individual who attributes the change to personal accomplishment.[1]

Davison and Valins (1969) reasoned that self-attributed behavior change should be maintained for a longer time than behavior change which the person believes to be due to an external agent, such as a drug. They tested this in a study where subjects were led to believe that their apparent increase in pain tolerance had been the result of a drug. One group was then disabused of this belief, being told that the pill had actually been a placebo, so that they now had to assume that their "increase in pain tolerance" (actually a surreptitiously reduced shock intensity) was the result of personal accomplishment. It was found that these subjects subsequently perceived shock as less painful and tolerated significantly more of it than those subjects who continued to attribute their behavior change to the drug.

[1] G. C. Davison, personal communication.

These writers speculate that the attribution of a drug effect is a major reason why positive behavior change so often disappears as soon as an effective psychoactive drug is withdrawn. They urge that whenever a drug is used to change a person's behavior, careful attention should be paid to the question of how the individual explains the change. When the person receiving the drug is also given something to do—such as exercising, relaxing, or following a set routine—so that the change can be attributed to that activity rather than the drug, the therapeutic change can be maintained after the drug has been withdrawn. This was demonstrated in a study by Davison, Tsujimoto, and Glaros (1973) based on work with adults who had trouble falling asleep.

While we know of no similar research in the area of hyperactivity-learning disability, it seems reasonable to assume that children who attribute their newly acquired ability to sit still and attend to lessons to the effect of a drug will have a different attitude toward this achievement than children who attribute the change to their having mastered their own behavior through learning. This difference may mean that children who attribute their change to the drug will maintain the change only for as long as they continue to take the drug. Indeed, drug treatment of hyperactive children may be required for as long as three to five years (O'Malley & Eisenberg, 1973); some have equated this with the long-term drug maintenance required by diabetics.

The studies by Davison and his colleagues (Davison et al., 1969, 1973) strongly suggest that drug treatment of hyperactive children should, when used, be combined with behavior therapy so that the child can come to view his increased ability to sit still and to attend as something *he* is learning to master. It might be that with such a combination of approaches (chemical and psychological), the improvement could be maintained when the drug is withdrawn after a relatively short time. Studies along these lines are urgently needed.

When a child's hyperactivity is treated solely by the administration of a drug so that he comes to attribute his improvement to the effect of the medication, this may not only make the maintenance of the improvement a function of continued and regular administration of the drug but the experience may also affect the child's perception of himself and his belief regarding the potency of drugs in solving personal problems. The children here under discussion frequently have a poor self-image and low self-esteem as a result of their many years of failure at tasks on which their peers succeed. When the complaints about their hyperactivity and poor school performance on the part of the adults around them cease as a result of a behavior change brought on by effective medication these children are likely to say, "The only reason I am doing so well is because of my medicine." In other words, they will attribute their success to an external, chemical agent instead of viewing the change as a personal achievement. The locus of control is thus shifted to the outside world, and in the long run this can induce an attitude of helplessness and passivity.

At the same time, having learned in childhood that a problem—such as trouble in school—can be solved by taking a drug, it is not unlikely that such a child may, in later years, resort to chemical means for the solution of other troubles. There are no data to support these speculations, but if they have some merit, it would follow that medication to reduce hyperactivity and to increase selective attention should always be accompanied by explicit psychological efforts to assure that the child recognizes his personal role in the improvement he notices. These efforts must parallel remedial education for, as we have said earlier, drugs can, at best, alleviate problems that interfere with learning; they do not produce learning or magically restore all the learning that did not take place in earlier years. Additionally, as O'Malley and Eisenberg (1973) have stressed, the child's parents and family may need help in understanding the changes in the child's behavior; as a "different child," he will need to be seen differently by those in his immediate environment.

Potential Abuses   Yet another issue raised by a pharmacological approach to learning disabilities involves the potential abuse of medications. Here again, in the absence of data, we must resort to speculations and assumptions; but the issue is too important to omit simply because we cannot cite research in support of cautionary statements. The very ease with which a drug can be dispensed (it takes but a few minutes of a physician's office time to write or renew a prescription) raises the danger of indiscriminate use, misuse, inadequate supervision, and lack of follow-up. Wolff and Hurwitz (1973) have pointed out that

> The indiscriminate use of amphetamines and methylphenidate without benefit of careful medical screening has raised justified suspicion among parents, particularly in some inner-city communities. that their children are being subdued pharmacologically because drugs are cheaper than providing an adequate learning environment (p. 113).

To this one can add that it is not simply a matter of carefully screening a child before a stimulant drug is administered to him but that careful continued supervision of the drug supply and the child's physical and psychological status are also essential. Making sure that a child for whom a drug has been prescribed receives his proper dosage (and no more) at prescribed times is a serious responsibility for his parents and for school authorities. One frequently hears stories of doubling the dose because the child is "acting up" or because the previous dispensing was missed or of giving some of that effective medicine to another child "who needs it" without giving that child the benefit of medical advice. Whether these anecdotes are true or not, the possibility of such occurrences is real and must be carefully guarded against.

Still another issue which must be raised in this connection is the effect widespread use of stimulant drugs for presumably medical reasons has on educational efforts to prevent drug abuse. On the one hand we tell our schoolchildren not to turn to drugs to solve personal problems; marijuana has been called a "chemical copout." But in the very schools where this kind of "drug education" is carried on there is a high percentage of children who are told to take their pills so that they will behave and learn better. Considering the fact that we know no more about the long-range effects of continuous use of stimulant drugs than we know about marijuana, this double standard is both cynical and irresponsible.

These then are some of the dangers in using stimulant drugs to help hyperactive children with learning disabilities. They should be recognized so that they can be reduced or avoided, but the existence of these risks does not mean that all drug therapy should be abjured. Particularly in conjunction with psychological and educational approaches, stimulant medication is an effective mode of treatment for a limited number of carefully selected children. It is the irresponsible, uncritical application of this or any other form of treatment which must be decried.

SUMMARY

Hyperactivity is often, but not always, associated with learning disabilities. It may be that this relationship is no more than the result of a selection bias in that the learning-disabled child who is also hyperactive is more likely to be referred for study than his equally learning-disabled classmate who sits quietly in his seat. At any rate, the presence of hyperactivity in some learning-disabled children has often been used in support of the contention that there is something wrong in the brains of such children. For some children hyperactivity may well be the result of brain abnormalities, but for others it may be a learned behavior or no more than the manifestation of one end of the normal distribution of human motility. High levels of motor activity may not be a problem in its own right, but the reaction of the child's environment to this activity may make it such.

Learning disability is primarily a problem for the child; hyperactivity is primarily a problem for the adults around the child. Since adults are "in charge," it is not surprising that the focus of intervention is more often on what is troubling the adult than on what the child really needs. That is, treatment is more often directed at the hyperactivity than at the learning problem. All too often, adults are satisfied once the child sits still, regardless of whether he or she is now getting something out of school. It seems that hyperactivity can often be reduced through the administration of certain amphetamine-related drugs. By a tortured logic, this has again been used as proof that learning disabilities have their basis in brain disorders.

There are many methodological issues that must be taken into account if one wishes to study the effectiveness of a drug. These have stood in the way of truly definitive studies in the realm of hyperactivity and learning disability. As a result, knowledge in this area is uncertain, and the widespread use of medication with children who are problems for the school borders on the irresponsible. Long-term physical and psychological effects of continued use of powerful chemical agents are unknown and the potential for their abuse is very high. In view of this, drugs should be used with much circumspection and drug-free alternative interventions for hyperactivity and learning problems should be given priority.

Chapter 6

Teaching the Learning-disabled Child — Cognitive Methods

Selective Attention or Impulse Control?

After many years of research on the problems of hyperactive, learning-disabled children, Douglas (1972, 1974a,b) reviewed the work she and her colleagues had done and sought to answer the question whether there is some basic dimension on which these children differ from normal youngsters. Their difficulty, she concluded, does not lie in intelligence level, perceptual or conceptual capacity, or short-term memory. Not even activity level seemed to her to be the critical aspect, for, although these children move around a lot, most of their behavior seems goal-directed, albeit their goals may not be those of their teachers. In summarizing, Douglas (1972) writes,

> As I looked back over our various studies, it struck me that one closely related group of characteristics can pretty well account for all of the deficiencies we found. These youngsters are apparently unable to keep their own impulses under control in order to cope with situations in which care, concentrated attention, or organized planning are required. They tend to react with the first idea that occurs to them or to those aspects of a situation which are the most obvious or compelling. This appears to be the case whether the task requires that they work with

visual or auditory stimuli and it also seems to be true in the visual-motor and kinaesthetic spheres. These same deficiencies—deficiencies which I have come to think of as the inability to "stop, look and listen"—seem also to influence the children's social behaviour. . . . in real life, several of our older hyperactives are beginning to get into trouble with the law because of their inability to control their impulsive tendencies (p. 275).

Elsewhere, Douglas (1974a) wrote, "I have become convinced that the fundamental cause of their maladaptive behavior lies in their inability to focus, sustain and organize attention and to inhibit impulsive responding" (p. 3). She thus conceives of the basic problem of the learning-disabled as residing in two difficulties: inability to sustain attention *and* problems in impulse control. How these two problems relate to one another—whether the fundamental cause lies in both or whether one is a derivative of the other—is not made clear.

It is not simply for the sake of theory that one would wish to ask whether the fundamental cause of learning disabilities is a problem of sustaining attention, a problem of impulse control, or a problem in both these areas. From the point of view of devising a training program, the answer to this question is of more than theoretical interest. If the child's problem is with attention *and* impulse control, both would have to be taught; if his impulsivity interferes with attention, he would have to learn control over his impulses before one could expect him to attend. Yet if what appears as impulsivity is simply a function of his problem with attention, attention training would have to be the primary focus of efforts to help.

What Is an Impulse? As is the case with other vague constructs used by psychologists, "everybody" knows what we mean by "impulse" because it is a term used in everyday language; yet when one has to define the term, one is limited to circumlocutions—such as "a sudden incitement to action"—which do not tell us anything more. When a child is given a problem to solve which requires careful attention and he immediately blurts out a wrong answer, we can say that he has acted in an impulsive fashion. When a child is working on a task and he suddenly turns away from it, we can say that this act was impulsive. When a child's mode of responding is pervasively impulsive, we might even describe him as an impulsive child.

In all these instances "impulse" is used to describe our observations: it is used in its adjectival form and communicates a quality of observed behavior. Yet when one asks why the child blurts out an answer or suddenly turns away from a task and offers the explanation "because he is impulsive" or "because of an impulse," one has no more than a pseudo-explanation, an explanatory fiction that may exist only in the head of the person seeking an answer to the question about motives.

That this is the case will become quickly apparent when one asks how one knows that the child was motivated by an impulse. The answer to this can only be in terms of the observation which "impulse" was supposed to explain in the first place; "because I saw him abruptly turn away from his task." This circularity underscores that nothing has been explained by invoking impulse as a cause of observed behavior. We might as well have stayed at the descriptive level and reported that the child blurted out the wrong answer or suddenly turned away from his task.

The question a scientist should ask when faced with an observation is not "why did this happen?" (answer: because he had an impulse), but "under what circumstances does this phenomenon occur?" The latter question will encourage further, more detailed observations and is likely to lead to the discovery that wrong answers are blurted out or tasks are suddenly terminated when the child lacks the skills needed to arrive at correct solutions.

Let us take another look at the statements by Douglas (1972, 1974a) which we cited earlier and see whether anything is contributed to our understanding of hyperactive, learning-disabled children by invoking the notion of impulse control. If one deletes references to impulse, the key sentences would read:

> These youngsters are apparently unable to . . . cope with situations in which care, concentrated attention, or organized planning are required. They tend to react . . . to those aspects of a situation which are the most obvious or compelling. . . . The fundamental cause of their maladaptive behavior lies in their inability to focus, sustain and organize attention. . . .

What we have done was to omit the motivational construct impulse, leaving a focus on problems of attention, a focus which seems to provide the necessary and sufficient conditions for dealing with learning disabilities.

When Douglas (1972) speaks of the learning-disabled child's inability to "stop, look, and listen" she concludes that remedial efforts should be directed at teaching such children to stop, look, and listen before answering a question or responding to a task. "Stop" is the injunction addressed at impulsivity; it could be worded as "Don't be impulsive." "Look and listen" instruct the child to attend to the relevant stimulus dimensions; they might be phrased as "Attend selectively."

From the point of view here advocated, one might say to a child, "Take your time so that you can attend selectively." Or one might simply say "attend selectively," since, in order to do so, the child would have to take his or her time. It would seem that if one succeeded in teaching a child to attend, the so-called impulsivity would be automatically taken care of. The notion that the principal problem of learning-disabled children is their impulsivity has spawned a number of studies dealing with remediation. We shall review some of these below and later seek to point out that the results would have been the same had the formulation been simply in terms of selective attention.

Remedial Efforts

"Stop, Look, and Listen"   In recent years methods have been developed and tested under research conditions that are designed to teach impulsive children to "stop, look, and listen" before responding. Palkes, Stewart, and

Kahana (1968) taught hyperactive children to use self-directed verbal commands designed to have them approach a task with reflection and deliberation. Verbally mediated self-control of this nature was pioneered by the Russian psychologist Luria (1961), who views internalized verbal commands as the principal means by which a child develops control over his own behavior. Luria has suggested that hyperactive children can be helped to improve their performance by incorporating their own speech.

In order to test Luria's hypothesis, Palkes, Stewart, and Kahana (1968) worked with 20 boys between the ages of 8 years, 2 months and 9 years, 11 months who were "under psychiatric care for hyperactive behavior disorder" (p. 818). None received medication while the study was in progress. Of these children, 10 were assigned to the experimental group who were to receive verbal training; the other 10 were assigned to a control group. The criterion task against which outcome was to be evaluated was the Porteus Maze Test, a graded series of mazes which the person being tested solves by tracing the correct path with a pencil. This test can be scored so as to provide an estimate of general intelligence (test quotient). In addition, the production can be examined from the standpoint of errors in style and quality, and the resulting qualitative (Q) score has been shown to distinguish between groups differing in impulsiveness (Porteus, 1942).

Prior to training, the two groups of boys did not differ on either the test quotient or the qualitative score. They made many errors—such as cutting corners, crossing lines, and moving in the wrong direction—reflecting a slap-dash quality of performance that might be described as "typical of an impulsive child." After completion of training (which will be described below), the mean of the experimental group's qualitative errors was significantly lower than that of the control group, while their test quotient was significantly higher. As the authors of the study conclude, their results are consistent with the hypothesis that training in self-directed verbal commands improves the overall performance of hyperactive boys on the Porteus Maze Test (Palkes et al., 1968, p. 825). They correctly point out that the improvement in test scores does not mean that the boys' intelligence was raised, but that, having learned a more prudent approach to a task such as a test of intelligence, they were able to achieve higher scores, thus permitting the test to give a more accurate reflection of their intellectual capacity. The fact that the training in self-directed verbal commands was accomplished in two 30-minute sessions makes this result particularly impressive.

The initial administration of the maze test took place on one day. Following this, each boy spent approximately 30 minutes with a person (other than the one who administered the maze tests) who presented a series of tasks which constituted the vehicle for training. These were Kagan's (1966) Matching Familiar Figures Test, the Embedded Figures Test, and the Trail Making Test. On the first of these tests, the child is required to identify which of a series of six representations of a familiar object matches a standard, standard

Figure 6-1 Sample item from Matching Familiar Figures (MFF). *(From Kagan, 1965. Copyright by The Society for Research in Child Development, and used by permission.)*

and variants being shown at the same time (see) Figure 6-1). The Embedded Figures Test involves the presentation of two line drawings of geometric designs, a simple one being embedded in another that is more complex. The child is asked to find the simpler design and to trace it with his fingertip. The Trail Making Test calls for the joining with a pencil line of a series of numbered or alphabetically labeled, irregularly spaced dots. These dots must be joined in the correct order and without lifting the pencil off the paper.

The children in the experimental group were required to emit a set of self-directed commands before responding to any part of a task. Those in the control group were given the same tasks but without self-directed-command training. The length of sessions was equalized by giving the control group an additional set of embedded figures. This procedure was repeated at the same hour on the following day, after which an alternate form of the maze test was administered by the same examiner who had tested the children on the previous day.

Since the self-command training procedure is the crux of this study and has direct applicability in a remedial program, it warrants detailed presentation. As a training aid, the experimenter provided the child with four visual reminder cards, 5 × 7 inches in dimension, on which instructions and appropriate illustrations were printed. These cards are illustrated in Figure 6-2. They were arranged on the desk in front of the child so as to be visible to him throughout the performance of the tasks. The experimenter directed the child's attention to these cards and pointed out that they were to serve him as a reminder of what he had to say before beginning any work. The child was asked to read Card 1 aloud, and its content was emphasized and reiterated by the trainer. Following this the folder containing the first task was placed before the child, but before it was opened, the experimenter pointed to the second item of Card 1, saying, "Now before we start a new task, what do you say?" The folder was then opened and the instructions were given. But before the child was allowed to begin, he had to verbalize the self-directed command on Card 4 ("I'll look and think before I answer"). Before turning to the next page for the next figure, the child had to say aloud, "Stop—listen." The experimenter would then present the next figure and give the instructions, "Point to the figure that is exactly like the one on top," whereupon the child had to say, "I look and think before I answer." Then he would point to his choice. This procedure was continued throughout the test and followed essentially the same form on the other two tasks. If the child failed to emit the pertinent verbalization, the experimenter would point to the relevant reminder card and insist that the child state the command before proceeding. Spontaneous use of the commands was reinforced by, "Good, you remembered the commands."

Through the use of this procedure, each child received a great number of rehearsals of the self-instruction statements. The significant improvement in the subsequent maze test performance strongly suggests that the instructions to "stop, listen, look, and think" had become sufficiently internalized to result

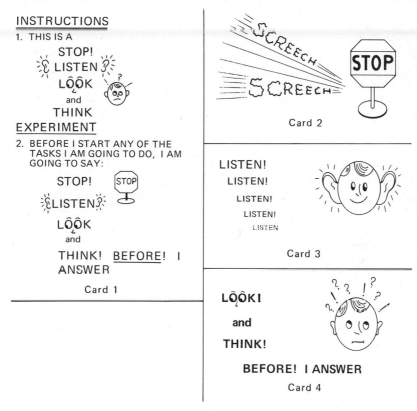

Figure 6-2 Training aid used in self-command procedure. *(From Palkes, Stewart, & Kahana, 1968. Copyright by The Society for Research in Child Development, used by permission.)*

in more careful and deliberate work, at least immediately after training. If, as Douglas (1974b) has concluded, the central problem of so-called hyperactive children is that they have not learned to "stop, look, and listen," a procedure such as that pioneered by Palkes, Stewart, and Kahana (1968) and replicated by Palkes, Stewarat, and Freedman (1971) might well help such children to acquire the needed control over their own behavior.

It obviously remains for further research to determine whether a method such as that used by Palkes et al. results in long-term changes in impulsive behavior and whether such changes generalize to school-related tasks and interpersonal behavior. The issue of whether improvement will hold over a period of time was one of the questions to which Meichenbaum and Goodman (1971) addressed a study which they entitled "Training Impulsive Children to Talk to Themselves: A Means of Developing Self-Control."

Instruction in Self-Guidance   Meichenbaum and Goodman (1971) view "private speech" as having a self-regulatory function which develops in the course of a child's interaction with the social environment. In the earliest phase of development, the speech of adult caretakers is mainly responsible for controlling and directing a child's behavior. A little later, his or her behavior comes to be regulated by the child's own overt speech, and eventually this overt speech is internalized to become covert, inner speech ("thoughts") which assumes a regulatory role over behavior. Assuming that impulsive children have failed to develop this covert self-control, these investigators decided to study whether it is possible to recapitulate this development, as it were, by presenting a child with an adult's instructions, then having the child verbalize these instructions, and—lastly—having the child state the instructions silently, that is, without overt verbalization. They reasoned that such covert self-verbalization should result in the child's own verbal control of his nonverbal behavior.

Two studies were conducted which applied this cognitive self-guidance training to impulsive schoolchildren. The first study used 15 second-grade children who attended a special class in which they had been placed because of their hyperactivity, poor self-control, and/or low intelligence test scores. There were eight girls and seven boys, ranging in age from 7 to 9 years. One group of five became the cognitive self-guidance treatment group; a matched group was assigned to an attention control condition which received the same amount of attention from the experimenters as the treatment group; and a third group served as a no-treatment control.

The behavior of all children was measured before and after the training period, using two general classes of assessments. The first class involved formal, individually administered tests; the Porteus (1942) Maze Test, Kagan's (1966) Matching Familiar Figures (MFF) test, and the Picture Arrangement, Block Design, and Coding subtests from the Wechsler (1949) Intelligence Scale for Children (WISC). The second class of assessments involved classroom measures designed to test the generalizability of the treatment to the classroom situation. One of these was a questionnaire, filled out by the teacher and assessing each child's self-control, activity level, cooperation, etc. The other measure consisted of time-sampling classroom observations. These were conducted for two school days one week before and immediately after treatment. These observations focused on inappropriate classroom behavior—defined as behavior not consistent with the task set forth by the teacher.

The treatment of the cognitive training group consisted of four individual half-hour sessions with each child, with the sessions spread over a two-week period. Using a variety of tasks of increasing difficulty—ranging from copying line patterns and reproducing designs to completing a pictorial series and solving conceptual tasks—the experimenter *(E)* would proceed as follows:

> First, *E* performed a task talking aloud while *S* (the child) observed (*E* acted as a model); then *S* performed the same task while *E* instructed *S* aloud; then *S* was

asked to perform the task again while instructing himself aloud; then S performed the task while whispering to himself (lip movements): and finally S performed the task covertly (without lip movements). . . . The following is an example of E's modeled verbalization which S subsequently used (initially overtly, then covertly).

Okay, what is it I have to do? You want me to copy the picture with the different lines. I have to go slow and be careful. Okay, draw the line down, down, good; then to the right, that's it; now down some more and to the left. Good, I'm doing fine so far. Now back up again, No, I was supposed to go down. That's okay. Just erase the line carefully . . . Good. Even if I make an error I can go on slowly and carefully. Okay, I have to go down now. Finished. I did it (Meichenbaum & Goodman, 1971, p. 117).

Following the two weeks during which the training sessions took place, all children were re-evaluated in order to ascertain whether this training in self-verbalization had been effective. One month later, the tests were repeated in order to assess whether any changes would hold up over this (limited) period of time. Comparisons between pre- and posttest scores for the experimental group and the two control groups on the formal psychometric measures indicated that the cognitive self-guidance training program significantly altered the behavior of these children in the direction of improved intelligence test scores and slower, more accurate responding on the MFF test. What is more, these improvements were maintained over the four-week follow-up period. While the performance of the trained group also showed significant improvement on the Porteus Maze Test, the group which had received an equal amount of attention but no training in self-verbalization displayed a similar improvement, so that self-verbalization did not seem to be the crucial independent variable for maze test performance.

While Meichenbaum and Goodman (1971) have thus demonstrated that a cognitive self-instruction training procedure can effectively improve the performance of impulsive children on selected subtests of the WISC and on Kagan's MFF test, there was no measurable effect on classroom behavior. As these authors suggest, this may be due to the limited number of training sessions or to a lack of sensitivity of the assessment measures used. A third possibility, also raised by them, that training simply did not generalize from paper and pencil activity to classroom behavior, appears to be the most likely.

Where significant results were obtained, the training focus had been on tasks calling for abilities and skills that are also required on the criterion measures. Thus, coloring figures within specified boundaries rehearses a skill that is involved in staying within the lines while following a paper-and-pencil maze; completing a pictorial series is related to solving the Picture Arrangement subtest of the WISC. While these children were clearly not trained on the specific tasks used for the dependent measures, the necessary generalization was over a limited range. On the other hand, learning to talk to oneself so as to proceed with care and deliberation on a paper-and-pencil task would seem to have little in common with being task-oriented, sitting still, and being cooperative in a classroom situation.

Behavior therapists have come to recognize (Ross, 1974) that treatment is most effective when its focus is on the target of intervention and takes place in the setting where the troublesome behavior is found. Thus, where children are in trouble because they fails to sit still and attend to their tasks in the classroom, treatment had best take place in the classroom and not in the therapist's consulting room. If for practical reasons, treatment cannot take place in the class, the locus of therapy should be as similar as possible to the classroom situation and the therapist must take explicit care to build generalization of behavior change to the classroom into the treatment program. We shall have occasion to return to this issue in the next chapter.

Modeling the Use of Self-Instruction   Before leaving the study by Meichenbaum and Goodman (1971), a brief review of their second experiment is called for. It will be recalled that in the first study the experimenter had not only instructed and rehearsed the child in overt self-instruction but that the experimenter had also served as a model for self-guidance behavior. The second study sought to test the relative efficacy of modeling alone versus modeling combined with self-instruction training. The criterion measure was the Matching Familiar Figures (MFF) test developed by Kagan (1966). As previously described, this instrument requires that the child select the exact match to a standard from among a series of highly similar variations. The performance is measured by two scores, one reflecting decision time, the other the number of errors. Short decision times in combination with high error scores is defined as impulsive responding, while reflective responding is found in relatively long decision times combined with low error scores. Impulsivity and reflection, thus defined, are viewed as the child's conceptual tempo or cognitive style.

While this test has attracted a good deal of attention on the part of investigators interested in studying impulsive behavior of children, it has a distinct disadvantage in that decision time and error scores do not inevitably covary (Block, Block, & Harrington, 1974). That is, while test performance will identify a group of slow responders who make few errors and a group of fast responders who make many errors (the "impulsives" and the "reflectives") two other groups also emerge. One is made up of children who manage to make few errors despite their fast responding, the other consists of children who make many errors no matter how slowly they respond. These two groups are often disregarded in research with the MFF test, which is thus not suitable for applications where one desires to categorize a heterogeneous group of children in terms of their cognitive style.

The fact that slow responding on the MFF test does not necessarily lead to a reduction in error scores has been shown in several studies in which researchers concentrated on having impulsively responding children delay their answer by a fixed amount of time (Kagan, Pearson, & Welch, 1966). This technique results in significant increases in decision time but without corresponding improvement in error scores. In other words, teaching a child to wait ("stop") before answering does not help in improving his accuracy if one does not also teach him a strategy ("look and listen") to use during the waiting period that will result in a more adequate response. This reasoning led Meichenbaum and Goodman (1971) to the decision to teach the children in their second study a strategy for solving the task posed by the MFF test—a strategy designed to find explicit differences among the alternatives presented and to check each variant against the standard for verification.

The children for the second Meichenbaum and Goodman (1971) study were selected from among kindergarten and first-grade children on the basis of their performance on the MFF test. There were 15 children defined as impulsive by their test scores, and these were divided into three groups of 5 children each. On a pretest given to see whether the children's performance could be improved by the simple instruction not to hurry—to go slowly and carefully—none of these children significantly altered their style of responding. One of these three groups was now exposed to a model who used tasks similar to the MFF and requiring the matching of visual stimuli. This model demonstrated self-verbalizations to the effect to go slowly, to look carefully at standard and variants, and to check out alternatives before announcing an answer. Following this demonstration, the child was asked to work with the training materials, to "do just like I did," and to remember to go slowly and carefully.

The second group of five children was exposed to the same modeling exemplar as the modeling-alone group but, in addition, they were explicitly trained to produce self-instructions along the lines used in the first study. The third group, an attentional control group, also observed a model, but her verbalizations consisted only of self-admonitions to go slowly and carefully; they did not include statements about scanning strategies. These children were also given an opportunity to perform on each of the practice items, but they received no training in self-instruction. In many ways this procedure is similar to that used by many parents and teachers who will give a child general admonitions ("now be careful") without providing instructions on the detailed steps needed to succeed on a task.

Immediately following the training sessions, all children were retested with an alternate form of the MFF test. The results indicated that modeling *plus* training in self-instruction, as experienced by the second group, was the most effective of the three procedures in increasing decision time and reducing errors. While the modeling-alone group showed an increase in decision time, their error scores did not change significantly. Neither measure underwent a change in the control group, which had received general admonitions but no explicit instructions.

Taken together, the results of the two studies by Meichenbaum and Goodman (1971) indicate that a cognitive self-guidance program which trains impulsive children to talk to themselves is effective in modifying their behavior on a variety of psychometric tests which assess cognitive impulsivity, Performance IQ, and motor ability. . . . the addition of explicit self-instructional training to modeling procedures significantly alters the attentional strategies of the impulsive children and facilitates behavioral change. The impulsive children were taught to use their private speech for orienting, organizing, regulating, and self-rewarding functions with the consequence of greater self-control (p. 124).

Film-mediated Modeling   In the studies just discussed, children were shown an adult model who was present during the training sessions. This approach not only introduces inevitable variations from child to child but also uses a potentially weak model, since it has been shown (Bandura, 1969) that observational learning can be enhanced if model and observer are similar, that is, if a child models for a child observer.

Ridberg, Parke, and Hetherington (1971) report a study in which a film-mediated model was of the same age and sex as the child observers. By using a filmed model, these investigators not only standardized the modeling from observer to observer but also opened the way for eventual practical applications in educational settings where the showing of films would be far more feasible than the use of live models. Ridberg et al. (1971) were interested not only in the question whether the response style of impulsive children could be made more reflective but also in the converse, whether reflective children could be made more impulsive through the observation of a model who responded in the style opposite to that used by the observer.

This two-sided question is relevant to a theoretical issue, namely, whether cognitive style is a fixed, unmodifiable dimension of behavior or a learnable response. The results of their research lend support to the learning formulation, since both groups of children modified their behavior after observing the model. Because it is of little interest in the present context that initially reflective children can learn to be more impulsive, we shall discuss only that portion of this investigation which deals with impulsive children.

As in studies discussed earlier, the measure of cognitive style (impulsive-reflective) was the Matching Familiar Figures test (Kagan, 1965), which was administered to a group of fourth-grade boys. Those who scored below the group median on response time and above the group median on errors were classified as impulsive. The 50 boys so selected had a mean IQ score near 115, those with IQs below 90 and above 140 having been excluded from the study.

Two to three months after the initial testing, these children were seen individually and shown a film in which a nine-year-old boy responded to MFF items in a reflective manner. The film was introduced by a statement to the effect that most of the boys in the class had experienced some trouble with the test the last time it had been administered and that the film was to help them by showing a boy who "did very well and made few mistakes."

In one experimental condition, the filmed model simply waited from 25 to 31 seconds before responding. In another condition, he verbalized his strategy in the interval before responding. He stressed that he responded slowly, avoided choosing the first picture that appeared correct without having checked the remaining stimuli, and that he frequently checked back with the comparison standard. In a third condition, the model demonstrated his scanning strategy by pointing with his finger but without making verbal statements; while in a fourth experimental condition the model combined a demonstration of the scanning strategy with the verbalization.

Immediately following the exposure to the modeling film and again one week later, all children were again given the MFF test, using alternate forms. The results revealed a significant increase in response latencies and a significant decrease in errors which remained stable over one week. The experimental conditions had varied the model's activity from a simple display of reflective behavior to verbalization, demonstration, and verbalization plus demonstration. All these conditions resulted in more reflective performance, but there was a differential effect which was a function of the observing child's intelligence level. The children with IQs below 115 (which had been the mean for the group) showed greater benefit from the model who combined verbalization and demonstration than those who had seen only the simpler modeling. On the other hand, the children with high IQs (above 115) did better in the simple conditions, the more complex modeling condition having apparently interfered with their performance.

This study thus shows not only that impulsive response style on the MFF test can be modified through observation of a film-mediated model. It also serves as a reminder that no one technique will be equally effective for all children and that individual characteristics, such as intelligence level, must be taken into consideration if one wishes to achieve optimal effect. At the same time, it is well to keep in mind that the Ridberg, Parke, and Hetherington (1971) study demonstrated no more than a short-range (one week) effect on the MFF test performance of presumably normal boys. Extrapolations to general academic performance of hyperactive, learning-disabled children may or may not be valid.

Teaching Response Strategies A somewhat more permanent effect of training impulsive children to be more reflective, together with an apparent generalization in terms of improved reading, was reported by Egeland (1974). He administered the MFF test to 260 second-grade children and, on the basis of short response time plus high number of errors, identified 72 "impulsive children" who ranged in age from 6 years 10 months to 8 years 11 months. These children were randomly assigned to one of two training groups or to a control group which received no training. The training groups received eight 30-minute training sessions over a four-week period. These sessions entailed exercises on match-to-sample tasks involving geometric designs and nonsense words, drawing geometric designs from memory, and describing geometric designs.

One training group was instructed to wait 10 to 15 seconds before responding; to "think about your answer and take your time." The other training group was given a set of rules and basic strategies which the children were to follow in responding to the training tasks. These rules were designed to induce the children to attend to the relevant features of the stimuli, to examine alternatives, to break the alternatives down into component parts, to look for similarities and differences, and to eliminate alternatives until only the correct alternative remained. This scanning strategy was designed to overcome the impulsive child's tendency to attend to only one alternative without considering others before deciding on the response.

The important difference between the two training groups used by Egeland (1974) is that one group was told to delay their responses while the other group was taught what to do during the delay. The former thus received a general admonishment, much like those often used by adults in hopes of improving a child's performance, "Take your time; pay attention; think," while the latter group was given explicit training in a specific skill that is applicable to the task at hand.

When an alternate form of the MFF test was administered upon completion of the four-week training period, the results revealed that both groups had increased response times and a corresponding decrease in errors, while no such changes were found with the control group. Two months later, however, when the children were once again tested on the MFF, only the group which had received training in the use of scanning strategies had maintained the improved performance. What is more, this group also achieved significantly higher scores on a test of reading comprehension (Gates-MacGinitie Reading Test) which was administered to the classes five months after completion of training.

As the author points out, these results prove most encouraging, since they indicate that impulsive children can be trained to alter the way in which they process information and solve problems. It is of interest to note Egeland's comment that when the children encountered a more difficult problem, they would revert back to an impulsive way of responding, as if they had learned to respond in that fashion in situations where they anticipated failure. This seems to suggest that the newly learned "reflective" response style was still too tenuous and that further training under conditions of intermittent positive reinforcement might have made it more resistant to extinction.

Impulse Control or Selective Attention?

Egeland's (1974) work strongly suggests that the basis of the performance deficit of the so-called impulsive child lies not so much in the precipitous nature of his responses as it does in his not using adaptive strategies of attention. We are thus led back to the question asked at the beginning of this chapter and to the issue raised by Douglas (1974a), whether one needs to invoke problems in selective attention *and* impulse control in elucidating the difficulties of learning-disabled children. Must such children be taught to "stop, look, and listen," or is it sufficient to teach them to "look and listen," inasmuch as that strategy perforce requires pausing between stimulus presentation and response emission?

Impulsivity as a Learned Response Style   The studies reviewed above would seem to suggest that simply teaching children to slow down (not to be impulsive) does little to improve their performance, but that when the intervention is aimed at teaching them to attend to the distinctive aspects of the stimuli (to attend selectively), the performance deficits which had been attributed to impulsivity can be overcome. This leads us to inquire into the nature of the abrupt and precipitous behavior which is often observed as a characteristic of learning-disabled, hyperactive children and which has given rise to the speculations about impulses and lack of impulse control.

Egeland (1974) reports that the children he had trained to use more adaptive attentional strategies reverted to the impulsive mode of responding when they encountered more difficult problems and appeared to anticipate failure. Could it be that impulsive responding is not the cause but the effect of failures on cognitive tasks; that impulsivity is not a conceptual tempo but a learned response style? A response style that is characterized by rapidly produced, unreflective answers which arc usually wrong (the operational definition of impulsivity used on the MFF test) might be typical of a child who has had a long history of failure experiences when he or she is faced with a cognitive task.

These failure experiences could be a function of the child's not having developed sufficient capacity to use selective attention in dealing with such a task. Repeated failures might result in making cognitive tasks aversive; such children might experience anxiety whenever they are faced with problems which they know they can't solve. The quickest way of reducing such anxiety, to get out of the unpleasant situation and thus to be reinforced, would be to come up with a quick answer. "Better to give a wrong answer quickly than to struggle for a long time only to find that the answer is wrong anyway," might be the logic by which such children would operate. Moreover, physically removing oneself from the situation or, at least, turning away from the task would further serve to reduce anxiety engendered by being faced with a problem one knows one is unable to solve. Such moving or turning away might well be the behavior which earns such children the labels "hyperactive" and "distractible."

It is only when these children are taught the attentional strategies required to solve cognitive problems that they will encounter sufficient success experiences to make it attractive for them to spend enough time on such problems to arrive at the right answers. Such performance will then earn them the label "reflective" on the MFF test, and observers will assume that they have acquired impulse control.

Implications for Remedial Programs

Almost all the research discussed in this chapter used performance on psychological tests as the criterion of improvement. Only Egeland (1974) reported that the children who had participated in a program of training in problem solving showed improvement on an academic achievement test. While it is interesting to know that training in self-guidance helps children obtain better scores on tests of tracing a maze or matching familiar figures, the educator wants to know what all this means in terms of classroom performance. Can a method such as that devised by Meichenbaum and Goodman (1971) be used in helping learning-disabled children?

The laboratory scientist, trained to make no statements unless they are supported by well-established facts, would wish to do further research and gather more data before answering that question. Meanwhile, however, there are children both in and out of school (whose numbers range into millions) who must have help and should have it now. These children and those charged with educating them cannot wait until painstaking research has furnished all the answers. The dilemma is threefold: Should one do nothing until the research has been completed? Should one continue to use available methods of questionable merit? Or should one take the research-based answers that are now available, few though these may be, and derive educational methods from them for immediate application? The third of these alternatives seems to have the greatest appeal. Provided one monitors the effect of such methods on the academic performance of the children so as to avoid following yet another educational fad despite its fruitlessness, some applications of the self-instruction methods detailed in this chapter would seem to be in order.

SUMMARY

The problem of learning-disabled children has sometimes been formulated as residing in their lack of impulse control. They seem to blurt out the first available answer (which is often wrong) instead of examining alternatives with care and planning. While lack of impulse control can also be interpreted as an inability to sustain selective attention, this formulation has led to considerable research designed to help children arrive at more adaptive modes of responding. These have taken the form of teaching them verbal statements involving self-instruction and self-guidance. Several investigators have reported that these methods have helped impulsive, learning-disabled children to improve performance on tasks requiring care, planning, and the consideration of alternatives. A particularly effective method appears to be the modeling of adaptive response strategies, and since this can be presented by film, it has exciting educational potential. Nonetheless, the ultimate effectiveness of this approach in terms of improved school performance has not been conclusively demonstrated and thus awaits the outcome of further research. We recognize the fact that this poses a dilemma for the educator who must try and help children now.

Chapter 7

Teaching the Learning-disabled Child — Behavioral Methods

In the previous chapter we discussed approaches which seek to teach learning-disabled children more adaptive cognitive strategies. Whether or not a child engages in a particular cognitive process can only be inferred from the nature of his or her performance; cognitive processes, such as selective attention, are not subject to direct observation. Behaviorally oriented psychologists prefer to use formulations and research strategies that do not necessitate making assumptions and drawing inferences about such nonobservable events as cognitions. Instead, they define their problems and focus their research on directly observable responses, such as motor movements, and seek to modify these responses through the manipulation of their antecedents and consequences.

In dealing with learning-disabled children such a research strategy demands that the children's problems be defined in terms of observable behaviors; the focus of intervention thus tends to be more on motor-activity level or disruptive behavior than on selective attention or comprehension. As we undertake to review the research based on behavioral approaches, it should be understood that we are not proposing to compare cognitive and behavioral methods so as to choose one over the other. These are not competing models but merely differences in emphasis; a comprehensive program of remedial work for learning-disabled children must draw on the contributions of both approaches if these children are to receive the best available and most appropriate help.

Increasing Attending Behavior

A demonstration of the use of behavioral principles in working with a disruptive, hyperactive child was presented by Patterson, Jones, Whittier, and Wright (1965), who treated a ten-year-old brain-injured, retarded boy who was enrolled in a special school for physically handicapped children. The boy's teacher described him as having a short attention span, being hyperactive, and being aggressive toward younger children. He was thus a severely impaired child whose problems were of greater magnitude than those of children usually classified as hyperactive or learning-disabled, but if one can demonstrate a method that is effective in increasing the attending behavior of such a child, it stands to reason that the principles involved should also be applicable with less severe problems.

In order to ensure that changes in the child's behavior were indeed the result of the experimental manipulation, Patterson and his co-workers (1965) also gathered data on a control subject, a child in the same class who had problems and behaviors similar to those of Raymond, the experimental subject. At the beginning of the project Raymond was spending most of his time in the classroom staring into space, walking about the room, almost continuously moving his arms or legs, and displaying other behavior incompatible with attending to the academic task. Using a checklist, observers placed behind a one-way screen in the classroom recorded such "non-attending behaviors" as swinging of arms, twisting in chair, looking out of window, wiggling feet, fingering objects, talking to self, and walking around. Baseline data were collected before any intervention was introduced. These showed that both boys engaged in a mean of approximately five nonattending responses per minute.

Following the baseline period, Raymond was introduced to the conditioning procedure, which was described to him as a way of teaching him to sit still so that he could study better. He would wear an earphone (connected to a small radio receiver strapped to his back) through which he would receive a signal that indicated when he had earned a piece of candy. He was given a series of training trials outside the classroom during which the experimenter would activate the earphone and deliver a piece of candy for each 10-second period during which the boy did not display any non-attending behavior. In other words, reinforcement was contingent on brief periods of attending to the work that had been assigned to him.

The reason for phrasing the contingency as a double negative (not displaying non-attending behavior) is that wiggling and other non-attending responses are readily observable while "attending" is difficult to define in such a way that one is not merely reinforcing a child for directing his glance toward the workbook. It must be recognized that reinforcing periods during which non-attending behavior does not occur will not automatically ensure that these periods are taken up with constructive, attending behavior. A test of whether attention has increased as a result of such a manipulation would require a demonstration of improved academic performance, and Patterson et al. (1965) do not provide information on this point, since their primary interest was in a demonstration of the reduction of hyperactivity via conditioning methods.

After the initial adaptation to and training with the conditioning apparatus, Raymond wore the equipment in his classroom, the rest of the children having been told that it was to help him learn things by telling him when he was sitting still. They were also told that he would be earning candy which he could share with the class at the end of the period. This involvement of the other children had led to much peer support and social reinforcement in earlier work conducted by Patterson, who reasons that many of a child's behaviors, both positive and negative, are maintained by the reactions they elicit from the social environment. The conditioning phase of this study lasted for three weeks, during which data were collected on eight days for both subjects, with actual conditioning carried out for periods ranging from five to eighteen minutes.

The results of this study showed that during the conditioning phase Raymond made significantly fewer non-attending responses than the control child. The mean number of such responses per minute was approximately 3.3 for Raymond while those for the other child remained at the baseline level, near 5.0. After the end of the conditioning phase, the observations were continued over a four-week period. This revealed that the difference between Raymond and the control child was maintained, although the latter's behavior also showed a decrease in the occurrence of non-attending behavior. This is an intriguing phenomenon which might be attributed to the fact that the two children sat close to each other in the class, so that Raymond's improved behavior may have reduced the number of distracting stimuli to which the other child had previously reacted with hyperactivity of his own. Such an influence on the part of a disruptive child on the rest of the class is not unknown to classroom teachers.

Working with Groups of Disruptive Children   Patterson, Jones, Whittier, and Wright (1965) have thus demonstrated that it is possible to strengthen the attending behavior of a brain-injured, hyperactive boy by a relatively simple conditioning procedure. However, the use of a radio receiver and the need for an observer who signals the delivery of reinforcements limit this approach to higly specialized situations. It is thus important to note that other investigators working in the behavior modification framework have demonstrated that behavioral principles can also be applied under more normal classroom conditions. These applications usually involve a token reinforcement program where the immediate reinforcer is a readily dispensable symbol (token) that can be exchanged for material prizes or special privileges, known as backup reinforcers.

With children who can comprehend verbal instructions, the relationship between backup reinforcer, tokens, and the means for earning these are usually announced in a clearly stated set of rules. When tokens—such as plastic disks, check marks, or paper scrip—are handed out, they are accompanied by statements of praise, approval, smiles, and other social gestures which, being paired with the more concrete reinforcer, come to acquire greater strength in their own right. This is an important aspect of such a program because the concrete reinforcers and their backups are scheduled for eventual withdrawal, at which point social reinforcement and more "natural" reinforcers, such as highly favored classroom or recess activities or privileges, must take the place of the token program.

Not only is it possible to apply behavioral principles with relatively little "hardware," such as radio receivers or electrically operated counters, it is also possible to enlist relatively untrained helpers in the operation of effective programs of behavior modification. Thus, Ryback and Staats (1970) gave parents of reading-disabled children four hours of training, after which they proved successful "therapy technicians" who worked with their own children.

Similarly, Drass and Jones (1971) demonstrated that learning-disabled children themselves can be trained to act as behavior modifiers for their peers. These investigators taught three such children to apply behavioral principles so that they were able to use them in tutoring individual schoolmates in letter recognition and in the beginning and completion of assignments. According to teacher reports, the modified behavior carried over into the classroom, suggesting that this might be a useful approach, worthy of further, more systematic investigation.

Yet another instance of the use of subprofessional therapy technicians in a behavior modification program is reported by Staats, Minke, Goodwin, and Landeen (1967), who enlisted adult volunteers and high school seniors to work with reading-disabled youngsters. A similar program was evaluated by Camp and van Doorninck (1971). Here 66 retarded readers were given reading therapy based on behavior modification principles by nonprofessional neighborhood aides who had been given special but limited training. After a mean of only 14 lessons, children in the reading group had surpassed their controls on sight vocabulary performance, although this improvement was not reflected in the scores on a standardized achievement test.

The effect of a token program on the behavior of seven disruptive children in a second-grade class of 21 children was studied by O'Leary, Becker, Evans, and Saudargas (1969). Following a six-week period during which baseline data were gathered, the teacher gradually introduced systematic changes in classroom management. These consisted of rules for behavior, structuring of the program, praising appropriate and ignoring disruptive behavior, and—

finally—the contingent delivery of tokens which were exchangeable for back-up reinforcers. The results showed that disruptive behavior did not manifest a decrease until the introduction of the delivery of tokens, thus demonstrating that changes in classroom management which usually accompany a token program (rules, structure, and social reinforcement) are not, by themselves, responsible for behavior change.

After five weeks, the token program was experimentally withdrawn, reinstated, and again withdrawn, and the disruptive behavior showed changes commensurate with these manipulations. As a final step, the token program was replaced by a procedure in which children received stars for appropriate behavior, with extra stars awarded to the best-behaved row of children. At the end of the week, one piece of candy was awarded to the child with the greatest number of stars and to each member of the group (boys versus girls) which had earned the most stars. This procedure added peer competition to the awarding of stars (tokens) and served to maintain the improvement for some of the children. While successful for the eight months during which this program was in effect, it is not known whether it resulted in any long-range changes in child behavior. What is more, the effects of this program, which was conducted only in the afternoon sessions of the class, did not generalize to the morning session when the token program was not in operation.

Generalization of Progress

The issue of the generalization (carry-over) of behavior changes achieved in token programs was discussed by O'Leary and Drabman (1971), who reviewed the use of token reinforcement programs in the classroom. They pointed out that generalization should not be expected to take place automatically but that it must be built into the treatment plan in the same careful and systematic manner in which one works toward treatment effect in the first place. These authors make a number of suggestions for achieving generalizations from a treatment setting, such as a special resource room where a token economy is operating, to the child's regular classroom.

Follow-through   The first of these suggestions stresses the importance of providing the child with a good academic program that is designed to teach the skills and knowledge commensurate with his level of achievement. This is important for any child who returns to the regular classroom after having had remedial help with academic work or special training in acquiring more adaptive behavior. Unless the regular classroom provides the child with the wherewithal to engage in constructive activity—if needed, by special tutoring—the probability that he will once again engage in disruptive behavior is quite high unless, as O'Leary and Drabman (1971) put it, "he has simply learned to sit 'doing nothing.' " It is also important to remember that "good" behavior is not the natural alternative to "bad" behavior; that a reduction in the frequency of undesirable behavior will not automatically result in desirable behavior taking its place.

Visualize a pie diagram that represents the total time in a child's school day. A "slice" representing one quarter of this time might be taken up with disruptive behavior. Under specialized treatment conditions, such as a token program, this quarter-slice of disruptive time might be reduced, but something—some other behavior—will have to fill that space; there cannot be a behavioral vacuum. If the person in charge of the treatment program does not make explicit and systematic plans to develop behavior to fill this "space," the behavior most likely to move into the vacant time is whatever behavior happens to be reinforced, often fortuitously, when it is emitted. Without a systematic plan, this behavior is very likely to be something the teacher or others find objectionable; it is unlikely to be constructive studying behavior.

When one works with a hyperactive child on reducing the hyperactivity by means of a reinforcement program, one can reward and thus increase the period of sitting still. But merely sitting still should not be the goal of the program, for sitting still is merely a necessary step toward attending to a task to be learned. For this reason, reinforcement should quickly be made contingent not merely on sitting still but on sitting still *and* working; otherwise one is apt to end up with a child who has simply learned to "sit and do nothing." Assuming that the child has learned to sit still and work while in the special teaching setting, it is incumbent on the regular classroom teacher to whom he is returned that the child be given suitable tasks so that the sit-still-and-work behavior can continue.

Attribution of Progress   The second suggestion for achieving generalization offered by O'Leary and Drabman (1971) deals with the expectations such children have for their own behavior. If these children attribute their improvement to the setting in which they are acquiring a desirable response repertoire, their "good behavior and ability to learn," they will expect that once they are out of that setting, all they have gained is likely to be lost. For this reason, it is important that these children be given the expectation that they themselves are capable of doing well, that their successes are their accomplishments, not something somebody else has done for them. In order to ensure that children will attribute improvement to themselves and not to others, one must explicitly structure the entire helping situation from the start as one designed to increase the children's sense of competence.

Attributions of success cannot be taken for granted, particularly not with children who have had long histories of failure experiences which, because adults will usually have blamed them, may have resulted in poor self-images and low self-expectations. Children who have come to be convinced that they "can't do it" are very likely to attribute success experiences to external causes. For this reason, O'Leary and Drabman (1971) advocate that one use exaggerated excitement when children succeed, pointing out that if they work they *can* succeed. Similarly, such children must be given the expectation that they will be able to work without a token program. Since a good token program is gradually faded by thinning out the schedule of reinforcement and shifting the burden of maintaining the behavior to such reinforcers as praise, approval and privileges, this expectation is given considerable support. A token program is a temporary crutch, not a permanent prosthesis.

Another way of making sure that the children attribute improvements to themselves and will thus be able to carry them to other settings is to involve them in planning the specifics of the program, making it "their" program rather than the teacher's. They can help in the selection of the behaviors to be reinforced, in evolving the rules under which the class is to function, and—as the program progresses—in the specification of contingencies.

Enhancing Generalization   Generalization is also enhanced if children receive reinforcement for desirable behavior not only in the specialized environment of the token classroom but also in a variety of other situations and settings. Furthermore, it is important that the treatment setting be as similar as possible to the regular classroom setting so that the discrimination between the two is reduced. The ideal setting where a child should learn adaptive classroom behavior is, of course, the classroom itself; but where this is not feasible, the special resource room or treatment class should not be so distinctly different as to have desirable behavior become associated with these distinct features. For example, if children in regular class are used to calling their teachers by their last names, the resource room teacher should not be addressed by the first name. As children are phased back from special to regular classes, their teachers should be prepared to make it a point to praise good behavior, thus providing a similarity of settings and maintaining the adaptive behavior. (It would, of course, be nice if the regular classroom teacher were to make it a practice to praise desirable behavior of all children most of the time.)

Participation of Parents   Yet another means of enhancing transfer of progress by building a "bridge" between the special and the regular classroom is to involve the child's parents in the treatment plan. The parents can provide a constant background factor, and their potential contribution to a treatment plan cannot be sufficiently stressed. Provided they are included in the planning from the start and given a thorough understanding of the principles and rationale involved, parents can be a primary source for the delivery of backup reinforcers. When this is done, the child brings home the tokens earned during a given period and there exchanges these for whatever it is that has been agreed upon. This has the advantage that backup reinforcers can be highly personalized and consistent with the family's values and standards. More importantly, however, the parents can add their own social reinforcement to the delivery of the tangible reinforcer. This social reinforcement can and should continue to be available long after the child has left the special treatment class and returned to regular class.

The effectiveness of involving parents in a token program was demonstrated in a study reported by McKenzie, Clark, Wolf, Kothera, and Benson

(1968). These investigators worked with 10 students, ranging in age from 10 to 13 years, who attended a special class for children with learning disabilities. All had an achievement level at least two years below grade in one or more academic areas and all were described as highly distractible and prone to engage in disruptive behavior. Completion of work assignments was selected as the criterion behavior to be reinforced.

During a baseline period, the children could earn free-time activities, teacher attention, and special privileges for completed work. In addition, they received weekly grades, reflecting the level of correctness of the work they had done. An observer seated behind a one-way mirror monitored the attending behavior of the children, and this was used as the dependent measure. "Attending" was defined as direct orientation toward work materials and contact with the teacher. It was recorded during the first three hours of every morning with a score obtained for each child once every three minutes.

At the conclusion of the baseline period, which lasted for 19 school days, the children's parents were enlisted in a plan whereby the weekly grades brought home by the child were to become the occasion for the awarding of a monetary allowance, the amount being contingent on the level of the grades. The children were paid for the average weekly grade for each subject area. For example, each "A" would earn 10 cents, each "B" 5 cents, each "C" 1 cent; an "incomplete" would result in the loss of 10 cents. The actual amounts used in this pay scale were set by the parents on the basis of the family economy and values. The parents were instructed that the weekly exchange of grades for money was to be structured as an important event and that the child should henceforth be expected to pay with his earnings for all items he valued highly.

With the introduction of parent participation and the pay for weekly grades, the mean attending scores in both reading and arithmetic increased significantly. Compared to the baseline period, the overall median for attending in reading increased from 68 percent to 86 percent. In arithmetic, it increased from 70 percent to 86 percent. Although observations were discontinued halfway through the school year, the weekly grading and contingent allowances were continued for all children, including those who returned to regular classes. In this manner the transition from special to regular class was eased and the likelihood of transfer of improved behavior was greatly enhanced.

At the end of the school year, all 10 students were working successfully one to four levels above their starting levels in all academic areas. Six of them were returned to full-time attendance in regular class, which was one grade higher than the ones they had been in during the previous year. All these students consistently earned at least "C" averages, with half of them obtaining "B" averages. At the close of the school year, all the returned students were promoted to the next grade.

While this study lacks certain controls which might permit one to draw definitive conclusions, it does appear that the use of grades as tokens which parents exchange for monetary backup reinforcers led to substantial gains in attending behavior and that this, in turn, was largely instrumental in improving academic performance. The importance of involving parents in the operation of programs designed to improve the school performance of their children cannot be overstressed, but this should probably be combined with another effective operation: having the children take an active part in the operation of the token program. Thus, it is possible to teach children to evaluate their own behavior and to keep their own records, thereby freeing the teacher to attend to the academic substance.

Self-Evaluation   Self-evaluation by children played an important role in a study conducted by Drabman, Spitalnik, and O'Leary (1973), who demonstrated reduction of disruptive behavior which generalized over brief periods of time. The children in this study were eight boys, ages 9 to 10, who attended "adjustment" classes for students with academic and emotional problems. All were at least one year below grade level in reading skills and their teachers viewed them all as very disruptive, even in their small, special classes. For the purpose of the study these children were enrolled in an after-school remedial reading class, which met for one hour five times a week, where the principles of token reinforcement were applied.

Programs of this nature had demonstrated improvements in behavior, but these had failed to generalize to situations other than those in which the token program was conducted (e. g., O'Leary, Becker, Evans, & Saudargas, 1969). For this reason Drabman, Spitalnik, and O'Leary (1973) wished to determine whether self-evaluation by children would lead to transfer of improvements in social and academic behavior to periods of the day when the token program was not in effect. The study was therefore designed to teach honest and veridical self-evaluation skills so that the teachers could transfer the responsibility for behavior evaluation to the students in a manner that would produce long-range maintenance of appropriate behavior.

To accomplish the goal of this study, Drabman and his colleagues (1973) proceeded in several phases. After recording baseline measures on disruptive behavior and the scores from the California Achievement Test Reading-Vocabulary and the Sullivan reading series, they had the teacher introduce a standard token program in which the children could earn points for "good behavior" and completion of assignments. Each hour-long class was broken into four 15-minute periods. During one of these periods, the token program was not in effect. At the beginning of each period the teacher would announce whether it was a token period or not, and the no-token episodes served as a control.

With the implementation of the conventional, teacher-administered token program, disruptive behavior decreased and academic performance improved.

After five days of this regime, the teacher announced that henceforth the children were to rate their own behavior and to attempt to match the ratings she was giving them. During this matching phase, the children could earn extra points if their ratings matched those of the teacher. After 10 days of this training in self-rating, the teacher's checking of the students' ratings was gradually faded out, thereby fading out the bonus points which accompanied successful matches. During the last 12 days of the study, all checking was completely discontinued and the earning of points depended solely on the ratings the children had awarded themselves.

Throughout the study, trained observers continued to record disruptive behavior. During the self-evaluation phase, such behavior showed an 88 percent decrease from baseline while points were in effect. For the no-token control periods, the improvement was even greater, disruptive behavior showing a 90 percent decrease. The group gained an average of 0.72 years on the reading vocabulary test during the 2½ months of the study, and similar improvement was reflected on the Sullivan reading series.

This work highlights the fact that honest self-evaluation can be taught to very disruptive children, who thus acquire sufficient self-control to maintain improved behavior even when this receives no extrinsic reinforcement. In discussing their work, Drabman, Spitalnik, and O'Leary (1973) write,

> Several factors may have contributed to this maintenance of appropriate behavior during the self-evaluation phase: (a) The teachers continually praised the students for appropriate behavior, and their praise may have become more reinforcing over the course of the study; (b) Similarly, peer reinforcement for appropriate behavior increased with time, and the children did not want to be bothered by other pupils; (c) Honest self-evaluation was socially reinforced by the teachers and later by peers. It is quite likely that these self-evaluations became cues which served as self-instructional or mediational statements which guided appropriate behavior; (d) The children's academic skills were improved; their involvement in academic activities was partly incompatible with inappropriate behavior. Particularly toward the beginning of the self-evaluation phase, when the rate of disruptive behavior was lowest, the children could easily see that they had made academic progress; (e) The self-evaluations may have become secondary reinforcers for appropriate classroom behavior (p. 15f)

Despite the impressive finding regarding self-evaluation, this study is not really very convincing on the issue of generalization. The test for generalization of improved behavior was based on the 15-minute control periods during which the token program was not in effect. For most of these time segments, a token period preceded and followed, so that the finding that disruptive behavior also decreased during the control sessions is not very strong evidence for generalization. It is more convincing if one can demonstrate that the positive effects of a token program are retained after a token program is terminated altogether. Such a demonstration was reported by O'Leary, Drabman, and Kass (1973), who found improved behavior to be maintained over a 20-day follow-up period after termination of a token program.

From Tokens to Praise

Most of the early token programs used with children in classroom situations used tangible rewards such as money, candy, and toys as backup reinforcers. This not only introduces a highly artificial element into the school setting but it has also been thought that the magnitude of these reinforcers might be one of the reasons why improvements in behavior are rarely maintained once the reinforcements are withdrawn. For these reasons O'Leary, Drabman, and Kass (1973) decided to test whether appropriate behavior, developed in a token program, could be maintained if the reinforcers used were those readily available to any classroom teacher, such as extra recess or free time in a special activity area of the classroom.

For this study, 22 third- and fourth-grade children were selected on the basis of their being the most disruptive in the school. All of them were deficient in reading and/or arithmetic. After they had been observed in their own classroom for the purpose of establishing a baseline for disruptive behavior, these children were assigned to three separate resource-room classes where they received special instruction in reading or arithmetic for one hour per day in supplementation of their regular academic program, which they continued in the home room. Following observations during a baseline phase in the resource room, token programs lasting for four months were introduced. As is the case in all studies by O'Leary and his colleagues, disruptive behaviors observed and recorded were: not sitting in the seat, inappropriate noise, playing, turning around, noncompliance, vocalization, aggression, and not attending to task.

When the token reinforcement program was initiated, the teacher announced the introduction of a point system. Points could be earned for completion of assignment, completion of homework, coming to class on time, and behaving well in class. The emphasis was on the academic tasks, which served as the largest single source of potential point-earning. Points were awarded at the end of the first 45 minutes of the one-hour resource-room period and the points thus earned were exchangeable (one point for one minute) for free time during the last 15 minutes of free-activity period. A variety of games—such as checkers, paints, and building blocks—were available during this free time.

The token programs in the resource room were continued for four months. During the last three weeks, all children were again observed in their home class to determine if the improved behavior developed in the resource room had influenced home-class disruptive behavior. In addition, the home-room teachers repeated a rating of each child which had been gathered at the beginning of the study. Finally, one of the resource-room classes was monitored for eight weeks following termination of the program in order to investigate maintenance of the appropriate behavior generated by the token system.

The results reported by O'Leary, Drabman, and Kass (1973) clearly show a decrease in disruptive behavior with the initiation of the token program. In one class, for example, the average frequency for disruptive behaviors decreased 57 percent, and this improvement was maintained throughout the fol-low-up period when the token program was no longer in effect. An interesting phenomenon was revealed in the investigation of generalization to the home-class situation. While the ratings by the teachers in the home rooms showed a reduction in disruptive behavior for a significant number of children, no sig-nificant generalization of appropriate behavior to the home-room classes was reflected in the independent observer recordings. These recordings showed that 14 of the 22 children manifested less disruptive behavior than they had during baseline, but this change did not reach statistical significance. It is likely that the teacher ratings were influenced by their expectations based on the knowledge that these children were participating in a special program.

This raises the question whether, for practical purposes, it is more impor-tant to demonstrate a statistically significant effect or to influence the percep-tions of teachers regarding the behavior of the children in their class. A statis-tically significant difference can have little practical significance. On the other hand, an event of practical significance may have little statistical significance. The two are not the same. At any rate, if 14 out of 22 disruptive children improve their behavior following a one-hour-per-day experience over a four-month period, the method used would seem to merit further investigation.

It is very likely that generalization to the home room could have been enhanced if certain steps which the investigators had planned could have been carried out. They had hoped that the home room teacher might also award points, based on home-room behavior, that could be exchanged for time in the special-activity area of the resource room. These ratings were then to be grad-ually faded out so that appropriate behavior might be maintained in the home-room without such special treatment. Administrative difficulties kept this plan from being implemented.

Another "bridge" between a special-class situation and a child's regular schoolroom would be the use of praise and teacher attention for desirable behavior. The special-class teacher usually pairs the awarding of points or tokens with much social reinforcement, and this is continued even when the artificial rewards are eliminated. If classroom teachers could be helped to see the merit of frequent and explicit praise and attention for constructive behav-ior, they would be using the reinforcers made effective in the special class, thus enhancing generalization of progress a child has made. Unfortunately, as O'Leary, Kaufman, Kass, and Drabman (1970) have documented, classroom teachers are much more likely to deliver reprimands and to attend to undesir-able behavior than they are to bestow praise and to attend to desirable behav-ior. The effect of this paradoxical behavior is that undesirable behavior is strengthened and maintained.

The Teacher's Role

In all the studies discussed in this chapter, the classroom teacher played a key role in the treatment programs. This is the logical consequence of the principle that treatment must take place where the troublesome behavior is found. If the trouble is in the classroom, then treatment must be in the classroom; the teacher thus becomes the principal agent of treatment. Yet in the studies which we have used to illustrate the operation of this principle, the teacher was usually an intermediary, since the treatment programs were designed and directed by psychologists who worked, as it were, behind the scenes.

While such specialized consultation should ideally be available to all classroom teachers, it is not necessary for a teacher to forego the use of behavioral methods in seeking to help a learning-disabled child simply because expert consultation is not readily at hand. A teacher who is familiar with the basic principles of behavior,[1] should have no difficulty in planning and implementing an effective program of therapeutic intervention provided the following procedural steps are conscientiously followed.

Steps in Implementing a Treatment Plan   Before one can hope to treat a problem, one must identify what it is one wishes to treat. This is neither as easy nor as obvious as it sounds. All too often we are troubled by something a child does without being able to make an objective statement of what it is that troubles us. It is not enough to say, "He is distractible." We must also be able to say what *observable* behavior it is that makes us use the word "distractible" in describing this child. What would we point to in showing someone else that the child is distractible? Does the child look up from a task every time there is a noise in another part of the classroom? Does the child ask questions or make statements that have nothing to do with the task at hand? Does the child wander away from an unfinished activity and begin to do something else? Before one can hope to introduce an intervention, one must have an objective statement of the behavior one wishes to change, and that behavior must be something someone else can also observe.

In some instances a child's problem is not that of engaging in troublesome behavior but of the inability to do something that is expected on the basis of his or her age and grade level. In that case, in addition to identifying the problem and defining it objectively, we must also undertake a task analysis so as to have a detailed, fine-grain description of the skills needed to accomplish the task.

Again, it is not enough to make a global statement such as, "He can't write his name." We must also be able to specify the many units of behavior that enter into the task we call writing one's name. This begins with knowing one's name, understanding the request to write it, picking up and holding the crayon or pencil, managing the left-to-right hand movement, and so forth. A child's inability to perform any one of these subskills would result in his not being able to write his name, and intervention will have to start with this subskill.

After one has identified and objectively defined the behavior that is con-

---

[1] An excellent outline of these can be found in O'Leary and O'Leary (1972).

sidered a problem and conducted a task analysis where this is essential, the next step in moving toward an intervention is to observe the circumstances under which the behavior takes place or should be taking place. Any given act occurs in a context; it has antecedents—events that take place immediately before the act—and it has consequences—events that take place immediately after the act. By careful observation one can usually discover that a defined problem behavior is almost always preceded and followed by the same or very similar events. In more technical terms, a given response is usually emitted under similar stimulus conditions. The antecedent stimuli can be assumed to control the behavior. That is to say, if these stimuli were not present, the behavior would be unlikely to occur. The stimuli which follow that behavior can be assumed to be maintaining it over time; without these consequences appearing at least some of the time, the behavior should ultimately cease to take place. Again, in technical terms, events which regularly follow a given response can be assumed to be reinforcing events (reinforcing stimuli) which, when removed, will lead to the extinction of the response.

We can take the distractible child as an illustration of the statements made in the preceding paragraph. We may have observed that this child looks up from a task whenever there is a noise in the back of the room and that when this happens, the teacher very often admonishes this child to "pay attention." Having identified these antecedents and consequences, we now have an idea of how we might go about reducing the looking-up-from-the-task behavior. In theory, the possibilities are twofold: We can remove the antecedents or the consequences. In practice, however, the likelihood of eliminating the noises from the back of the room is very slim; hence, we should concentrate the intervention on the consequences. Strange as it may seem, the teacher's admonition or reprimand appears to serve as a reinforcer that maintains the looking-up behavior. If one withdrew this consequence, never again admonishing the child under these particular circumstances, the troublesome behavior should disappear, particularly if we concurrently increased praise statements and other reinforcements when the child is engaging in desired behavior, such as working on a task without looking up.

The above formulation provides the teacher with a starting point. Whether it is correct can only be determined by putting it to a test. Before one can do that, however, another important step is required. That is to obtain a record of the frequency with which the identified problem behavior occurs. We can't determine whether an intervention results in change (improvement or deterioration) unless we have an objective way of ascertaining change. It is remarkable how easy it is to fool oneself into believing that a program works if one has no more to go on than an impression. Without a written record based on observations of behavior that has been counted, one cannot possibly know whether an intervention is effective.

It will now be clear why we insisted on an objective, observable definition of the problem. Without that, one would be reduced to reporting the impression that the child "seems less distractible"; with it, we can report the fact that the frequency of the child's looking up from reading was reduced from eight times per 10 minutes to two times per 10 minutes. It is therefore necessary to count and record the frequency of the problem behavior before any intervention takes place. We must obtain a baseline from which to note later changes.

Next we should define the goal of the intervention. It is the rare behavior where one would wish to work toward a zero frequency. Never looking up from work, never getting up from the seat, or always finishing every assignment are probably not reasonable expectations. We should thus set outselves a reasonable goal or even an intermediate goal toward which to work and against which to measure our progress. One cannot say whether an intervention has been successful unless one has a basis for comparison; hence the importance of a baseline and a goal.

Only now are we ready to enter upon intervention, ready to modify antecedents or consequences while continuing to count and record. Why make such a fetish of counting? The approach we have outlined is not a treatment package that can be "plugged in" wherever problems are identified. It is far better viewed as a hypothesis to be tested in each and every case. We can only assume that the antecedents and consequences we have identified are indeed responsible for the behavior, and we can only hope that we have correctly identified the circumstances surrounding the behavior. Whether the assumption is correct and the hope justified must be put to test, and this test requires continued counting and recording.

If the hypothesis we are testing is correct, one should see some change in behavior reflected in our records rather soon after initiation of the program. If the record reflects no change within about a week, it is well to assume that something is wrong with our formulation or with the implementation of the program. At this point one should return to the step of observing the behavior in its context to see whether the antecedents and consequences have been identified correctly. Failure of an intervention program is almost always the result of an incorrect formulation of the problem, a faulty definition of the conditions maintaining the problem, or an unsystematic, inconsistent application of the intervention procedure. The cause of treatment failure should always be sought in the treatment or its application, never in the child!

Before we summarize the steps in intervention which have been discussed above, one other point bears emphasis. When one tries to reduce the frequency of a troublesome behavior, one should always plan on what behavior one wishes to see in its place and take steps to strengthen that replacement behavior. Working toward the absence of a problem behavior is not enough; we must also work toward the presence of something constructive that is to take its place. Thus, if we wish to reduce the frequency of children's looking up from their work, we should explicitly strengthen their looking at their work. Though the latter appears to be the logical opposite of the former, one cannot assume that it will automatically appear as the result of the elimination of the looking up. If one makes that assumption, one might find that the children no longer look up from their work but that they now close their eyes every time there is a noise in the back of the room. Careful attention to strengthening desired behaviors through rewarding them in a systematic fashion is as important as working toward reducing undesired behavior.

In summary then, the steps of an intervention program are as follows:

1 Identify and objectively define the problem and, where necessary, do a task analysis of behavior to be strengthened.
2 Observe the circumstances under which the problem occurs and note the antecedents and consequences.
3 Obtain a baseline of the problem behavior by counting and recording its frequency.
4 Define the goal of intervention in objective terms.
5 Begin the intervention program and continue counting and recording the frequency of the problem.
6 Strengthen desirable behavior alternatives to the problem if the program involves elimination of a problem.
7 If no change is noted, return to stage two.
8 Continue until goal is reached or seek expert advice.

RELEVANCY OF TRAINING METHODS

Despite the fact that there is no training method which has been shown to be universally effective when used with heterogeneous groups of children (whether they be categorized as reading-disabled, learning-disabled, hyperactive, or—for that matter—"normal"), one continues to find advocates of specific methods who would want all children in a given category treated by their approach. This uncritical championing of a method is sometimes based on enthusiasm unbridled by available research results, but one also suspects that commercial interests may occasionally play a role in the desire to "sell" a certain technique, particularly once it has been packaged by a publishing house.

While it can certainly not be claimed that we have conclusive research which points in a given direction, it does appear that the studies discussed in this and the preceding chapters suggest the need to use remedial methods and training techniques which are specifically designed to help a given child (or group of children) with the specific aspect of learning or behavior which creates difficulty. Some learning-disabled children have trouble sitting still, thus disrupting both their own and their classmates' ability to attend to academic tasks which, by their nature, require a certain amount of sedentary behavior. Such children can no doubt benefit from the approaches discussed above. Other learning-disabled children seem to have difficulty orienting their sense receptors to the stimuli which must be perceived if they are to be processed. Such children would seem to need the kind of visual training advocated by Rosner (1970). Other, and possibly many learning-disabled children have difficulty sustaining selective attention, and they seem to benefit from programs of training that follow the suggestions of Douglas (1972) or Meichenbaum and Goodman (1971).

It may also be that carefully dosed and selectively administered medication is of help to some of these children (Conners, 1971). Again, there are children with learning difficulties who lack adequate preparation in spoken language, and these can be helped by remedial programs designed to strengthen the language base (Blank, 1970). In the area of reading disabilities, there are children who have difficulty with the decoding process; for them a method which emphasizes the teaching of sound-letter association may be appropriate (Spalding & Spalding, 1957).

Last, there are children who have no difficulty with any of the subsidiary skills just mentioned but who nonetheless fail to get meaning from written material. For these, training methods that focus on comprehension are probably the most logical (Serafica & Sigel, 1970). Myers and Hammill (1969) present a comprehensive overview of the various methods that have been developed for helping children with learning disabilities. Most of these methods have a very specific focus on one or another deficit, but few of their advocates seem to restrict themselves to a circumscribed target population with specific disabilities.

When training in a prerequisite subskill—such as sitting still, right-left discrimination, or selective attention—is indeed suitable for a particular child because careful assessment has revealed that he or she is deficient in that skill, it must be remembered that such training does no more than to provide the subskill; it does not teach reading or other academic subject matter. It seems so obvious, but it is often forgotten that teaching a child to walk on a balance beam in order to improve coordination or prescribing a drug designed to faciliate concentration will not automatically teach such a child to read or do arithmetic. If needed subskills are to be provided, it is crucial that the plan include concurrent remedial teaching or tutoring designed to give the child the academic substance he or she needs in order to respond to the demands and expectations of the school.

By the time a child's learning disability is recognized, months and years have passed during which the child failed to benefit from the instruction to which he or she was exposed. If one now introduces subskill training without taking steps to help compensate for all the missed learning, the help is bound to be of little avail and the child will continue to do poorly in school (Ross, 1967). It is not a fair test of the efficacy of any intervention at the subskill level (and certainly unfair to the children involved) if one gives training at that level without concurrent academic help and then assesses whether the subskill training improved academic performance. The effect of subskill training must be assessed in terms of the subskill itself. Thus, if a child is given training in letter-sound association, one must assess whether there is an improvement in attaching the right sound to the various letters; one should not expect that he or she will spontaneously learn to read words. That skill must also be taught, and such teaching should be closely coordinated and paced with progress in the phonics training. We shall have more to say about this in the following chapter.

SUMMARY

Behaviorally oriented psychologists prefer to focus on responses they can observe. Therefore, instead of concentrating on such constructs as selective attention, they focus their research on attending behavior, which they operationalize as directing the glance at the presented task. By delivering reinforcements contingent on the specified response, one can demonstrate an increase in the desired behavior. This approach was illustrated by several studies which showed its success with both individuals and groups of children.

It is not enough to demonstrate that a child's behavior and performance improve while a program of intervention is in effect. One must also be able to show that the improvement carries over to the regular classroom setting, where the specialized reinforcement program is not in effect. There are various ways of enhancing such generalization which one must build into a program of intervention if it is to be of practical value. One such way is to involve the child's parents in a remedial program, for they can provide an important link between the special and the regular classroom. Another way is to give major responsibility for the operation of a remedial program to the children themselves. If they learn to evaluate their own behavior during the remedial phase of a program, they are more likely to maintain improved behavior than when evaluation is in the hands of others.

Remedial programs based on behavioral principles often use such artificial reinforcers as points or tokens in the earlier stages of the intervention. Since such reinforcers are not usually present in a regular classroom, praise statements and similar social reinforcers are paired with tokens. Thus, if the regular classroom teacher uses praise (as any good teacher would), the child's improved behavior and performance have a chance to generalize.

Because the treatment principles used by behavioral psychologists are relatively simple and thus easy to learn, their application does not require a highly trained specialist. Teachers can use these methods and should do so, because the best place for a child to learn adaptive behavior is in the place where such behavior is expected—the classroom. For this reason the steps required in the implementation of a treatment plan were outlined and illustrated.

Reading and Reading Disorders

What Is Reading?

Before one can engage in a meaningful discussion of reading disabilities, it is necessary to explore just what is meant when a behavior is called reading. When one observes accomplished readers, all one can see is that they look at a printed page. Closer observation also shows that their eyes move from side to side, but beyond that, the behavior in question defies direct observation. Silent reading, like learning, involves nonobservable internal events. Thus, if we see someone looking at a printed page and moving his or her eyes, we can't be sure whether that person is reading; the topography of reading behavior can be mimicked by a nonreader. The only way in which an observer can monitor reading is by asking the presumed reader questions about the content of the reading material, questions whose answers could only have been acquired by having read the writing on which the questions are based.

Because a teacher must be able to monitor reading more directly in order to give immediate feedback, beginning reading is taught by having the student read aloud. While this step is probably essential for the teaching process, learning to read by vocalizing the material represents a detour to the goal behavior, which is silent reading. Therefore the student must learn to transfer the skills acquired in reading aloud to reading silently. Many fail to master this step and therefore go through life subvocalizing what they read and reducing their reading speed.

Meaning and Understanding   A reader who vocalizes what he reads not only permits a teacher to monitor his behavior but also permits us to observe just what it is that we call reading. It is a process of decoding a set of symbols. The language we speak is itself a set of symbols. We have evolved a common code of vocal sounds which stand for (symbolize) objects, events, relationships, and ideas. In addition, we have developed a code—called writing—which permits a different way of denoting the same objects, events, relationships, and ideas. Since speech developed before writing, it is probable that writing is actually an encoding of speech. But it is logically possible to develop the two codes independent of one another, so that the written code could be a means of communication (a language) in the absence of a verbal code.

The logical independence of speech and writing makes it possible to teach at least the rudiments of reading to a subject who does not know "the language" and who thus learns to decode the written symbol directly into its referent in "the real world." But is that reading? If we teach a monkey to find a grape under a lid marked with the word "grape" and a banana under a lid marked with the word "banana," has he learned to read these words? Does he know the meaning of the words? Does he understand what he reads?

A further example will highlight another aspect of the difficulty involved in defining "reading." If one knows the rules of pronunciation of a phonetically regular language, it is possible to learn to vocalize a written text without understanding a word of it. Is that reading? Now take a language with phonetic irregularities: English, for example. Encountering the grapheme "tear" in a sentence ("He had a tear on his collar"), the phonetic reader would be unable to know how to pronounce it because it is necessary to know from the context whether the person had wept or torn his shirt.

Knowing the context is, of course, a matter of understanding the meaning, and we can thus conclude that a definition of "reading" must include a reference to meaning. Reading is not simply a decoding of written symbols but the identification of the meaning of these characters. We shall return to this issue in the course of an examination of the basic skills required for the acquisition of reading and after discussion of how insufficient mastery of these skills may contribute to reading disabilities.

READING DISABILITIES AND BASIC SKILLS

There are a number of capacities and skills a person must possess and master in order to read visually presented material. Among these are visual acuity, motor control over eye movements, ability to discriminate among stimuli, and knowledge of the language. At one time or another, individuals concerned with reading disabilities have implicated defects in one of these necessary skills as *the* cause of defective reading. Persuasive arguments have been advanced favoring one or the other of these presumed causes, and remedial programs have been developed aimed at alleviating the "basic" problem in hopes of enabling reading-disabled children to overcome their deficit.

What he calls the *perceptual deficit hypothesis* has been analyzed by Vellutino (1974), who concludes on the basis of research in his own and others' laboratories that the problem of disabled readers is not one of basic perceptual processes but of incorrect decoding of grapheme (letter) to phoneme (sound). That is to say, the problem of the disabled reader is one of reading, so that it would follow that remedial programs should concentrate not on learning to balance on a walking beam but on learning to decode written material; yet, visual training, perceptual-motor training, body-image training, and language training have each had and continue to have their enthusiastic advocates, all claiming success for their remedial method and hence validity for their causal theory. Aside from the fact that the success of a remedial method does not permit one to infer that the theory on which the method is based is correct (the *post hoc ergo propter hoc* fallacy), most of the studies on which these claims are based suffer from gross methodological or logical weaknesses.

If one takes a group of children who are selected on the basis of their low scores on a reading test and compares them with a control group of so-called normal readers, it is a safe prediction that the poor readers will perform worse than the normals on almost any test or task one might choose to give them. Their history of failures has led them to approach such tasks with expectations of failing, and this negatively affects their performance. What is more, poor readers may indeed share a common and basic deficit which, though not the one the experimenter seeks to assess, detracts from their ability to perform well on the presented task. If, for example, reading-disabled children were to share a problem in sustaining selective attention, this would be reflected in tasks used to assess any of the other skills, deficits in which have been advanced to explain reading problems.

A Hierarchy of Reading Skills

In their analysis of reading and reading difficulty, Wiener and Cromer (1967) pointed out that reading requires a sequence of skills which can be conceptualized in a hierarchical fashion, such that a problem encountered at any one level of this hierarchy will create difficulties at all subsequent, higher levels. Comprehension is the ultimate goal of reading, but before comprehension can occur, the reader must decode the written message and this, in turn, presupposes that the symbols of which the message is composed are discriminated.

For discrimination to take place, the reader must selectively attend to the stimuli so that orderly sensory input can occur. This implies that the visual stimuli must be attended to in a sequence, from beginning to end, requiring a skill called *scanning* which involves systematic eye movements from left to right. While the skilled reader does not scan all of the written material from left to right and line for line and need not attend to each symbol on the page in order to comprehend the content, the beginning reader must master each level of this conceptual hierarchy. Reading difficulties can derive from a failure to acquire competence at any one of these skills.

Figure 8-1 presents the hierarchy of reading skills in a schematic fashion. This is undoubtedly an oversimplification, and there are other necessary skills—such as vision—which are not included in this schema. The discussion to follow will deal with each of the skills in turn; the graphic presentation is meant not as a definitive theory but merely as an aid in visualizing the relationship of the various skills.

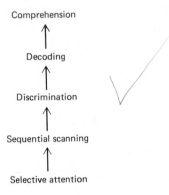

Figure 8-1 Schematic representation of the hierarchy of skills required in reading.

Selective Attention   If one imagines the multitude of objects and events in a child's environment which compete for his or her attention with the print on the page, one can appreciate the importance of selective attention as a basic requisite of reading. Not only are there the external objects and events but there are also internal events, from the stimuli emanating from the child's digestive system to the thoughts produced in his head, to which attention could be directed in preference to the print to be decoded.

External and internal events are all potential stimuli, and a person's information-processing capacity would be totally overwhelmed unless one were capable of selecting from among these potential stimuli a limited number to which to attend. This limited number of stimuli which become the focus of selective attention may be those a teacher expects to be the center of a child's attention; if they are not, the teacher will say that the child is "not paying attention," and this use of the term tends to confuse the issue. Selective attention entails a capacity to inhibit stimuli which are irrelevant to the task at hand. For some children this capacity may be limited because they have not yet arrived at a developmental level where it can be fully utilized. This issue was discussed in greater detail in Chapter 3.

Man seems to have a relatively limited capacity for processing information. This demands that we have a way of selecting out of the mass of stimuli impinging on our sensory systems those stimuli to which we must attend if we are to cope adaptively with the task set before us. This limited capacity is probably a function of the way in which the human organism has evolved, a "given" which does not appear susceptible to change through either maturation or training. On the other hand, the capacity to select stimuli and to make them the focus of attention does appear to change in the course of a child's development, probably through an interaction between physiological maturation and experiential learning. We have previously argued that a major basis of learning (and reading) disabilities may be a discrepancy between a child's ability to attend to stimuli selectively and the demands the teaching situation makes on his or her use of selective attention. Though he uses information processing synonymously with attention, Senf (1972) makes a similar point when he writes,

> Because the information-processing capacity is limited, the organism must select which information it will process (attend to). Though an obvious notion, the assumption that the processing system has limited capacity has very important ramifications for the distribution of this limited capacity. Improper management of an adequate amount of information-processing capacity can result in failure on certain tasks just as severe as that caused by limited capacity itself. The paradox of learning disabilities may find some resolution in this notion. Though not mentally retarded . . . the learning-disabled child has adequate resources, i. e., processing capacity, but seems unable to achieve the desired complex behavior, as for example reading (p. 310).

Having the capacity to attend to stimuli selectively does not, of course, guarantee that a child will be a good reader. Selective attention is a necessary but not a sufficient requisite for reading. Conceivably, a child can selectively attend to stimuli that have nothing to do with the task of reading, so that this capacity can either advance or retard good reading. Whether selective attention enhances or hinders reading performance is apparently a function of the material presented in interaction with the reader's competence.

Willows (1974) conducted a well-controlled study in which she related reading ability and selective attention and found that good and poor readers seem to focus their attention on different aspects of the reading task. The subjects were 104 sixth-grade boys who had been selected from a public school population on the basis of the relationship between their intelligence test and reading achievement test scores. Good readers were those whose reading achievement score was above the level expected on the basis of their intelligence test score. Conversely, poor readers were those where the discrepancy between expectation and performance was in the opposite direction.

The reading task involved eight stories at varying levels of difficulty which the child was instructed to read aloud. For the children in the control condition, these stories had been typed on cards in double-spaced form and black type. The children in the selective reading condition had to read the same stories, but for them these had been typed in such a manner that words typed in red appeared between the lines of black type. Though relevant to the story content, these words were different from those used in the story. For example, if the story dealt with truck drivers who haul dangerous explosives on mountain roads, the distractor words would include "transport drivers," "dynamite," and "slippery roads." These words would not make a story by themselves, and they were repeated several times in the various lines between the story typed in black.

All children were instructed to read the black passage aloud and to remember what they read so that they could answer questions about it later. In addition, the subjects in the selective reading group were told to pay no attention to the red words, that these had been put there as a distraction. After a child had read a story, he was asked to read four multiple-choice questions which included the distractor words. Thus, the question "About whom is this paragraph?" would, for the example cited above, give the following choices: transport drivers, van drivers, truck drivers, semi-trailer drivers, pickup-truck drivers, bus drivers. The data collected included the answers to these questions and the time taken to provide them, plus number of reading errors and reading time for each story.

Selective attention should permit an individual to focus on the story typed in black and to ignore the distractor words typed in red. If poor readers have difficulty in attending selectively to the stimuli relevant to the task, they should have more trouble than the good readers with the stories used in the selective reading condition (where they had to "screen out" the red distractor words).

The results showed that the reading times (and error scores) of the good readers were not affected by the selective reading condition, while the poor readers took significantly longer to read the paragraphs with distractors than those without. What is more, the poor readers tended to take more time answering the questions about the selective passages than about the control passages, while there was no such trend for the good readers. Thus far, the results are in line with the predictions one would make on the basis of considerations involving the role of selective attention in reading. The analysis of the answers the children gave to the questions, which represent a measure of comprehension, produced an interesting and—to some extent—unexpected finding.

If, in answer to the multiple-choice questions, a child selected a word which had appeared in the red interstitial lines, this was scored as an intrusion error; if the answer was otherwise wrong, it was scored as a nonintrusion error. Willows (1974) reports that

> Under the selective reading condition, good readers made substantially more intrusion errors than they did under the control condition. Poor readers, on the other hand, tended to choose the intrusion items less often under the selective than under the control reading condition. . . . poor readers made more nonintrusion errors than good readers under both selective and control reading conditions (p. 412).

This the author correctly calls "a surprising and provocative result." Good and poor readers, it would seem, attend to different aspects of a reading task; their reading strategies differ. In a distracting situation, the poor readers have to concentrate their attention on the words and lines to be read; they read these more slowly and make more errors than they do under non-distracting conditions. But working as hard as they do, they do not read (attend to) the distractor words. These words *are* distractors, but for the poor reader, they are not words. As a result the distractors do not appear in the poor readers' answers to the multiple choice questions, although their comprehension (as indexed by the non-intrusion errors) is much less adequate than that of the good readers.

While the plodding of the poor readers protects them from the intrusions, the reading strategy developed by the good readers makes them vulnerable to the distractors *under this atypical reading situation*. Were they to read word by word and line by line (as the poor readers do), the good readers would have few intrusion errors. Instead, they apparently scan the total page and extract meaning by a strategy Neisser (1967) calls "analysis-by-synthesis." Willows (1974) suggests that the good reader

> analyzes enough of the symbols on the page to allow him to formulate a general idea of what the passage is about. He then simply scans the text, taking in a few fragments of words and phrases here and there to be sure that he is "on the right track." To proceed rapidly, the good reader need only detect words that fit with his expectancies of the information content of the text (p. 413).

Since the words in the interstitial lines were consistent with the meaning of the text, it was possible for the good reader to validate his or her expectancies in either the black or the red lines, thus leading to intrusion errors.

Selective attention is essential for reading, but the question is, to what aspect of the stimulus array a reader must be attending in order to read competently. A good reader seems to attend to the message (meaning) to be extracted from the writing, while a poor (and beginning) reader attends to the medium (letters and words) in which the material is presented. Under ordinary conditions, their strategy serves the good readers well, but when distractors set a trap for them, as in the case of Willows's experiment, their approach can reduce the adequacy of their performance.

The question remains whether the strategy which the good reader has probably spontaneously adopted should be the one to teach to the beginning reader, or whether one must first learn to attend to letters and words before one can be expected to attend to meaning. It is likely that once the rudiments of reading skill have been taught, an emphasis on using analysis by synthesis would be helpful. But whether this can be done during reading acquisition requires further investigation.

There is some evidence to suggest that poor readers can be helped to improve their performance if, in addition to direct training in reading, they are exposed to a situation aimed at enhancing attention to words and letters. In a preliminary study conducted by Heiman, Fischer, and Ross (1974), a small group of problem readers who were concurrently receiving tutoring in reading were enrolled in a "booster program" in which they were systematically reinforced for attending to and identifying combinations of letters and words.

The child would watch a screen on which would be projected a series of 10 paragraphs of varying length and difficulty. These had been composed to contain repeated letter clusters, repeated words, and repeated word clusters. The child would be asked to read the paragraph aloud and to give a signal when he or she saw specified letters or words. Points, later to be traded for prizes, could be earned for correct identifications. A control group went through the same procedure except that they had no task other than to read the paragraphs and they received no reinforcement for attending to a particular aspect of the reading material.

The children participated in from 7 to 10 sessions lasting 30 minutes each over a period of seven weeks. Standardized reading tests had been administered to all children before and were repeated after the 7-week period. Since both experimental and control children had participated in a reading tutoring program, their average reading scores showed improvement, but the experimental group who had been exposed to the attention-enhancing procedure showed significantly greater improvement than the control group.

Specifically, where the control group had gained 0.67 years (grade levels) on the Spache Diagnostic Reading Test, the experimental group had gained 1.67 years. This group had been an average of 1.60 years below grade level at the beginning of the program but scored 0.07 years above grade level at the end. The authors point out that attention was a necessity in order for the children in the experimental group to win points; since all of them did earn points, one can conclude that they were selectively attending to the written material. Since attention was necessary for the successful completion of the task, these children can thus be said to have been trained to attend and this training appears to have contributed to their improved reading performance.

It must again be stressed that this special training in attending was paralleled by tutoring in reading, and that it used reading material as stimuli to which the child had to attend. It is unlikely that training in attention given in isolation or using material unrelated to reading would lead to the same results. This, however, remains an assumption to be put to experimental test.

Sequential Scanning   Given that a child is able selectively to attend to the shape of the segment of print on a page which is to be read (instead of attending to the space between the lines, the picture on the facing page, the texture of the paper, the size of the letters, the color of the print, etc., etc.), the child must now direct his or her gaze to (look at) the stimuli in left-to-right sequence if that is the order in which the language is printed.

While there is no direct way of monitoring selective attention—because it is an internal, covert event—it is possible to observe eye movements. These are therefore the first manifest indications of whether the child is making task-relevant responses in a situation requiring him or her to read. Many students of reading have therefore focused on eye movements as a convenient anchoring point for their observations. The next point where an observer has access to the reading process does not come until the child verbalizes what he or she has decoded in oral reading, and there are several covert processes which occur before this.

While it is reasonable to assume that there is a close relationship between reading and eye movements and that children who manifest deficient reading skills should therefore have atypical eye movements, the research literature on this relationship is equivocal. Oculomotor patterns change as reading improves (Tinker, 1958), but, as Taylor (1965) noted, "Eye movements are neither the cause nor the effect of good or poor reading" (p. 199). This statement was addressed at the mistaken notion that a poor reader can be helped simply by giving him eye-movement exercises. The relationship between reading and eye movements is not that direct.

Evidence is beginning to accumulate which suggests that eye movements, particularly the rapid lateral movements called saccades, are related to attention (Amadeo & Shagass, 1963; Heiman & Ross, 1974; Weitzenhoffer & Brockmeier, 1970) and that records of eye movements permit one to determine to which aspect of a stimulus array a person is attending. Nodine and Lang (1971) summarized some of the research on eye movements and their relationship to reading by concluding that learning to read is largely a matter of learning to sample information from written material in a selective fashion. As the child learns to control visual input, he or she becomes progressively more and more attuned to the information patterns contained in the written language. Control of visual information, as reflected by the eye movements, is thus a learned strategy at which some become more, some less proficient. The more efficient a person's visual scanning strategy, the more efficiently will he or she extract meaning from written material; that is, the better a reader such a person is likely to be.

While efficient strategy will be reflected in rapid visual scanning (eye movements), giving a poor reader eye-movement exercises aimed at speeding up these movements will do little or nothing to improve reading skill because good reading is not a matter of rapid eye movements. Rather, it is a matter of rapidly selecting information from written material—a process which, in turn, will be reflected in rapid movements of the eyes. What the child must learn is not the making of rapid eye movements but to be efficient in the information-processing activity we call reading.

Nodine and Lang (1971) studied the development of visual scanning strategies by comparing nonreaders (kindergarten children) with readers in third grade. They concluded that the development of perceptual strategies is a direct result of increasing cognitive control over eye movements. "With increased cognitive control of eye movements there is greater specificity and economy in the selection of visual inputs. As a consequence, extraction of written information becomes more efficient" (p. 231). They point out that the proficient reader thus actively controls visual inputs, attending selectively to information in the reading display, processing information details, and ignoring those which are irrelevant or redundant (Nodine & Lang, 1971).

Further support for the relationship between reading and eye movements comes from a study conducted by Heiman and Ross (1974), who obtained a record of saccadic eye movements of children with reading difficulties before and after a seven-month remedial tutoring program. Before this program, the rate of eye movements of the problem readers was markedly lower than that of a comparison group of normal readers. After the program, however, the problem readers had attained or surpassed the rate of their normal peers. This finding suggested the conclusion that one of the consequences of learning to read is a change in the size and timing of saccadic eye movements so as to make these more functional for the task of reading.

The fact that these eye-movement changes are specific to reading was shown in the fact that Heiman and Ross (1974) found no similar changes when the stimuli were not words but pictures. For non-written stimuli, the scan rate was relatively lower for both problem readers and normals, and the rate was unaffected by exposure to the remedial reading program. The saccadic eye movements studied in this research can thus be seen as a response, modifiable through learning, which serves an information-gathering function and varies with the nature of the visual stimulus presented.

Directionality and Laterality The proficient reader does not necessarily scan a line of writing from left to right and a page from top to bottom but succeeds in extracting meaning by less rigid though nonetheless systematic scanning. The beginning reader, however, must learn the left-to-right, top-to-bottom strategy on the way toward more efficient processes. To assume that reading can be acquired by teaching a child the scanning strategy used by an adult is analogous to assuming that a young child can learn to walk stairs by taking two steps at a time. Since beginning readers must learn to direct their glance from left to right, one of the prerequisites they must have developed before that is the ability to differentiate between left and right. Some reading-disabled children, it appears, have difficulty in this area. This has, at times, been used to substantiate the hypothesis that reading-disabled children have brain dysfunctions, but it may entail no more than a developmental retardation.

Croxen and Lytton (1971), for example, studied right-left discrimination in a group of nine- to ten-year-olds whose reading quotient was 80 or less. They found a significantly greater incidence of difficulty in this discrimination in this group than in a control group of normal readers and concluded that *for some children* reading disability is associated with such perceptual problems as right-left confusion. Similar findings were reported by Belmont and Birch (1965), who reported that confusion in right-left identification of own body parts was associated with reading retardation. On the other hand, Benton (1968), upon conducting a review of the available literature, concluded that right-left discrimination did not relate in any important way to reading ability.

Such contradictory conclusions are not uncommon in this field of research. They are a function of differences in sampling methods (whether one examines all children in a school or only those referred for reading problems), methods of testing (which vary along lines of sophistication from asking children to hold up their right hands to observing their behavior in situations requiring right-left discrimination), and the age of the children studied. Similar contradictory conclusions can be found in the related area of laterality. This is the issue of eye-hand dominance where one examines the question whether a child who is right-eye dominant is also right-hand dominant, the presumably normal combination. Here Forness and Weil (1970) report crossed dominance to be associated with reading retardation, while Capobianco (1967) found no differences in reading performance between children with and without established laterality. This led him to conclude that the determination of laterality preferences possesses dubious practical value from the standpoint of helping children with reading problems.

The reason for discussing the ambiguous areas of right-left discrimination and laterality in this context is that so much has been made of these in the literature on learning disabilities and reading problems. Some remedial programs, in fact, are founded on the assumption that a child's difficulties in this area are the cause of his reading or learning problem, and they recommend training in the localization of body parts and right-left discrimination. Observed confusions in directionality and laterality in some children with reading problems has also been used as proof that these problems are caused by something that is wrong in the brain, because children with known brain damage sometimes display similar difficulties. The unsound logical base of this reasoning has been discussed in detail in Chapter 4.

Discrimination The next skill level which must be mastered by a child learning to read involves the discrimination of the visual stimuli with which he or she is presented. If reading is taught by the phonics method and the child cannot tell letters apart and learn to associate the appropriate sound to each letter or letter combination, the child will have trouble reading. This is equally if not more true if reading is taught by the word-recognition method, for while a misperceived letter does not necessarily result in a misread word, a misperceived word—that is a word which is incorrectly discriminated from another word—is likely to result in a misread sentence.

Studies on discrimination learning (Stevenson, 1972) demonstrate developmental changes in the capacity for performance as well as individual differences in the rate at which this skill develops and the relative level that is reached at maturity. A child who has not yet reached a level in discrimination-learning capacity required by reading instructions or one whose capacity for this skill is less than is expected for his age—that is, a child whose discrimination-learning capacity is either retarded or deficient—would find reading acquisition difficult.

Whipple (1970) conducted a study which is relevant to this issue. His experimental group consisted of 60 fourth- and fifth-grade students whose reading level ranged from 8 to 21 months behind their grade level. Controlling for speech problems, hearing loss, and cultural disadvantage, he matched this group with children who were normal readers and of the same age, sex, grade level, and intelligence as the experimental group. The experiment included two kinds of discrimination-learning tasks, one where the stimuli to be discriminated were presented simultaneously, the other where they were presented successively. The length of stimulus exposure varied, one group receiving a two-second, the other a ten-second view.

On the successive discrimination task, the retarded readers displayed significantly greater difficulty than the normal controls, requiring nearly twice as many trials (66.6 as against 35.2) to learn the discrimination. The simultaneous discrimination was somewhat easier for them, but here too they performed significantly less well than the normal readers. In one condition the mean number of trials-to-learning was 33.26 for the retarded readers and 21.33 for the normal readers. Whipple (1970) found similar differences between these groups on a perceptual-learning task, where the performance of the retarded readers was inferior to that of the normal readers.

A study such as the one just discussed does not, of course, permit us to conclude that reading retardation is the result of difficulty in discrimination learning, since all it can tell us is that retarded readers also do less well than their normally reading peers on a task requiring simultaneous or successive discriminations. It may be that the difference between the two groups is due to differences in selective attention, in memory, in anxiety level about taking tests and anticipation of failure, or a host of other unknown variables. As Senf (1972) reminds us, one can find significant differences in performance between learning-disabled and so-called normal children on almost any task one chooses to introduce.

Paired-associate learning is a case in point. Unlike discrimination learning, where the task is to learn which of two or more stimuli is the correct one (as defined by the experimenter), paired-associate learning requires one to learn which two stimuli "go together." Both types of learning are related to reading. Discrimination learning is involved when a child has to learn to tell "b" and "d" apart; paired-associate learning is required when the child has to attach the sound "bee" to the letter "b."

Gascon and Goodglass (1970) compared young retarded and normal readers on several paired-associate learning tasks to test the hypothesis "that reading retardation might be caused by impairment in forming associations between stimuli of low information content" (p. 418). As might have been expected, they found differences between their groups in that the retarded readers had difficulty, particularly with visual stimuli; but this finding does not justify the conclusion that problems with paired-associate learning cause reading difficulty. The causal relationship could as readily be the other way around, in that reading difficulty could bring about difficulty on tasks requiring paired-associate learning. For that matter, both difficulties might have a common base, such as retarded development of selective attention, so that they would not be causally related at all. A demonstration that two variables are correlated does not permit one to conclude that one variable is the cause of the other, and statements about the direction of that causality are certainly not justified.

In order to venture a statement about the cause of reading disabilities, one would have to demonstrate that a specific skill problem precedes the development of reading difficulties and that it does so for problem readers and not for normal readers. This can be done only if one conducts a longitudinal study on a large group of randomly selected children for whom skills in selective attention, sequential scanning, discrimination, and association are validly tested before they acquire reading and whose development is followed at least through the elementary school years. Such a study has never been conducted and the cause of reading problems therefore remains unknown.

Decoding and Comprehension   We now arrive at the two related skills that are the crux of reading: The ability to take the written or printed visual stimulus, decode it into its verbal equivalent, and comprehend the meaning of the message contained in the writing. The issue of meaning in the context of reading is complex and one of the most promising but most difficult areas for psychological research. Largely because the processes by which a person extracts meaning from sensory information is not subject to direct observation and partly because behavioral psychologists had, for a long time, shown little or no interest in the so-called cognitive processes, experimental research in this area is of relatively recent origin (Neisser, 1966).

Studies which show that a person perceives a letter in a briefly presented word more accurately when he attends to the whole word than when he focuses only on the letter to be identified (Johnston & McClelland, 1974) or that letters in a word are perceived more accurately than a single letter presented alone (Reicher, 1969) go counter to what "common sense" would lead one to expect and open up a whole host of questions related to the teaching of reading which beg to be investigated.

Meaning is also implicated when it is shown that words on a previously learned list are more likely to be remembered in terms of their connotation than in terms of their actual form. Thus, if a person learns a list that includes the word "ham" in the semantic context of Virginia ham and is later asked which of a series of nouns he or she recognizes as having been on the original list, "ham" is less likely to be recognized if it now appears in the context of radio ham (Light & Carter-Sobell, 1970). The adjective thus biases recognition in the direction of a different semantic interpretation, suggesting that memory is organized (stored) according to meaning (Schvaneveldt & Meyer, 1971). Further research in this area should provide a great deal of information for the study of learning disabilities and replace with facts much of what is now speculation.

Thus we arrive at the end of our discussion of the hierarchy of skills required in reading. We have pointed out that the ability to attend selectively to the relevant visual stimuli (writing) is the most basic of these skills, so that defective or retarded development of that skill would cause difficulty at all subsequent levels. It is conceivable that some reading-disabled children are able to sustain selective attention but have difficulty at one of the higher levels in the hierarchy. Careful study of each individual child is necessary if one is to ascertain the specific nature of the problem and decide on the kind of remedial help required. If it is correct to hypothesize that selective attention represents the first level on the skill hierarchy, then the first question one should ask about a reading-disabled child is whether that skill is adequately developed. Only when problems at that level are ruled out does it make sense to explore skill adequacies at the higher levels.

Inasmuch as comprehension of written material is the aim of all reading, one further assumption underlies all other considerations about reading ability. It is the assumption that the child knows the language which is encoded in the writing. Linguistic skill is not so much another, even more basic level in the skill hierarchy as it is the context in which the entire hierarchy is embedded. We thus turn to a discussion of that, the most important of all the skills required for reading.

LINGUISTIC SKILL

Some years before normally developing young children learn to acquire the skill of reading, they will have differentiated objects and sensations out of the mass of sensory experiences impinging on them from their environment. A child will have learned to recognize (know the meaning of) his or her mother some time before learning to make a consistent vocalization that "stands for" (symbolizes) the person he or she has come to know. The acquisition of language is a complex process about which there exist several equally plausible theories. It is likely that modeling by others and rewards for appropriate verbal labeling play an important role, but we cannot enter into a detailed discussion of these issues. Suffice it to say that children must have had experiences with primary sense data for which they have learned a verbal code before one can expect to present them with a written code and expect that they will be able to use it constructively by translating it into the verbal code and ultimately refer that back to the primary sense data.

All this would be rather abstract theorizing were it not for the fact that in asking ourselves why a child has difficulty in learning how to read we should first of all inquire whether this child possesses the sensory experiences and the verbal code to which the written code refers. One of the principles of various preschool programs is to present the children with experiences they might otherwise have missed (such as seeing a cow or a horse), so that, when they are later shown the written codes for these concepts, they will be able to "make sense out of them," that is, to understand their meaning.

Because the verbal code is already available to the beginning reader, he will decode the written material first into the verbal code, say the word to himself silently or aloud, and, hearing himself say the word will, in turn, decode that into its meaning in terms of the primary sense data he has stored in memory from past experiences. The facile, accomplished reader may well skip the verbal stage and decode directly from the written word into meaning and, what is more, gather meaning from the written material itself as when he uses books to gather information about concepts with which he has had no previous direct experience.

From the standpoint of studying the child who experiences difficulty in learning to read, these later skills are irrelevant and much confusion can result if the adult who is an accomplished reader seeks to teach a child to approach the task in the way that is suitable for the adult. The argument between those who advocate the teaching of reading by the phonics methods with those who promote the sight-recognition method is, at least in part, based on attempts to extrapolate from the behavior of the skilled reader to the task of reading acquisition.

Two Methods of Teaching Reading

If reading consists of decoding written symbols into their verbal equivalents, how should this skill be taught? Students of perception (Gibson, 1965) suggest that learning to read can be broken down into four processes: (1) learning to communicate by means of the spoken language; (2) learning the differentiation of graphic symbols; (3) learning the decoding of graphic symbols (graphemes) to sounds (phonemes); and (4) learning the use of progressively higher-order rules, such as those of spelling, semantics, and syntax.

It is often assumed that this analysis of the components of reading skills requires that the skill must be taught sequentially; that a child must learn all grapheme-phoneme combinations before he can encounter the higher-order rules. In other words, it is assumed that phonetics must be mastered before letters and words can be encountered in context and thus with meaning. There is nothing in perception theory that demands this kind of rigid serializing of reading instruction. While a child must have acquired some capacity to communicate in verbal language before reading can be introduced, reading instruction and continuing expansion of language capacity can obviously go on at the same time. Similarly, as soon as the child has learned a few grapheme-phoneme combinations, these can be combined into simple words which, in turn, can be used in the context of meaningful sentences (higher-order structures).

There is thus no reason to argue whether one should emphasize phonics or content, since the two are not incompatible. This argument is often based on comparisons between two methods of teaching reading: the phonics method (which emphasizes letter-sound combinations) and the sight-recognition method (which holds that the beginning reader should learn to recognize words).

Proponents of the sight recognition ("look-and-say") method hold that since reading involves obtaining meaning from written material, the whole-word approach introduces meaning from the start, while pure letter-sound combinations are essentially meaningless. It is true that the quickest way of having beginning readers get meaning from written symbols is to teach them to recognize words as whole units without first subdividing them into component elements (letters or letter combinations) and "sounding them out." The question, however, turns on what one gives up for the presumed benefit of early introduction of meaning. Research comparing the two approaches provides an answer to this question. We shall review some relevant studies after some further discussion of the two methods.

Accomplished readers undoubtedly obtain meaning from printed material by a method that is very similar to sight recognition; they perceive whole words and combination of words and do not decipher a word letter by letter *unless it is a totally unfamiliar word.* The sight-recognition method seeks to teach children to read the way adults do their reading, but it ignores the fact that for beginning readers every word is totally unfamiliar and that they therefore need a way of tackling these words. This way is provided from the start and as an essential tool by those who teach reading by the phonics method; it is only gradually introduced (almost as an afterthought) by those who use the sight-recognition method. The latter method is thus based, in part, on an unwarranted extrapolation from the accomplished to the beginning reader.

In addition, sight-recognition is strongly influenced by the Gestalt school of perception, which stressed that we see the world in constellations (*Gestalten*) and not as a sum of subunits and that, in fact, the whole is different from the sum of its parts. The once major influence of the Gestalt approach in psychology has declined considerably, but its impact on the teaching of reading continues to be felt in the dominance of the sight-recognition method. As so often, there is a lag between laboratory research and practical application.

Sight Recognition   In teaching by the sight-recognition method, the emphasis is on reading for understanding; hence whole words are learned before the alphabet is introduced. Each word must thus be individually memorized for later recognition. To aid in this process, the children are given various clues such as the shape the word makes (the "y" at the end of "monkey" makes a "tail"). They are also encouraged to use context and picture clues; in other words, to guess at what the word might be (Russell, 1961). One of the chief criticisms leveled against this approach is that the limited capacity of a young child's memory for recognizable words of necessity limits his or her reading vocabulary. Instead of being able to attack new words they might encounter on their own, these children have to pass them by because they do not "know" them. One of the major principles of learning, that of transfer, is thus ignored, and the child practices skills which have very little relevance to the goal task of independent reading.

The limited reading vocabulary of a child taught by the whole-word method is made dramatically clear by the fact that the speaking vocabulary of a third grader has been estimated to be 44,000 words, while by that time a popular basal reading series (Scott-Foresman) will have introduced only 1,778 words. As a result, textbooks in other subject areas must also be limited to this meager vocabulary, and the content of the stories that can be created with it becomes boring; hence the child may well discover that reading is boring and unrewarding.

Phonics   The phonics method is based on the recognition that beginning reading is not the same as skilled reading; it thus emphasizes the decoding of the word by teaching the alphabet and the sounds of letters and letter combinations. The children practice letter-sound combinations in isolation (devoid of meaning) and they learn the rules of phonics. A new word will be introduced as a problem to be solved, not as a shape to be memorized. This approach permits the introduction of a larger vocabulary than is possible in the look-say method, but there is a limitation. This is imposed by the fact that English is phonetically irregular so that, in the early stages of reading instruction, the vocabulary is for the most part phonetically regular. The phonetic irregularity of English is, however, not as great as is often believed. At least 85 percent of English words are phonetically regular (Francis, 1958); a rather substantial vocabulary is thus opened up to the child who has acquired the ability to "sound out" an unfamiliar word, so that the world of writing presents a challenge and not a bewildering forest of unfamiliar shapes he has "not yet learned."

Sight Recognition or Phonics?   Whether the sight-recognition method or the phonics method is better for teaching reading is, of course, not an issue that should be decided by argument or opinion but a question to be put to the empirical test of research. There have been many comparative studies on the relative efficacy of these two methods in the teaching of beginning reading, but the seemingly simple question is not easily answered because, as Nelson (1972) has pointed out, there is no global measure of reading skill that might permit one to state unequivocally which method is superior to the other.

In the absence of a measure of "reading," one is forced to rely on a variety of assessments, none of which can be judged to be more basic than the others. Thus one can measure word recognition, oral reading, spelling, reading speed, word-attack skills, or comprehension. Since learning to read has its ultimate "payoff" not in the early elementary grades but in a student's competence at reading some years later, there is the added problem of the relationship between early measures and later skills. Thus, a method found superior on a particular measure at grade 1 may or may not maintain its superiority at a later grade. Because it is difficult to control uniformity of reading experience over a number of years, very few longitudinal studies which compare teaching methods have been done past grade 4.

Chall (1967) reviewed a series of studies which compared the phonics and sight-recognition methods. She concluded that at the end of first grade, children trained by the phonics method have a decided advantage over children trained by the sight-recognition method on measures of phonics skill, word recognition, oral reading, and spelling. On the other hand, children trained by the sight-recognition method are superior on measures of vocabulary, comprehension, and rate of reading. The advantage of the sight-recognition group on vocabulary and comprehension is lost by grade 2, by which time the children trained by the phonics method are superior on these tests as well as on tests of word recognition, oral reading, and spelling. The two groups do not differ on reading rate; phonics skills are no longer measured at later grades.

Nelson (1972) cites several other studies which also point to the superiority of the phonics method over the sound recognition method; her own research lends further support to this conclusion. She compared two groups of kindergarten children who had been given instruction in reading, one by the phonics method (as represented by the Lippincott Basic Reading Series) the other by the sight-recognition method (as represented by the Scott-Foresman Series). Instruction was given in groups of four children over a total of 49 sessions, each lasting 20 minutes. At the end of this period, standardized tests of reading revealed that the phonics group had acquired better knowledge of letter-sound combinations, while the sound-recognition group had acquired better word-recognition skills. In other words, each group was superior on the particular skill which had been the focus of the teaching method used with them. That alone would not be too surprising. What is of more general interest, however, is the fact that in Nelson's study the word-recognition skill of the group who had been trained on this method did not generalize to words on which they had not been specifically taught, so that their "reading" was limited to a restricted vocabulary.

It is obviously important to ask how a given skill is to be presented to a child who is expected to acquire mastery of that skill. For reading, research results strongly suggest that the presentation of grapheme-phoneme combinations is the method of choice. There is, however, the problem that learning these combinations in isolation is not only meaningless but also dull and unrewarding for a young child. For this reason it is not only important to introduce words into a meaningful context as soon as a child has succeeded in decoding a few of them, it is also essential that one inquire into the nature of the consequences of the reading response being acquired. Teaching involves the presentation of discriminative stimuli and reinforcing stimuli. Research on methods of teaching reading has usually focused on the discriminative stimuli, which have become quite standardized, as in the various published reading programs. The matter of reinforcing stimuli has been left largely to the individual teacher's initiative and implicit hopes that the "intrinsic interest" of reading will be its own reward. Since there is little of intrinsic interest in the simple stories one can prepare for the beginning reader, it is necessary to pay particular attention to motivational aspects. This is especially true since not all children can be assumed to arrive at school with the concept that reading is a good and important thing, a concept acquired in the context of the value system of their home environment.

Reading and Reinforcement

When a child looks at a word printed on a page and says that word aloud, it is easy to view this sequence as the presentation of a stimulus and the emission of a verbal response. If, following the correct response, the teacher says "good," the typical sequence of stimulus-response-reinforcement of the operant conditioning paradigm will have taken place. One would therefor predict that the next time this child is presented with that word, the child will again emit the correct reading response. Reading can thus be seen as operant behavior, and several investigators have studied the topic from this point of view (Staats, Minke, Finley, Wolf, & Brooks, 1964; Staats, Minke, Goodwin, & Landeen, 1967).

The operant approach to reading does of course entail more than the systematic delivery of reinforcement contingent on a correct response. At least as important is the stress on analyzing the behavior to be taught into its component skills and the emphasis on teaching these skills in a carefully designed hierarchical sequence, from the most simple to most complex. Because different children will progress along this sequence at different rates, with some needing more, some less training at a given level, reading programs based on operant principles tend to emphasize individualization of teaching and the use of mechanical devices, so-called teaching machines, for the transmission of some of the more routine skills.

Remedial Reading Based on Operant Principles   When a teaching strategy is broken down into objectivly defined component steps, as one does for a program based on operant principles, it is possible to teach these steps to relatively untrained individuals who can then assist the teacher in the task of teaching. Accordingly, Staats and his colleagues have involved adult volunteers and high school seniors (Staats, Minke, Goodwin, & Landeen, 1967) or parents (Ryback & Staats, 1970) as "therapy-technicians" in remedial reading programs. Because a careful analysis of component skills permits one to detect where a given child is having trouble, and because individualization is especially important when a child cannot benefit from group instruction, operant approaches to the teaching of reading have usually been applied for remedial work with disabled readers (Goldiamond & Dyrud, 1966; Staats & Butterfield, 1965; Sibley, 1967; Heiman, Fischer, & Ross, 1973).

The reinforcers used in such programs are usually tokens or points (Sibley, 1967), which are initially delivered on a continuous or near-continuous schedule and then "thinned out" so that they may be given as infrequently as once for every 30 correct responses. Both the reinforcement schedules and the nature of the reinforcer must be individualized, since it is well known that something that is reinforcing to one child is not necessarily reinforcing to another. Sibley (1967) found that the less successful, less persevering children performed best under lower reinforcement ratios (1 reinforcement for every 2 responses) while the more able readers performed better at higher ratios (1 reinforcement for ever 30 responses).

The effectiveness of these approaches can be demonstrated in number of new words learned, reading rate, or standardized test scores. Staats, Minke, Goodwin, and Landeen (1967), for example, report that reading-deficient junior high school students learned a mean of 593.5 new words during 28.2 daily half-hour training sessions, while Heiman, Fischer, and Ross (1973) found that retarded readers improved by an average of 1.2 years on standardized reading tests after a seven-month program of individual tutoring based on operant principles.

The details of the study by Ryback and Staats (1970), who used the reading-disabled children's own parents as therapy technicians, highlight both the method and the results of a remedial program based on principles of operant reinforcement. There were four children between the ages of 8 ½ and

13, all of whom were significantly retarded in reading at the start of the program. Their scores on the Spache Diagnostic Reading Scales are shown in Table 8-1. Also shown in that table are their scores on a 100-word reading test which the authors developed from the reading material used in the program, the scores reflecting the number of words on this list which the child was able to read correctly.

The training program made use of reading material contained in the Science Research Associates Reading Laboratory, material which was modified into a method called the Staats Motivation-Activating Reading Technique (SMART). This requires that a list of all new words appearing in a story about to be read be made up. These words are presented individually to the child, who is prompted if he cannot read one. A word is deleted from the training series only when the child can read it at least once without prompting. Following this, the full story is presented to the child to be read aloud. Prompts are again given for any words he or she cannot read. If necessary, a paragraph is reread until it is completed without mistake, and then the child is presented with the entire story to be read silently. Comprehension is tested by questions about the story and when a question is missed, the child rereads the relevant paragraph so that he or she can answer it. Following every 20 lessons, a vocabularly review tests the extent of retention of words that were previously learned.

Using a system of tokens, representing points which could eventually be

Table 8-1
Pre- and Posttest Results in Reading Ability
(after Ryback & Staats, 1970)

Subject	Test	Spache Diagnostic Reading Scales reading grade level			100-word test	
		Word recognition	Instructional level	Independent level	Score	Gain (percent)
A						
Age 13,	pre	2.8	2.5	2.5	43	81
ungraded	post	4.5	4.5	4.5	78	
B						
Age 11,	pre	3.8	3.0	3.75	61	44
fifth grade	post	5.0	4.5	5.0	88	
C						
Age 10 1/2,	pre	3.3	2.75	3.5	50	66
fifth grade	post	3.5	4.5	4.5	83	
D						
Age 8 1/2,	pre	2.3	2.25	2.25	29	224
third grade	post	5.0	4.5	5.0	94	

traded for pennies, the child was rewarded for all efforts. These reinforcements were carefully graded so that a word read with prompting earned a less valuable token than a word read correctly without prompt; answering comprehension questions earned more than silent reading. All stimuli presented, responses made, and reinforcement delivered were carefully recorded by the child's tutor (parent), who had also been instructed to provide positive social reinforcement in the form of praise statements but not to criticize or urge the child to do better.

The length of the training period varied for the different children and ranged from five to seven months, with an average of 51 ¼ hours of training. The intensity of the experience is reflected in the fact that during that period the children made an average of 74,730 single-word reading responses. The results in improved performance on both the standardized reading test and the special 100-word test are shown in Table 8-1. The increases in reading grade level and in percent of words correct are statistically highly significant. While the absence of a formal control group makes it impossible to say whether these results were a function of the training program, improvement of at least one grade level over at most a seven-month period of training is impressive. In fact, the pre- and posttesting of two of the children's siblings who had not been in the program showed no improvement or very little gain, thus providing a partial control for the effect of the program.

The training program used by Ryback and Staats (1970) entails a number of variables, each of which or combinations of which might have been responsible for the improvements in the children's reading performance. Compared to the child's previous experience with reading, there was novelty in the manner in which the material was presented, the parents were highly involved, the approach was systematic, the child's responses earned him rewards. The effectiveness of tangible reinforcers in working with retarded readers has been demonstrated by Loiry (1970), but it is not clear whether reinforcers serve the function of providing motivation, information, or both.

It is likely that when one works with children for whom reading has acquired many negative connotations because of a history of repeated failure on this task, the use of explicit positive reinforcement has important motivational aspects. As such a child begins to experience success in reading, the frequency of the delivery of these explicit reinforcers can be reduced (as was done by Ryback and Staats), since the more intrinsic rewards of reading "for the sake of reading" become effective. At the same time, it may be helpful to provide the child with information regarding the accuracy of his responses, and this can be done by pointing out errors (criticism). Nelson (1972) found that in teaching reading to kindergarten children, criticism for incorrect responses was slightly more effective than praise for correct responses. She suggests that the motivational and informational functions of response consequence might be separated by providing praise for the occurrence of reading responses (rewarding effort) while giving information as to response accuracy by providing criticism for errors. At this point, these issues remain unsolved and subject to continuing research.

Comprehension   Before leaving this topic, a word about comprehension. When, as in the Ryback and Staats (1970) study, the report focuses on the number of words a child has learned because these are concrete responses which are easily counted, the question arises whether saying a word correctly is tantamount to reading. Reading, after all, consists of obtaining meaning from the content of the material one reads; it is not merely the pronouncing of individual words. While Ryback and Staats tested for comprehension and reinforced correct answers to these questions, they did not report these results, although the fact that the child could not go on to the next story until comprehension questions were correctly answered implies that satisfactory answers were obtained.

The issue of comprehension was studied more directly by Lahey, McNees, and Brown (1973), who worked with two sixth-grade children whose reading comprehension was tested and found to be two years below grade level. They had these children read a passage orally and then asked them questions about the content. When they gave the children praise and pennies for correct answers, the percentage of correct answers increased to the point where that percentage was approximately at the same level as that of children whose reading performance was at grade level. Inasmuch as no direct training in reading or in reading comprehension had been given to these reading-disabled children, one must conclude that comprehension (or at least the giving of correct answers to comprehension questions) can be increased when reinforcement is made contingent on such behavior. Since comprehension is not likely to develop without training if a child has defective comprehension, this result suggests that what seems like poor comprehension in at least some poor readers is more a function of low test validity than of actual comprehension deficits. This again relates to the difficulty one invariably encounters when one seeks to assess covert events, such as comprehension, to which we can have only indirect access. In the case of comprehension, we must ask questions and infer the presence or absence of comprehension from the answers the child is willing or able to give.

When one provides reinforcement contingent on correct answers to comprehension questions and finds an increase in the frequency of such answers, one may not have increased comprehension but merely the motivation of the child to emit responses, the capacity for which had been present right along. If, for example, a child who has a long history of failure experiences is asked a question about the meaning of a story he has just read such a child may have so little confidence in the adequacy of his response that he prefers to say, "I don't know" to risking failure, yet once again, by giving an answer. If one now increases his motivation to produce an answer by providing reinforcement and discovers an increase in the frequency with which correct answers are given, one must take care not to interpret this as reflecting an increase in the child's ability to comprehend.

A study by Kass (1966) lends some support to this speculation, for, testing a group of children with reading problems, she found that they had difficulty in the skill of relating grapheme to phoneme and not in comprehension. Difficulties in verbal coding were also implicated in reading problems in a study conducted by Bryden (1972), again suggesting that difficulties at the level of comprehension may be more apparent than real and that the problem lies further down in the skill hierarchy.

Reading Is Its Own Reward   In discussions of programs of remedial reading based on operant principles, the objection is sometimes heard that one should not provide a child with extrinsic reinforcers, such as candy or trinkets, for a behavior as pleasurable as reading which carries its own reward. Reading, it is argued, permits one to obtain information which is such a basic human need that extrinsic reinforcers are not only unnecessary but will, in fact, detract from and interfere with the intrinsic reinforcer entailed in gathering information. We need not concern ourselves with the question of whether information is a basic need; it may well be, but this is irrelevant for the point is that the reading-disabled child has trouble in obtaining information from the printed page. Not only that, but in all likelihood such a child's previous experiences with the printed page have been fraught with unpleasantness, frustration, and anxiety—if not punishment, so that the very sight of such a page will be aversive to him. To expect that such a child will work on learning how to read "for the sheer pleasure of it" is quite absurd.

Others will argue that the motivation for a child's working on remedial reading should come from his relationship with the remedial teacher or tutor. This supposes that the child's incentive is either to please the teacher or to obtain the teacher's praise and approval, and there is no reason to assume that a child (who may have had all sorts of negative experiences with teachers of reading) will care either about pleasing that adult or about obtaining his or her approval. In other words, neither of these consequences are necessarily positive reinforcers. Aside from the fact that working to please the teacher is a peculiar motivation on which to base behavior that should be pleasing to oneself, both these incentives will usually require that child and teacher develop a relationship; that is, that the teacher become a source of social reinforcement. An individual tutor may be able to do this, but it will take time. A reading specialist working with a group of children may never reach that point. It is here that extrinsic reinforcers serve as a potent shortcut.

Extrinsic (artificial) reinforcers—such as candy or trinkets or privileges—are introduced only where social reinforcers such as praise or the natural reinforcers (getting information from reading) are not effective. They serve as a crutch until such time as first the social and then the natural reinforcers take over. No one expects a child who is learning to read in a program based on operant principles to require the delivery of prizes for the rest of his or her life: In fact, in any properly administered token reinforcement program, it is emphasized that the tokens be delivered together with a smile, a praise statement, and other social rewards which thereby acquire reinforcing properties they may previously have lacked. In this way, the tokens can be phased out as soon as social reinforcers are effective.

Ultimately, since the child will be learning to read in the process and to discover that interesting things can be garnered from the page, reading will become "its own reward." Then the child will be at the point where extrinsic reinforcers will no longer be needed. Such a child will now be reading for the same reasons most people read, but to assume that a disabled reader *should* be reading for the same reasons that motivate most people is to overlook the fact that the disabled reader *is* disabled and is thus not like most people. A judicious, temporary use of artificial reinforcers can help make reading its own reward.

SUMMARY

Reading involves the decoding of combinations of visual symbols (letters and words) into a previously acquired verbal code (language) which symbolizes objects, events, relationships, and ideas. It is only when the visual symbols and their combinations correctly evoke the associations which underlie the verbal code that one can say that reading has taken place. In other words, the reader must understand the meaning of what is read. There is a hierarchy of skills that enter into the process of extracting meaning from the printed words, and children may have difficulty with one or more of these skills. The prevalence of reading disabilities may well be a reflection of the fact that many of these skills cannot be directly monitored, because they entail internal, covert processes.

Selective attention is probably the most basic of the skills required for reading. The child must be able to select from the many stimuli in the environment the limited few that are critical for what we call reading. If a child has not yet acquired the capacity for sustaining selective attention, reading will be difficult or impossible. Good, advanced readers eventually learn to attend not so much to the individual letters and words but to the context, while beginning and poor readers attend to the details of the printed material. This early stage is probably essential; one should not try to skip it by teaching a beginner the strategy of the advanced reader. On the other hand, it seems possible to enhance selective attention to reading material by selectively reinforcing responses entailing selective attention.

Once a child is able to attend selectively to the task at hand, sequential scanning becomes the next crucial skill. This can be monitored by observing the reader's eye movements, the nature of which changes as the child becomes more proficient in reading. This observation has led some to seek improvement in reading by giving eye-movement exercises; but for most cases of reading disability, this is probably based on a confusion of cause and effect. There is no evidence that such exercises alone will improve reading, nor is there support for the often prescribed training in right-left discrimination or localization of body parts.

The next level on the hierarchy of skills essential for reading is discrimination. The child must learn to tell similar letters or words apart. Only after having learned that—and many reading-disabled children find this difficult—can the last level, decoding and comprehension, be attained.

Two methods of teaching reading have for some time vied for adoption in our schools: the phonics method and the sight-recognition method. It is not easy to decide which method is better, because there is no global measure of reading skill. The question to be asked is probably not "Which method is better?" but "Which method is better for what purpose and for what kind of child?" Research studies in which groups of children were compared (thus obliterating the needs of the individual child) have generally favored the method of phonics; from the standpoint of helping a reading-disabled child acquire basic reading skills, this approach is to be preferred over sight recognition.

For the accomplished reader the act of reading is rewarding in and of itself but it is a mistake to assume that this is also true for the problem reader, to whom the act of reading may, in fact, be repugnant. For this reason it is important to reward the reading behavior of these children with such extrinsic, artificial reinforcers as points or tokens. Programs of remedial reading which used this approach have demonstrated impressive results. Only after a child has acquired the skills that make reading possible will he or she experience the joy of reading, and at that point the artificial reinforcers will no longer be needed.

Conclusion

In the Preface to this book I spoke of my hope to build a bridge connecting the land of the psychological laboratory, where learning is being studied, with the land of the classroom, where children are being taught and where some children fail to learn. I trust that I have succeeded in building some sort of bridge, however makeshift and ramshackle. I expect that others will come along who will strengthen it and adjust its serpentine roadway. This is not the last word on the matter of learning disabilities, for the body of knowledge that is psychology is open-ended and self-correcting. It is thus constantly subject to revision, addition, and change. If one wants to base one's approach to learning disabilities on a science, one cannot expect to be handed an immutable set of procedures. Too many methods currently used in the field of learning disabilities are taught as if they were eternal verities, but they are based on the untested hunches of a few "recognized authorities," not on the results of research.

It will be apparent to anyone who has read to this page that there is but a limited number of principles so well established that one can feel comfortable in advocating their classroom application. Yet there are children who need help now, and neither they nor their teachers can wait until the scientific investigators are certain of their facts. With that in mind—and fully aware of the rickety nature of our bridge—let me review some of the lessons the teacher of learning-disabled children can draw from available knowledge.

Consider the learning-disabled child to be a child whose development has progressed more slowly than that of other children, particularly in the area of selective attention. Don't consider such a child as damaged, deficient, or permanently impaired. Learning-disabled children *can* learn!

If a child fails to learn, look for a different way of teaching. Don't look for something that is wrong inside the child. Chances are that your teaching method and the child's way of learning are out of phase. Neither the child nor you are to blame for that, but you *can* be blamed if you don't try something else.

Don't be awed by fancy labels. "Dyslexia" is an attempt to say in Greek that the child can't read! "Hyperactivity" means the child moves around more than some of us would like. Neither word explains anything.

Don't accept as true the things "everybody knows." Be skeptical. Ask not "Who said so?" but "How do they know?" Ask about their facts, not their reputations. So-called authorities can be wrong.

Don't look for ready-made methods to apply to an individual child's problem. Just because two children carry the same label does not mean that their needs are the same.

Don't encourage the use of behavior-altering drugs. There are many unanswered questions about their effectiveness and long-term consequences. In making life easier for yourself, you may be damaging the life of the child.

If the goal is to teach a child to read, teach reading and the subskills directly relevant to it. The goal is not improved performance on a test of spatial relations or auditory association; the goal is getting the child to read. Nobody ever learned to read by balancing on a walking beam.

Adapt your teaching to the child's developmental level. Don't take your cue from the way an accomplished student attacks a task. Take your cue from the child you are trying to teach.

Give specific instructions; not general admonitions. Don't say, "Pay attention"; tell the child what in particular you want him or her to attend to.

To enhance selective attention, emphasize the distinctive features of the stimulus; provide verbal labels, teach self-instruction; use novelty, change, and surprise in presenting material. Don't leave long pauses between an alerting message ("Now look here") and the material to be presented.

Provide meaningful connecting links through words or pictures when a task involves rote associative learning.

Present easily confused letters in contrasting pairs and under various circumstances.

Solicit the participation of a child's parents in a remedial program.

Define your goals objectively and strengthen desired behavior systematically through praise and other rewards so as to move the child toward that goal. Remember that you can't tell whether you are making progress unless you keep an objective record.

And finally, don't look for easy answers readily packaged by somebody else. Be inventive and rely on your own good sense, for you probably know at least as much about the child in your classroom as anyone else. Try different approaches, but constantly check on the effectiveness of whatever you do.

References

Amadeo, M., & Shagass, C. Eye movements, attention and hypnosis. *Journal of Nervous and Mental Disease,* 1963, **136,** 139–145.

Anderson. W. F. The relative effects of the Frostig program, corrective reading instruction, and attention upon the reading skills of corrective readers with visual perceptual difficulties. *Journal of School Psychology,* 1972, **10,** 387–395.

Bandura, A. *Principles of behavior modification.* New York: Holt, Rinehart & Winston, 1969.

Barsch, R. H. *Achieving perceptual-motor efficiency: A space-oriented approach.* Seattle: Special Child Publications, 1967.

Bateman, B. D., & Schiefelbusch, R. L. Educational identification, assessment, and evaluation procedures. In *Minimal brain dysfunction in children,* U.S. Public Health Service Publication #2015. Washington, D.C.: U.S. Department of Health, Education, and Welfare, 1969. pp. 5–20.

Battle, E. S., & Lacey, B. A context for hyperactivity in children, over time. *Child Development,* 1972, **43,** 757–773.

Beery, J. W. Matching of auditory and visual stimuli by average and retarded readers. *Child Development,* 1967, **38,** 827–833.

Belmont, L., & Birch, H. G. Lateral dominance, lateral awareness, and reading disability. *Child Development,* 1965, **36,** 57–71.

Benton, A. L. *The revised visual retention test: Clinical and experimental applications.* New York: The Psychological Corp., 1963.

170

Benton, A. L. Right-left discrimination. *Pediatric Clinics of North America,* 1968, **15,** 747–759.

Berlyne, D. E. *Conflict, Arousal and Curiosity.* New York: McGraw-Hill, 1960.

Berlyne, D. E. Attention as a problem in behavior theory. In D. I. Mostofsky (Ed.), *Attention: contemporary theory and analysis.* New York: Appleton-Century-Crofts, 1970. Pp. 25–49.

Birch, H. G., & Belmont L. Auditory-visual integration in normal and retarded readers. *American Journal of Orthopsychiatry,* 1964, **34,** 852–861.

Blank, M. Implicit assumptions underlying preschool intervention programs. *Journal of Social Issues,* 1970, **26,** 15–33.

Block, J., Block, J. H., & Harrington, D. M. Some misgivings about the Matching Familiar Figures Test as a measure of reflection-impulsivity. *Developmental Psychology,* 1974, **10,** 611–632.

Broadbent, D. E., & Gregory, M. Stimulus set and response set: The alternation of attention. *Quarterly Journal of Experimental Psychology,* 1964, **16,** 309–317.

Bryden, M. P. Auditory-visual and sequential-spatial matching in relation to reading ability. *Child Development,* 1972, **43,** 824–832.

Camp, B. W., & van Doorninck, W. J. Assessment of "motivated" reading therapy with elementary school children. *Behavior Therapy,* 1971, **2,** 214–222.

Campbell, S. B., Douglas, V. I., & Morgenstern, G. Cognitive styles in hyperactive children and the effect of methylphenidate. *Journal of Child Psychology and Psychiatry,* 1971, **12,** 55–67.

Capobianco, R. J. Ocular-manual laterality and reading achievement in children with special learning disabilities. *American Educational Research Journal,* 1967, **4,** 133–138.

Caron, A. J. Conceptual transfer in preverbal children as a consequence of dimensional training. *Journal of Experimental Child Psychology,* 1968, **6,** 522–542.

Chall, J. *Learning to read: The great debate.* New York: McGraw-Hill, 1967.

Clements, S. D. *Minimal brain dysfunction in children.* NINDB Monograph #3 (USPHS Publication #1415). Washington, D.C.: U.S. Department of Health, Education, & Welfare, 1966.

Conners, C. K. Recent drug studies with hyperactive children. *Journal of Learning Disabilities,* 1971, **4,** 478–483.

Crane, N. L., & Ross, L. E. A developmental study of attention to cue redundancy introduced following discrimination learning. *Journal of Experimental Child Psychology,* 1967, **5,** 1–15.

Crinella, F. M. Identification of brain dysfunction syndromes in children through profile analysis: Patterns associated with so-called "minimal brain dysfunction." *Journal of Abnormal Psychology,* 1973, **82,** 33–45.

Croxen, M. E., & Lytton, H. Reading disability and difficulties in finger localization and right-left discrimination. *Developmental Psychology,* 1971, **5,** 256–262.

Czudner, G., & Rourke, B. P. Age differences in visual reaction time of "brain-damaged" and normal children under regular and irregular preparatory interval conditions. *Journal of Experimental Child Psychology,* 1972, **13,** 516–526.

Davison, G. C.. Tsujimoto, R. N., & Glaros, A. G. Attribution and the maintenance of behavior change in falling asleep. *Journal of Abnormal Psychology,* 1973, **82,** 124–133.

Davison, G. C., & Valins, S. Maintenance of self-attributed behavior change. *Journal of Personality and Social Psychology,* 1969, **11,** 25–33.

de Hirsch, K., Jansky, J., & Langford, W. S. *Predicting reading failure.* New York: Harper & Row, 1966.

Delacato, C. H. *The diagnosis and treatment of speech and reading problems.* Springfield, Ill.: Thomas, 1963.

Day, H. Looking time as a function of stimulus variables and individual differences. *Perceptual and motor skills,* 1966, **22,** 423–428.

Douglas, V. I. Differences between normal and hyperkinetic children. In C. K. Conners (Ed.), *Clinical use of stimulant drugs in children.* Princeton, N.J.: Excerpta Medica, 1974. (a)

Douglas, V. I. Stop, look and listen: The problem of sustained attention and impulse control in hyperactive and normal children. *Canadian Journal of Behavior Science,* 1972, **4,** 259–281.

Douglas, V. I. Sustained attention and impulse control: Implications for the handicapped child. In J. A. Swets & L. L. Elliott (Eds.), *Psychology and the handicapped child.* Washington, D.C.: U.S. Department of Health, Education, and Welfare, 1974. (b)

Drabman, R. S., Spitalnik, R., & O'Leary, K. D. Teaching self-control to disruptive children. *Journal of Abnormal Psychology,* 1973, **82,** 10–16.

Drass, S. D., & Jones, R. L. Learning disabled children as behavior modifiers. *Journal of Learning Disabilities,* 1971, **4,** 418–425.

Dykman, R. A., Ackerman, P. T., Clements, S. D., & Peters, J. E. Specific learning disabilities: An attentional deficit syndrome. In H. R. Myklebust (Ed.), *Progress in learning disabilities,* Vol. 2. New York: Grune & Stratton, 1971. Pp. 56–93.

Egeland, B. Training impulsive children in the use of more efficient scanning techniques. *Child Development,* 1974, **45,** 165–171.

Ellis, M. J., Witt, P. A., Reynolds, R., & Sprague, R. L. Methylphenidate and the activity of hyperactives in the informal setting. *Child Development,* 1974, **45,** 217–220.

Forness, S. R., & Weil, M. C. Laterality in retarded readers with brain dysfunction. *Exceptional Children,* 1970, **36,** 684–695.

Francis, W. N. *The structure of American English.* New York: Ronald, 1958.

Freeman, R. D. Controversy over "patterning" as a treatment for brain damage in children. *Journal of the American Medical Association,* 1967, **202,** 385–388.

Frostig, M., Lefever, D. W., & Whittlesey, J. R. B. *The Marianne Frostig developmental test of visual perception.* Palo Alto, Calif.: Consulting Psychologists Press, 1964.

Frostig, M., & Maslow, P. *Learning problems in the classroom: Prevention and remediation.* New York: Grune & Stratton, 1973.

Fuller, G. B. The Revised Minnesota Percepto-Diagnostic Test. *Journal of Clinical Psychology,* Monograph #16, 1969.

Gagné, R. M. *The conditions of learning* (2d ed.). New York: Holt, Rinehart & Winston, 1970.

Gagné, R. M. *Essentials of learning for instruction.* Hinsdale, Ill.: Dryden, 1974.

Gallagher, J. J. Children with developmental imbalances: A psychoeducational definition. In W. M. Cruickshank (Ed.), *The teacher of brain-injured children.* Syracuse, N.Y.: Syracuse University Press, 1966. Pp. 23–43.

Gascon, G., & Goodglass, H. Reading retardation and the information content of stimuli in paired associate learning. *Cortex,* 1970, **6,** 417–429.

Gibson, E. Learning to read. *Science,* 1965, **148,** 1066–1072.

Gibson, E. *Principles of perceptual learning and development.* New York: Appleton-Century-Crofts, 1969.

Gibson, E. The ontogeny of reading. *American Psychologist,* 1970, **25,** 136–143.

Goldiamond, I., & Dyrud, J. E. Reading as operant behavior. In J. Money (Ed.), *The disabled reader: Education of the dyslexic child.* Baltimore, Md.; Johns Hopkins, 1966. Pp. 93–115.

Goldstein, K. *Aftereffects of brain-injuries in war.* New York: Grune & Stratton, 1942.

Hagen, J. W., & Hale, G. H. The development of attention in children. In A. D. Pick (Ed.), *Minnesota Symposium on Child Psychology,* Vol. 7. Minneapolis, Minn.: University of Minnesota Press, 1973. Pp. 117–140.

Haider, M. Neuropsychology of attention, expectation, and vigilance. In D. I. Mostofsky (Ed.), *Attention: Contemporary theory and analysis.* New York: Appleton-Century-Crofts, 1970. Pp. 419–432.

Hallahan, D. P., & Cruickshank, W. M. *Psychoeducational foundations of learning disabilities.* Englewood Cliffs, N.J.: Prentice-Hall, 1973.

Heiman, J. R., Fischer, M. J. & Ross, A. O. A supplementary behavioral program to improve deficient reading performance. *Journal of Abnormal Child Psychology,* 1973, **1,** 390–399.

Heiman, J. R., & Ross, A. O. Saccadic eye movements and reading difficulties. *Journal of Abnormal Child Psychology,* 1974, **2,** 53–61.

Holroyd, J., & Wright, F. Neurological implications of WISC verbal-performance discrepancies in a psychiatric setting. *Journal of Consulting Psychology,* 1965, **29,** 206–212.

Johnson, D. J., & Myklebust, H. R. *Learning disabilities: Educational principles and practices.* New York: Grune & Stratton, 1967.

Johnston, J. C., & McClelland, J. L. Perception of letters in words: Seek not and ye shall find. *Science,* 1974, **184,** 1192–1194.

Kagan, J. Reflection-impulsivity and reading ability in primary grade children. *Child Development,* 1965, **36,** 609–628.

Kagan, J. Reflection-impulsivity: The generality of conceptual tempo. *Journal of Abnormal Psychology,* 1966, **71,** 17–24.

Kagan, J., Pearson, L., & Welch, L. The modification of an impulsive tempo. *Journal of Educational Psychology,* 1966, **57,** 359–365.

Kass, C. E. Psycholinguistic disabilities of children with reading problems. *Exceptional Children,* 1966, **32,** 533–539.

Kephart, N. C. *The slow learner in the classroom* (2d ed.). Columbus, Ohio: Merrill, 1971.

Kirk, S. A. Behavioral diagnosis and remediation of learning disabilities. In *Conference on exploration into the problems of perceptually handicapped children.* Evanston, Ill.: Fund for Perceptually Handicapped Children, 1963. Pp. 1–7.

Kirk, S. A., & Bateman, B. Diagnosis and remediation of learning disabilities. *Exceptional Children,* 1962, **29,** 73–78.

Kirk, S. A., McCarthy, J. J., & Kirk, W. D. *Illinois Test of Psycholinguistic Abilities* (rev. ed.). Urbana, Ill.: University of Illinois Press, 1968.

Koenigsberg, R. S. An evaluation of visual versus sensorimotor methods for improving orientation discrimination for letter reversal by preschool children. *Child Development,* 1973, **44,** 764–769.

Koppitz, E. M. *The Bender Gestalt Test for young children.* New York: Grune & Stratton, 1963.

Koppitz, E. M. *Children with learning disabilities: A five-year follow-up study.* New York: Grune & Stratton, 1971.

Lahey, B. B., McNees, M. P., & Brown, C. C. Modification of deficits in reading for comprehension. *Journal of Applied Behavior Analysis,* 1973, **6,** 475–480.

Laufer, M. W., & Denhoff, E. Hyperkinetic behavior syndrome in children. *Journal of Pediatrics,* 1957, **50,** 463–474.

Light, L. L., & Carter-Sobell, L. Effects of changed semantic context on recognition memory. *Journal of Verbal Learning and Verbal Behavior,* 1970, **9,** 1–11.

Loiry, D. A. Reinforcer effectiveness and the performance of academically retarded readers on a word recognition test. *Dissertation Abstracts International,* 1970, **30,** (8-B), 3871.

Lovaas, O. I., & Schreibman, L. Stimulus overselectivity of autistic children in a two-stimulus situation. *Behaviour Research and Therapy,* 1971, **9,** 305–310.

Lovaas, O. I., Schreibman, L., Koegel, R., & Rehm, R. Selective responding by autistic children to multiple sensory input. *Journal of Abnormal Psychology,* 1971, **77,** 211–222.

Luria, A. R. *The role of speech in the regulation of normal and abnormal behavior.* New York: Liveright, 1961.

Martin, G. L., & Powers, R. B. Attention span: An operant conditioning analysis. *Exceptional Children,* 1967, **33,** 565–570.

McIntosh, W. J. Clinical and statistical approaches to the assessment of brain damage in children. *Journal of Abnormal Child Psychology,* 1973, **1,** 181–195.

McKenzie, H. S., Clark, M., Wolf, M. M., Kothera, R., & Benson, C. Behavior modification of children with learning disabilities using grades as tokens and allowances as back up reinforcers. *Exceptional Children,* 1968, **34,** 745–752.

Meichenbaum, D. H., & Goodman, J. Training impulsive children to talk to themselves: A means of developing self-control. *Journal of Abnormal Psychology,* 1971, **77,** 115–126.

Minde, K., Webb, G., & Sykes, D. Studies on the hyperactive child. VI—Prenatal and paranatal factors associated with hyperactivity. *Developmental Medicine and Child Neurology,* 1968, **10,** 355–363.

Mostofsky, D. I. (Ed.) *Attention: Contemporary theory and analysis.* New York: Appleton-Century-Crofts, 1970.

Myers, P. I., & Hammill, D. D. *Methods for learning disorders.* New York: Wiley, 1969.

Neisser, U. *Cognitive Psychology.* New York: Appleton-Century-Crofts, 1967.

Nelson, R. O. The effect of different types of teaching methods and verbal reinforcers on the performance of beginning readers. Unpublished doctoral dissertation, State University of New York at Stony Brook, 1972.

Newsom, C. D., & Lovaas, O. I. Studies of overselective attention in autistic children. Paper presented at the American Psychological Association meeting, Montreal, August 1973.

Nodine, C. F., & Lang, N. J. Development of visual scanning strategies for differentiating words. *Developmental Psychology,* 1971, **5,** 221–232.

O'Donnell, P. A. The effects of Delacato training on reading achievement and visual-motor integration. *Dissertation Abstracts International,* 1969, **30(A),** 1079–1080.

O'Leary, K. D., Becker, W. C., Evans, M. B., & Saudargas, R. A. A token reinforcement program in a public school: A replication and systematic analysis. *Journal of Applied Behavior Analysis,* 1969, **2,** 3–13.

O'Leary, K. D., & Drabman, R. Token reinforcement programs in the classroom. *Psychological Bulletin,* 1971, **75,** 379–398.

O'Leary, K. D., Drabman, R., & Kass, R. E. Maintenance of appropriate behavior in a token program. *Journal of Abnormal Child Psychology*, 1973, **1**, 127 130.

O'Leary, K. D., Kaufman, K. F., Kass, R. E., & Drabman, R. The effects of loud and soft reprimands on the behavior of disruptive children. *Exceptional Children*, 1970, **37**, 145–155.

O'Leary, K. D., & O'Leary, S. G. *Classroom management: The successful use of behavior modification.* Elmsford, N.Y.: Pergamon, 1972.

O'Malley, J. E., & Eisenberg, L. The hyperkinetic syndrome. In S. Walzer & P. H. Wolff (Eds.), *Minimal cerebral dysfunction in children.* New York: Grune & Stratton, 1973. Pp. 95–103.

Omenn, G. S. Genetic issues in the syndrome of minimal brain dysfunction. In S. Walzer & P. H. Wolff (Eds.), *Minimal cerebral dysfunction in children.* New York: Grune & Stratton, 1973. Pp. 5–17.

Otto, W. The acquisition and retention of paired associates by good, average, and poor readers. *Journal of Educational Psychology*, 1961, **52**, 241–248.

Owen, F. W., Adams, P. A., Forrest, T., Stolz, L. M. & Fisher, S. Learning disorders in children: Sibling studies. *Monographs of the Society for Research in Child Development*, 1971, **36** (Serial #144).

Palkes, H., Stewart, M. A., & Freedman, J. Improvement in maze performance of hyperactive boys as a function of verbal-training procedures. *Journal of Special Education*, 1971, **5**, 337–342.

Palkes, H., Stewart, M., & Kahana, B. Porteus maze performance of hyperactive boys after training in self-directed verbal commands. *Child Development*, 1968, **39**, 817–829.

Patterson, G. R., Jones, R., Whittier, J., & Wright, M. A. A behaviour modification technique for the hyperactive child. *Behaviour Research and Therapy*, 1965, **2**, 217–226.

Piaget, J., & Inhelder, B. *The psychology of the child.* New York: Basic Books, 1969.

Pick, A. D., Christy, M. D., & Frankel, G. W. A developmental study of visual selective attention. *Journal of Experimental Child Psychology*, 1972, **14**, 165–175.

Porteus, S. E. *Qualitative performance in the maze test.* Vineland, N.J.: Smith, 1942.

Reicher, G. Perceptual recognition as a function of meaningfulness of stimulus material. *Journal of Experimental Psychology*, 1969, **81**, 274–280.

Ridberg, E. H., Parke, R. D. & Hetherington, E. M. Modification of impulsive and reflective cognitive styles through observation of film-mediated models. *Developmental Psychology*, 1971, **5**, 369–377.

Rosner, J. Screening for perceptual dysfunction. *Journal of the American Optometric Association*, 1970, **4**, 858–866.

Ross, A. O. *The practice of clinical child psychology.* New York: Grune & Stratton, 1959.

Ross, A. O. Learning difficulties of children: Dysfunctions, disorders, disabilities. *Journal of School Psychology*, 1967, **5**, 82–92.

Ross, A. O. *Psychological disorders of children: A behavioral approach to theory, research, and therapy.* New York: McGraw-Hill, 1974.

Rourke, B. P., Dietrich, D. M., & Young, G. C. The significance of WISC verbal-performance discrepancies for younger children with learning disabilities. *Perceptual and Motor Skills*, 1973, **36**, 275–282. (a)

Rourke, B. P., & Czudner, G. Age differences in auditory reaction time of "brain-damaged" and normal children under regular and irregular preparatory interval conditions. *Journal of Experimental Child Psychology*, 1972, **14**, 372–378.

Rourke, B. P., Orr, R. R., & Ridgley, B. A. The neuropsychological abilities of normal and retarded readers: a three-year follow-up. Unpublished manuscript, University of Windsor, 1973.

Rourke, B. P., & Telegdy, G. A. Lateralizing significance of WISC verbal-performance discrepancies for older children with learning disabilities. *Perceptual and Motor Skills,* 1971, **33,** 875–883.

Rourke, B. P., Yanni, D. W., MacDonald, G. W., & Young, G. C. Neuropsychological significance of lateralized deficits on the grooved pegboard test for older children with learning disabilities. *Journal of Consulting and Clinical Psychology,* 1973, **41,** 128–134. (b)

Routh, D. K., & Roberts, R. D. Minimal brain dysfunction in children. Failure to find evidence for a behavioral syndrome. *Psychological Reports,* 1972, **31,** 307–314.

Russell, D. *Children learn to read.* Waltham, Mass.: Ginn, 1961.

Ryback, D., & Staats, A. W. Parents as behavior therapy technicians in treating reading deficits (dyslexia). *Journal of Behavior Therapy & Experimental Psychiatry,* 1970, **1,** 109–119.

Safer, D., Allen, R., & Barr, E. Depression of growth in hyperactive children on stimulant drugs. *New England Journal of Medicine,* 1972, **287,** 217–219.

Salapatek, P., & Kessen, W. Prolonged investigation of a plane geometric triangle by the human infant. *Journal of Experimental Child Psychology,* 1973, **15,** 22–29.

Sameroff, A., & Chandler, M. Reproductive risk and the continuum of caretaking casualty. In F. D. Horowitz, M. Hetherington, S. Scarr-Salapatek, & G. Siegel (Eds.), *Review of Child Development Research,* Vol. 4. Chicago: University of Chicago, 1974.

Satterfield, J. H. EEG issues in children with minimal brain dysfunction. In S. Walzer & P. H. Wolff (Eds.), *Minimal cerebral dysfunction in children.* New York: Grune & Stratton, 1973. Pp. 35–46.

Satz, P., Rardin, D., & Ross, J. An evaluation of a theory of specific developmental dyslexia. *Child Development,* 1971, **42,** 2009–2021.

Schachter, S., & Singer, J. E. Cognitive, social and physiological determinants of emotional state. *Psychological Review,* 1962, **49,** 379–399.

Schreibman, L. Effects of within-stimulus and extra-stimulus prompting on discrimination learning in autistic children. *Journal of Applied Behavior Analysis,* 1975, **8,** 91–112.

Schreibman, L. Within-stimulus versus extra-stimulus prompting in discriminations with autistic children. Unpublished doctoral dissertation, University of California, Los Angeles, 1972.

Schreibman, L., & Lovaas, O. I. Overselective response to social stimuli by autistic children. *Journal of Abnormal Child Psychology,* 1973, **1,** 152–168.

Schvaneveldt, R. W., & Meyer, D. E. Retrieval and comparison processes in semantic memory. Paper presented at the Fourth International Symposium on Attention and Performance, Boulder, Colorado, 1971.

Senf, G. M. An information-integration theory and its application to normal reading acquisition and reading disability. In N. D. Bryant & C. E. Kass (Eds.), *Leadership training institute in learning disabilities: Final Report,* Vol. 2. Tucson, Arizona: University of Arizona, 1972. Pp. 305–391.

Serafica, F., & Sigel, I. E. Styles of categorization and reading disability. *Journal of Reading Behavior,* 1970, **2,** 105–115.

Severson, R. A. Early detection of children with potential learning disabilities: A seven-year effort. *Proceedings, Eightieth Annual Convention, American Psychological Association*, 1972. Pp. 561–562.

Sibley, S. A. Reading rate and accuracy of retarded readers as a function of fixed-ratio schedules of conditioned reinforcement. *Dissertation Abstracts*, 1967, **27**, 4134–4135.

Siegel, A. W. Variables affecting incidental learning in children. *Child Development*, 1968, **39**, 957–968.

Spalding, R. B., & Spalding, W. T. *The writing road to reading.* New York: Morrow, 1957.

Sprague, R., Barnes, K., & Werry, J. Methylphenidate and thioridazine: Learning, activity, and behavior in emotionally disturbed boys. *American Journal of Orthopsychiatry*, 1970, **40**, 615–628.

Sroufe, L. A. Age changes in cardiac deceleration within a fixed foreperiod reaction time task: An index of attention. *Developmental Psychology*, 1971, **5**, 338–343.

Sroufe, L. A. Drug treatment of children with behavior problems. In F. D. Horowitz, M. Hetherington, S. Scarr-Salapatek, & G. Siegel (Eds.), *Review of Child Development Research*, Vol. 4. Chicago: University of Chicago Press, 1975.

Sroufe, L. A., Sonies, B. C., West, W. D., & Wright, F. S. Anticipatory heart rate deceleration and reaction time in children with and without referral for learning disability. *Child Development*, 1973, **44**, 267–273.

Sroufe, L. A., & Stewart, M. A. Treating problem children with stimulant drugs. *New England Journal of Medicine*, 1973, **289**, 407–413.

Staats, A. W., & Butterfield, W. H. Treatment of nonreading in a culturally deprived juvenile delinquent: An application of reinforcement principles. *Child Development*, 1965, **36**, 925–942.

Staats, A. W., Minke, K. A., Finley, J. R., Wolf, M. M., & Brooks, L. O. A. Reinforcer system and experimental procedure for the laboratory study of reading acquisition. *Child Development*, 1964, **35**, 209–231.

Staats, A. W., Minke, K. A., Goodwin, W., & Landeen, J. Cognitive behavior modification: "Motivated learning" reading treatment with sub-professional therapy-technicians. *Behaviour Research and Therapy*, 1967, **5**, 283–299.

Stevenson, H. W. *Children's learning.* New York: Appleton-Century-Crofts, 1972.

Stevenson, H. W., Friedrichs, A. G., & Simpson, W. E. Interrelations and correlates over time in children's learning. *Child Development*, 1970, **41**, 625–637.

Stewart, M. A., Pitts, F. N., Craig, A. G., & Dieruf, W. The hyperactive child syndrome. *American Journal of Orthopsychiatry*, 1966, **36**, 861–867.

Sykes, D. H., Douglas, V. I., Weiss, G., & Minde, K. K. Attention in hyperactive children and the effects of methylphenidate (Ritalin). *Journal of Child Psychology and Psychiatry*, 1971, **12**, 129–139.

Taylor, S. E. Eye movements in reading: Facts and fallacies. *American Educational Research Journal*, 1965, **2**, 187–202.

Thomas, A., Chess, S., & Birch, H. G. *Temperament and behavior disorders in children.* New York: New York University Press, 1968.

Tinker, M. A. Recent studies of eye movements in reading. *Psychological Bulletin*, 1958, **55**, 215–231.

Tuddenham, R. D., Brooks, J., & Milkovich, L. Mothers' reports of behavior of ten-year-olds: Relationship with sex, ethnicity, and mother's education. *Developmental Psychology,* 1974, **10,** 959–995.

Vande Voort, L., Senf, G. M., & Benton, A. L. Development of audiovisual integration in normal and retarded readers. *Child Development,* 1972, **43,** 1260–1272.

Vellutino, F. R., Steger, B. M., Moyer, S. C., Harding, C. J. & Niles, J. A. Has the perceptual deficit hypothesis led us astray? An examination of current conceptualizations in the assessment and treatment of exceptional children. Paper presented at Annual International Convention of the Council for Exceptional Children, New York, N. Y., April, 1974.

Vurpillot, E. The development of scanning strategies and their relation to visual differentiation. *Journal of Experimental Child Psychology,* 1968, **6,** 632–650.

Wagner, R. F., & Guyer, B. P. Maintenance of discipline through increasing children's span of attending by means of a token economy. *Psychology in the Schools,* 1971, **8,** 285–289.

Wechsler, D. *Wechsler Intelligence Scale for Children.* New York: The Psychological Corp., 1949.

Wechsler, D. *Wechsler Intelligence Scale for Children—Revised.* New York: The Psychological Corp., 1974.

Weiss, G., Minde, K., Douglas, V., Werry, J. S., & Nemeth, E. Studies of the hyperactive child. VIII—Five-year follow-up. *Archives of General Psychiatry,* 1971, **24,** 409–414.

Weitzenhoffer, A. M., & Brockmeier, J. D. Attention and eye movements. *Journal of Nervous and Mental Disease,* 1970, **151,** 130–142.

Wender, P. H. *Minimal brain dysfunction in children.* New York: Wiley-Interscience, 1971.

Werner, H., & Strauss, A. A. Pathology of figure-background relation in the child. *Journal of Abnormal and Social Psychology,* 1941, **36,** 236–248.

Werry, J. S. Organic factors in childhood psychopathology. In H. C. Quay & J. S. Werry (Eds.), *Psychopathological disorders of childhood.* New York: Wiley, 1972. Pp. 83–121.

Werry, J. S., Minde, K., Guzman, A., Weiss, G., Dogan, K., & Hoy, E. Studies on the hyperactive child. VII—Neurological status compared with neurotic and normal children. *American Journal of Orthopsychiatry,* 1972, **42,** 441–451.

Werry, J. S., Weiss, G., & Douglas, V. Studies on the hyperactive child. I—Some preliminary findings. *Canadian Psychiatric Association Journal,* 1964, **9,** 120–130.

Wheeler, R. J., & Dusek, J. B. The effects of attentional and cognitive factors on children's incidental learning. *Child Development,* 1973, **44,** 253–258.

Whipple, C. I. Discrimination and perceptual learning in the retarded reader. *Dissertation Abstracts International,* 1970, **30(B),** 3419.

Wiener, M., & Cromer, W. Reading and reading difficulty: A conceptual analysis. Cambridge, Mass.: Harvard Educational Review, 1967, 620–643.

Willows, D. M. Reading between the lines: Selective attention in good and poor readers. *Child Development,* 1974, **45,** 408–415.

Wolff, P. H., & Hurwitz, I. Functional implications of the minimal brain damage syndrome. In S. Walzer & P. H. Wolff (Eds.), *Minimal cerebral dysfunction in children.* New York: Grune & Stratton, 1973. Pp. 105–115.

Name Index

Name Index

Ackerman, P. T., 74–75, 80
Adams, P. A., 70–71
Allen, R., 100
Amadeo, M., 149
Anderson, W. F., 83

Bandura, A., 118
Barnes, K., 99
Barr, E., 100
Barsch, R. H., 13
Bateman, B., 1, 9, 13
Battle, E. S., 91–92
Becker, W. C., 126, 131
Beery, J. W., 72
Belmont, L., 71, 72, 74, 151
Benson, C., 129
Benton, A. L., 44, 69, 72–73, 151
Berlyne, D. E., 39–42, 60
Birch, H. G., 71, 72, 74, 89, 151
Blank, M., 139
Block, Jack, 116
Block, Jeanne H., 116
Broadbent, D. E., 44
Brockmeier, J. D., 149
Brooks, J., 86
Brooks, L. O. A., 159
Brown, C. C., 163
Bryden, M. P., 164
Butterfield, W. H., 59, 160

Camp, B. W., 126
Campbell, S. B., 100
Capobianco, R. J., 151
Caron, A. J., 57
Carter-Sobell, L., 154
Chall, J., 158
Chandler, M., 90, 91, 94
Chess, S., 89

Christy, M. D., 48, 49
Clark, M., 129
Clements, S. D., 63, 65–67, 74–75, 80, 85
Conners, C. K., 139
Craig, A. G., 87–89
Crane, N. L., 33
Crinella, F. M., 68
Cromer, W., 143
Croxen, M. E., 151
Cruickshank, W. M., 12
Czudner, G., 46–49

Davison, G. C., 102, 103
Day, H., 42
deHirsch, K., 13
Delacato, C. H., 82
Denhoff, E., 87
Dieruf, W., 87–89
Dietrich, D. M., 79, 80
Dogan, K., 86, 95
Douglas, V. I., 51, 52, 85, 100, 107–109, 113, 121, 139
Drabman, R. S., 127, 128, 131–134
Drass, S. D., 126
Dusek, J. B., 59
Dykman, R. A., 74–75, 80
Dyrud, J. E., 160

Egeland, B., 119–122
Eisenberg, L., 99, 103, 104
Ellis, M. J., 100
Evans, M. B., 126, 131

Finley, J. R., 159
Fischer, M. J., 59, 148, 160
Fisher, S., 70–71
Forness, S. R., 151

Subject Index

Subject Index